the family meal solution

One Handed Cooks is a baby, toddler and family food website that features a wide range of simple, healthy and clever recipes to help parents make food a source of enjoyment and nourishment for their children. Written with an Accredited Practising Dietitian (APD) as part of the team, it also offers friendly and realistic nutrition information, as well as tips and strategies to help manage fussy eating behaviours. They have written a collection of much-loved magazines and in 2016 they published their bestselling, self-titled cookbook *One Handed Cooks: How to raise a healthy, happy eater – from baby to school age*, followed in 2019 by *Boosting Your Basics: Making the most of every family mealtime – from baby to school age*. They have since become an Australian leader in the area of baby, toddler and family food. Join the friendly and engaging One Handed Cooks community on social media and say hello.

onehandedcooks.com.au
@onehandedcooks

Allie Gaunt

Formerly a professional nanny and advertising copywriter, Allie, now a mum of three gorgeous children, is the creator and co-director of the hugely successful One Handed Cooks blog. When her first child, Harry, started solids in 2012 she found herself preparing food with a baby on one hip and was keen to connect with other parents and share her positive experiences. Allie is passionate about feeding children nutritious, homemade food and making mealtimes happy, and she has inspired families around the world to make positive, healthy changes for their children.

Jessica Beaton

Jessica is an Accredited Practising Dietitian with a passion for starting solids and inspiring families to enjoy happy mealtimes and a healthy love of food. She is a co-director of One Handed Cooks, a keen cook and combines her personal journey as a mum of four fun-loving boys with twenty years of evidence-based training and experience as a dietitian to simplify the science and educate parents in a friendly and practical way. Since joining One Handed Cooks in 2012 Jessica has undergone further training in 'Picky Eaters vs Problem Feeders: The Sequential Oral Sensory (SOS) approach to feeding' and 'Making SENSE of Mealtimes'.

Sarah Buckle

Sarah is a dedicated primary-school teacher and much-loved aunty of five with a passion for baking. A co-director of One Handed Cooks, she is also the photographer, capturing the enjoyment of childhood and cherished food moments while showcasing simple, wholesome food to perfection.

the family meal solution

a flexible and achievable approach to feeding your family each week

Allie Gaunt, Jessica Beaton and Sarah Buckle

VIKING
an imprint of
PENGUIN BOOKS

contents

introduction

ONE HANDED COOKS ARE BACK, and so excited to share with you our new book, *The Family Meal Solution: A flexible and achievable approach to feeding your family each week.* As busy parents ourselves, we were becoming overwhelmed by the daily struggle of feeding our growing families – trying to cater to different age groups and food preferences, from babies starting solids to ravenous school-aged children, and also wanting to enjoy flavoursome meals ourselves. We felt the need for a simple and adaptable guide that could help us optimise the pockets of time we had and assist our future selves in those busier moments. We wanted a collection of recipes that were versatile and provided leftovers. We wanted to fill our freezers and have a repertoire of fast meals that we could whip up as needed. Finally, we wanted to stop the expensive top-up shops, increase our veggie intake and offer varied and nutritious meals every week. Is that all too much to ask?

We don't think so. We practised these things with our own families as this book was developed, and we are never going back. While each family's routine is unique, there are similarities we can work with that will give you the confidence and the tools to take back control and simplify feeding the family. This book contains meal-planning guides and hacks, and more than 85 new family-friendly recipes that include baby and toddler notes and allergy/intolerance suggestions, to help you make the most of your time in the kitchen, stock your freezer and save money. All we suggest is that you're careful who you lend it to, as it may never come back!

This book is a practical and flexible guide to help busy families spend less time buying, prepping and cooking food, so they can spend more quality time together. When we asked our online community of busy families what they most wanted help with, answers included spending less time in the kitchen and more time being present with family after a busy day at work or running around; enjoying the meal being eaten instead of always thinking about the next one; and establishing a simple structure to help manage mealtimes, while reducing waste and maximising nutrition. We have found that, instead of spending their weekend cooking for the week ahead, busy parents and carers would rather use the snippets of time they can find to create multiple meals, be it through batch cooking, creating freezer dump bags or cooking meals two ways. For this reason **we have created a simple meal-plan formula you can adapt to your own lifestyle (p. 12),** to help you look at your week as a whole and find those gaps of time. Or, if you aren't quite at that point, you will still find little time-saving hacks you can include in your routine to make preparing good food simpler and easier.

As with all changes, those that are smaller are more achievable and easier to maintain than complete overhauls of your routine (or lack thereof). Start slowly and, once you're in the swing of things, add in another change or two. Over time, and with some consistency, these time-saving habits will become second nature.

The chapters in this book can be read and enjoyed on their own or pieced together to create a weekly meal plan. There is no better feeling than helping your future self – than opening your fridge after an exhausting day and seeing a veggie grab box that will help fill multiple lunchboxes, or having a simple recipe that shows you exactly what to do with the leftovers in the fridge. We have included all of the trusted tips and tricks that keep us ahead of our week and that will help you stay ahead of yours, too.

Enjoy cooking the wide variety of meals in this book, filling your freezer as you go and adding some delicious fast meals to your weekly rotation. You'll feel in control and set up for success, find it easier to stick to your budget, be able to ensure variety in your family's meals/food intake, and spend your time in the kitchen far more efficiently.

plan *and* stocktake

Taking stock of your fridge and pantry is a great first step to getting your mealtimes under control. After a big declutter you will find that doing a weekly sweep of your fridge and pantry right before your weekly shop will be all you need to keep on top of them.

pantry and fridge clean, declutter and stocktake

Both pantries and fridges come in all shapes and sizes and need to be well organised to be used effectively.

Aspiring to perfection may be the single thing holding you back, so we suggest starting small by following this simple task list to get on track today.

AIM   To remove expired food from your pantry and fridge, take stock of what you are left with, and incorporate this into your future meal plans.

STEP 1   Clear and clean: remove all items and give the pantry or fridge a good wipe.

STEP 2   Categorise and cull: time to simplify! Categorise like foods into groups, throw out any items past their use-by date, consolidate multiple packets/containers, then give away or donate any items you know you will not use.

STEP 3   Dedicate and display: zone the different sections of your pantry and fridge into the groups of like items you have created. Follow the golden rules of visibility and accessibility, making sure the items you use the most are the easiest to grab. And remember that if you can't see it, you won't use it!

STEP 4   Modify and maintain: regularly tweak this system until you find what works for you. Spend 5–10 minutes each week maintaining your organisation, and do a complete fridge and pantry refresh every 3–4 months.

pantry:

- Some pantries consist of drawers while others have long thin shelves. Look at the space you have and work with it as best you can. Simple, affordable grab-tubs will help you to categorise items.
- Choose a system that works for you. If you are an avid baker, organise this section to save yourself time in the kitchen.
- Try to have everything on display and/or labelled effectively. Doing this will mean you aren't rummaging around for that tin you thought you had or buying more than you need.
- Make the most of hanging space too – a hanging spice rack or under-shelf/floor storage can create so much extra room.

fridge:

- Use tubs to categorise 'floaters' – for example, have a tub for condiments, spreads and creams.
- Store all bottles and sauces in the door shelves or wherever they belong in your fridge.
- Wash and pre-chop any veggies you have bought straight away. Read more in our fruit and veggie grab boxes section (p. 27).
- Invest in a few 'leftovers' containers that stack nicely in the fridge.
- Create a 'finish me' tub in which to throw all of the bits and pieces that need to be eaten first. Think apples with one bite taken out, half-eaten tubs of yoghurt, and lunch leftovers. This will reduce food waste and is a great way to throw together last-minute snacks.

freezer:

The freezer is about to become your biggest asset, if it's not already. It will be the place where you keep all of the wonderful leftovers, batch meals and baking boxes you are about to create. Having a well-organised freezer is absolutely crucial to reducing your time and energy in the kitchen.

Spend some time clearing and decluttering your freezer and remove expired and freezer-burnt food. Take stock of what you are left with and write down any meals that you add to the freezer on a stash inventory that can be taped to the side of your freezer.

Purchase some quality freezer-proof reusable bags, or freezer-suitable containers with lids. Choose containers and bags that fit your freezer perfectly so you can maximise space and see most of the items. Finally, remember to label and date everything you freeze! Writing with a simple whiteboard or chalk marker directly onto the container lid or freezer bag will do wonders to reduce food wastage and keep your freezer well ordered.

TIP There are a range of ingredients that you can prep and freeze to reduce your waste:

- Citrus juice (lemon, lime, orange) – juice your fruit and freeze it into ice-cube trays. Once frozen, pop them out and store in a freezer-proof bag. You can even store citrus fruits whole in the freezer, if you are short on time.
- Bread and breadcrumbs, frozen in 1-cup amounts
- Chopped onions and chillies
- Simple tomato sauces, such as those for pizza bases or pasta
- Bananas, peeled and chopped
- Curry leaves, makrut lime leaves and bay leaves
- Vegetables, chopped and blanched*
- Poached chicken strips
- Cookie dough
- Leftover stock, frozen in 1-cup amounts

* Blanching is a process by which you quickly heat and cool vegetables prior to freezing them. This simple step can improve the texture and colour when you defrost and cook the vegetables later. Simply bring a saucepan of water to the boil, submerge the prepared veggies for 1 minute, then remove them to a bowl of ice-cold water to stop the cooking process. Remove them from the water and pat dry before freezing.

set up *for a* successful week

Forming positive, simple habits at the beginning of each week will set you up for success when it comes to meal planning, prepping and running an organised kitchen. When you have a busy family, the daily tasks of prepping, cooking and cleaning can quickly build up to a state of chaos. Limited time and no real break can leave you feeling unsure where to start. Creating a clean slate by sorting out your pantry, fridge and freezer is a great place to begin, and then there are other tasks you can work on over time that will soon become habits, tasks that can be efficiently ticked off once a week to keep a tidy and well-managed kitchen. Establishing a short routine to start your week that incorporates small, achievable tasks will do wonders for your mental load and help you keep on top of each day. (And don't worry, we're not talking about hours of cooking here!) Plus, when there is a solid routine in place, and a clear spot for everything, other family members are likely to be more proactive in keeping it running smoothly. To keep your kitchen under control, you can:

1   Give your sink a quick clean and sanitise it once a week, ideally before you bring your shopping home and the prepping begins.

2   Do a quick sweep of the fridge and pantry to remove any expired food, move produce nearing its use-by date to the front and incorporate it into your meal plan.

3   Wash your fruits and veggies (in your clean sink!) under running water and dry with a clean tea towel, or alternatively air-dry, before you pack them all away. This will save you time later and reduce the risk of someone crunching into an unwashed apple.

4   Unwrap, peel, chop and categorise as much as you can before packing produce away. This will help you to store it neatly and efficiently in the fridge and/or in tubs in the pantry, and will also increase the chance you will see it and use it, and reduce waste.

5   Set yourself one 10-minute kitchen-organising task a week. The things we find the most satisfying are: sorting the tupperware/plastic containers; tidying under the sink; cleaning and organising the cutlery drawer; cleaning and organising the cooking utensils; sorting the baking tin cupboard; reorganising the pots and pans; wiping down the microwave/oven; sorting and labelling the spices; wiping down the kitchen cabinets; polishing any stainless-steel surfaces; and cleaning the rangehood and exhaust.

meal planning *on a* budget

One of the many reasons people are inspired to meal plan is that they want to cut down on costs and save money. The weekly shop, top-up shops and incidentals can all add up pretty quickly. Setting yourself a realistic budget and planning the weekly shop around that is a great place to start.

Ways to significantly reduce your weekly spend:

- Write down your meals for the week and the ingredients you need, and double-check your fridge, freezer and pantry before you start your shop to make sure you aren't buying extra of what you already have.

- Shop the weekly specials, particularly for quality meats. Buy meat when it's on sale and create a freezer dump bag (p. 89) or batch cook it (p. 121) to ensure it all gets used. You can also buy meat in bulk and freeze 500 g portions to integrate into upcoming meal plans.

- Include meat-free meals in your weekly plan and/or try halving the meat and replacing the rest with vegetables, grains or legumes. This simple swap can not only boost your family's vegetable intake with next to no effort, but can also bulk up meals in a nutritious and affordable way.
- Choose seasonal produce and imperfect picks. Seasonal fruits and vegetables not only taste better but are far more affordable than out-of-season or imported produce. Always check out the weekly specials and imperfect picks, as these are fantastic to chop up and use in lunchboxes.
- Reduce top-up shops by meal planning. We have all been in the situation where the kids are hungry and time has gotten away from us. Enter the top-up shop, which is often an expensive impulse buy with a few extras added to the trolley that you might not even need. Create a simple meal plan each week to guide you, and only head to the shops when essentials such as bread, milk or fresh fruit need replenishing.
- Resist the temptation of expensive takeaway, opting for homemade 'fast food' instead. It can sometimes be very tempting to default to takeaway meals when life demands it, and while there's nothing wrong with having a break from cooking and including takeaway in your plan, it can sometimes creep into your week more than you might like or than your budget allows. The Fast Meals chapter (p. 163) was designed for exactly this! It's fast food without the price tag.
- Make use of affordable pantry staples such as pasta, tinned fish, rice and eggs by choosing to cook a few simple meals each week. We believe in balance when it comes to cooking homemade meals. Not every meal you make needs to be extravagant or time-consuming. There's nothing wrong with a simple meal or three each week and, if planned for, you will find this is a great way to save money too.
- Limit waste by having a reason for each ingredient you buy. It can be pretty tempting to grab that vibrant bunch of rhubarb or bag of salad mix, but without a plan you might find it wilts before you use it. If you know what you're cooking you will be more focused at the shops and only buy what you know you'll use.

variety *for* family mealtimes

Variety is the key to good health and wellbeing and having a positive approach to food and eating. It means enjoying a wide range of nutritious foods, textures and flavours throughout the week. It means being able to have our cake and eat it too (see more in the Desserts chapter, p. 203). Meal planning is the most important factor in ensuring our families are offered variety day to day and week to week. It allows us to safely and sensitively stretch our more reluctant eaters to enjoy new family meals. When we plan our meals and look at the week as a whole we can see gaps where certain foods, textures and flavours might be missing or where we can try a new meal or two. Referring to the family recipe list (p. 9) and having a child or three around to offer their ideas when you're planning for the week can help keep everyone happy, and space loved meals out among meals they are 'learning to love'. We like to keep a list of meals for the week ahead where it can be seen – it reduces anxiety for older kids who can read and certainly reduces the number of times they ask, 'What's for dinner?' For a week of varied, nutritious meals that the kids are (mostly) happy about, consider these five simple tips when meal planning:

1 Choose your meals for the week

Start by choosing some meals your kids enjoy, some they regularly refuse, plus one or two that may be new. To take the pressure off, allocate your chosen meals to suit your schedule: plan leftovers (p. 103), freezer meals (p. 121), slow-cooker meals (p. 89) or fast meals (p. 163) for the busiest days, and prep meals that require more attention or that you may not have cooked before on the weekend or on days where you have more time. More challenging meals are almost always suited to calmer days when you are able to sit down and eat together as a family.

2 Start with a variety of proteins

Aim to spread your protein base throughout the week – red meat, chicken, pork, fish, eggs, tofu, lentils and legumes are all excellent choices. They each lend themselves to different types of sauces and sides and offer a wide range of nutrients required for your children's development and family's wellbeing. Offering a variety of texture is equally important for little kids learning to eat meat (more on meat refusal in Marinades, p. 219). Offer minced, slow-cooked, grilled, barbecued and shredded meats and flaked fish. And whether you are a vegetarian or just looking for new ways to use lentils and legumes, try adding quick and easy-to-cook red lentils into casseroles or soups, roasting and tossing tinned chickpeas through salads or simmering them in curries, and using brown lentils in place of or in addition to minced meats in sauces and dishes such as bolognese, lasagne, shepherd's pies, burgers, meatballs, pastry pies and sausage rolls.

3 Choose your carbohydrate

Provide fibre for gut health and B vitamins for energy production, among many other nutrients, by serving high-quality carbs at mealtimes. Try starchy vegetables such as potato and sweet potato as well as pasta, quinoa, rice, bread, wraps, lentils and legumes. Choose wholegrain options wherever you can. If plain pasta is your child's go-to, or the only option they accept, offer that regularly until they become more accepting of other foods on the table – however, try for no more than every second day to prevent food jags (p. 86). You can then begin to offer this option less and less, increasing the variety and frequency of other nutritious options.

4 Add in some fruits and vegetables

Planning your meals for the week means you are better able to plan the sides to match. Be sure to buy fruits and vegetables in a range of colours and textures and enjoy them grated through your meals as well as steamed, baked and raw. If you are stuck on veggie sticks at mealtimes you could try deconstructed salads, such as our Gado Gado (p. 192) or Quinoa and marinated feta (p. 196) salads, or slicing them in different ways to ensure they're not the same day in and day out. Kids will often surprise you and they won't try foods if they're not on offer, so spice things up with make-your-own salad bars or veggie and fruit skewers, or alternatively drizzle steamed or roasted veggies with olive oil, butter or sauces to help encourage acceptance. Some children love having condiments made available, while others prefer not to have them. We have heaps more tips and recipe inspiration in our Salads chapter (p. 185).

You are responsible for when and where your child eats and what foods are on offer. Your child is responsible for what foods they choose to eat and how much they eat from what's on offer.

We love the Division of Responsibility in Feeding by registered dietitian Ellyn Satter to help make mealtimes calm, safe, secure and more diverse. Whether you serve up regular meals or tasting plates (p. 86) or offer buffet-style deconstructed meals (p. 87), the important thing is to always include a food or two you know your child will eat and enjoy. It will all come together in good time with some patience, positivity, persistence and consistency.

task zone *vs* transition zone

When you're in the kitchen, you're usually doing one of two things: working on a task, or transitioning into or out of that task. Once you know the tricks to making the most of your time in the former, you can reduce the latter as much as possible. This is the key to becoming more efficient, saving time and giving your future self a helping hand.

Think of everything you do in the kitchen as falling into either the task zone or the transition zone. The task zone includes anything that you are actively doing to get to your end goal of a meal – things like chopping, prepping, cooking and searing. The transition zone includes all of the other often time-consuming steps you need to take to get into the task zone, such as finding ingredients, pulling out utensils, cleaning up, wiping benches down, washing up or stacking the dishwasher. The time spent in the transition zone adds up, becomes monotonous and increases our mental load.

The more you can do while you have those ingredients immediately to hand, while the oven is on and the spices are out, the less time you will have to spend in the transition zone, which will hugely reduce the effort required to prepare meals over the space of a week.

All of the recipes in this book consider ways of maximising active cooking time in the kitchen. Some of the best ways to use your time in the task zone include:

Meal planning (p. 12): if you have an idea of what you want to cook for the week you can save time and help yourself by planning ahead.
Premixes (p. 69): these are so valuable for reducing your transition time and getting on task quicker. For example, if you're making a Mexican spice mix (p. 104), make double or triple the quantity and keep the rest for next time. Cooking up some pancakes? Double the dry ingredients and pop half the mixture in a jar ready for the next batch.
Batch cooking (p. 121): if you are making the family's favourite soup, double the ingredients and make two lots, and freeze one for later. Having a whole meal ready in the freezer will reduce your mental load significantly, and while all the ingredients are out and the chopping board is there, you might as well take a few extra minutes to get it done.
Meals 2 ways (p. 133): choose two recipes that have similar ingredients and make them at the same time. The Meals 2 Ways chapter has some brilliant examples but you can use the same strategy for many of your own recipes too.

meal planning time saviours

We have found that making a few small changes at a time to your meal planning approach can have the biggest impact, and is much more sustainable than trying to do a big overhaul. Including all family members in meal planning can be a positive experience for everyone, and giving kids the option of including their favourite meals in the weekly rotation will only encourage food enjoyment and acceptance.

our family recipe list

Taking just a few minutes to write a list of your family's favourite recipes is a great first step towards more organised mealtimes. Find a simple way to collate all of these favourite recipes, whether in a master spreadsheet with links, in a physical folder with print-outs, or – as we do – on a piece of paper stuck on the fridge! Spending time making a list may also highlight variety gaps, which will inspire you to fill those gaps in upcoming meal plans.

Fussy eating tip: a working list is a wonderful way to include your child's favourite meals too. Every time they enjoy something, add it to the list! The whole family will enjoy seeing it grow over time, and deciding 'what's for dinner' will become even easier.

Tips for writing a favourite-recipes list:

- Ask the kids to think of their three favourite meals.
- Start with your 'hit list' of meals the family loves and enjoy adding to it when a new favourite comes along.
- Add some recipes you want to try – to fill a gap or just to include something new. Add one of these recipes every couple of weeks. Your children might even enjoy exploring some cookbooks or magazines for ideas with you.
- Include some 'fast meals' (p. 163) that are easy to make from fridge and pantry staples. This can help you avoid takeaway and take the stress out of unexpectedly busy evenings.

meal preparation boxes

Meal prep boxes are boxes of pre-gathered and/or pre-prepped items that can save your future self a lot of time. These are some of our favourite boxes that you won't be able to live without once you've tried them:

- **Baking box:** streamline your snack and lunchbox game with this freezer hack. When you bake any sweet or savoury snacks, flash freeze them (p. 20) and dump them into a sweet or savoury baking box. Continue to top up the box with something new once or twice a week. Grab the frozen snacks to pop in lunchboxes as needed. Read more about this and see it in action on p. 28.
- **Breakfast box:** not a morning person? Simplify the breakfast routine by collecting your most used cereals, spreads and breads etc. and placing them in the one breakfast box. Pull it out before you go to bed and love how smoothly your mornings begin.

- **Dinner box:** making a chicken drumstick and couscous tray bake (p. 152) for dinner? Gather all of the ingredients together, chop and prep any that you can (i.e. make the marinade, cut up the vegetables), then place them in a container in the fridge to pull out and assemble with the pantry items at dinner time.
- **Premix box:** flick over to the premix recipe section (p. 69) and become an organisational genius. In this box you can keep your premixed dry staples that will be waiting for you to simply measure out and add wet ingredients to. Think pancakes, mug cakes and slices almost ready to go.
- **Baby box:** do you have a baby or young toddler in the house with their own specific foods? Maybe you've made or chosen lower-sugar and -salt varieties, or you have special cereals and breakfast toppers just for them, or a couple of food jars and pouches for occasional meals. Instead of keeping these things within reach of the rest of the family, we love to have a designated baby box, which saves rummaging around and prevents little rusks from being stolen.
- **Finish-me box:** this is a dedicated space in your fridge for items that need to be used, such as an opened hummus container, a hard-boiled egg, the half of a lemon you needed, or some sliced veggies from the night before, all of which can be added to lunchboxes or snack plates. This is the ultimate in reducing incidental kitchen waste.

food preparation tips

Food preparation is a simple act of kindness to your future self that can save you time when you need it most. Imagine pre-grated cheese, pre-chopped onions and garlic, and portioned sauces ready to stir through pasta. With the following list on hand you can make so many meals in half the time.

Our top time-saving food prep ideas are:

- **Grated cheese:** having pre-grated cheese on hand is an absolute game changer. The first time you grate cheese for the week, grate an extra few cups. This will make dinner toppings and sandwiches a joy.
- **Grated vegetables:** just like the cheese, grated vegetables can help to continually boost the nutrition in meals, add nutrients to your baking and help with sandwich and salad making during the week. We love pre-grating carrots and zucchini and storing some in the fridge and some flat in the freezer to snap off and use as required. You can use a food processor to grate your weekly veggies really quickly and you won't have to bring it out again that week.
- **Chopped onion and garlic:** chopped onion and garlic are used in so many meals that it makes sense to keep them on hand. We like to pre-chop and store them in small portions to use as required.
- **Sauces and pestos:** whenever we are making a sauce or pesto we double the quantity or save any leftovers. Keeping portioned sauces in the freezer means that for many meals half the work is already done. Our favourites are tomato-based sauces, pestos (p. 58) and spice mixes (p. 104).

prepping a meal in advance can save you lots of time

baked risotto with garlic prawns (p. 168) dinner box

designing a meal plan *that* works

We can't design a plan that suits your individual needs but we can show you how to do it. By simply looking at your weekly schedule, including activities and routines, you can quickly come up with a plan or formula that suits you and your family and then find recipes to include in it. You can plan to make a lasagne on an activity-free night and keep a 10-minute pasta meal for that busy afternoon you dread.

Our general rules for creating a meal plan that offers flexibility while continually filling the freezer look a little like this:

Cook 5 core meals a week

Include 2 easy-to-prep meals – such as a tray bake (p. 151) or a fast meal (p. 163) that uses pantry staples

One meal must have leftovers – choose a dinner + leftovers recipe (p. 103), or double a component of your meal

One meal must have a serve for the freezer for next week – choose a dump bag meal (p. 89), batch meal (p. 121) or meal 2 ways/meal couple recipe (p. 133)

Bake at least 2 snacks each week – this will keep your baking boxes topped up for lunchboxes and snacks

This meal plan formula will ensure you have at least one frozen meal and a leftovers meal each week – meaning next to no cooking on those days. This, combined with a fast meal or two using batched frozen pestos or sauces, will considerably lighten your cooking load.

If you were to use the recipes in this book, your meal plan might look like this:

MEAL 1   Butter chicken + freezer dump bag for next week (p. 93)

MEAL 2   Mexican beef with dumplings + leftovers (p. 104)

FROZEN MEAL   Last week's freezer dump bag

LEFTOVERS   Nachos with leftover Mexican beef (p. 104)

MEAL 3   Tray-baked salmon and potatoes with creamy feta sauce (p. 154)

MEAL 4   Zucchini slice (and optional meal-2-ways Zucchini nuggets) (p. 136)

MEAL 5   Sandwich press fold-ups (fast meal) (p. 170)

sample family meal plan

Using the above formula, this plan allows a busy family to continually have leftovers and frozen meals in the fridge while topping up baking boxes in the freezer. You might want to make a note to transfer dump bags or leftovers from the freezer to the fridge the day before you intend to use them.

	M	T	W	T	F	S	S
What have I got on?			Work	Work	Activity	Sport	Busy family day
What meal works for my day?	Meal 1 + freezer dump bag Butter chicken (p. 93) + freezer dump bag for next week	Meal 2 + leftovers Mexican beef with dumplings (p. 104) Extra Mexican beef for Thursday	Reheat a frozen meal Last week's freezer dump bag	Eat leftovers Nachos with leftover Mexican beef (p. 104)	Meal 3 Tray-baked salmon and potatoes with creamy feta sauce (p. 154)	Meal 4 Zucchini slice (and optional meal-2-ways Zucchini nuggets) (p. 136)	Meal 5 Fast meal Sandwich press fold-ups (p. 170)
What food-prep tasks can I fit in?	Make a veggie grab box (p. 28)	Make an extra Mexican spice mix (p. 104)	Make an oat premix (p. 72)			Freeze any leftover slices for lunchboxes	Make a pesto to freeze with any wilting herbs (p. 58)
What can I bake/ freeze?	No-bake 'snickers' slice (p. 40)				Pick 'n' mix bulk biscuits (p. 34)		Tuna and pesto balls (p. 58)
Tasks to keep me on track	Weekly shop, wash and prep				Write next week's meal plan		Clean and organise fridge

sample snack plan

This meal plan shows you how to make or prepare at least one recipe a day during the week to end up with a full baking box in the freezer ready for packing lunchboxes, plus some premixes in the pantry to ensure you have quick and easy snacks on hand. Many of the snacks will have similar ingredients, so as shown below you can maximise task time while the ingredients are out of the pantry and the inevitable mess is being made, which means one set-up and one clean-up. We love to do this at the beginning of each school term or season to set ourselves up for the next month or two.

	M	T	W	T	F
Recipe	Tuna and pesto balls (p. 58)	Spelt and sunflower biscuits (p. 44)	Spinach and cheese 'croissants' (p. 52)	Banana, apple and cinnamon loaf (p. 50)	No-bake 'snickers' slice/bliss balls (p. 40)
Extra prep	Make extra pesto and freeze for pastas	Make the oat premix (p. 72) while ingredients are out	Grate extra cheese for the freezer	Double the mixture and bake a batch of muffins for the freezer	Freeze some smoothie bags (p. 37) (similar ingredients)

entertainer's meal plan

Feel cool, calm and collected at your next mingle with family or friends thanks to this simple meal plan to feed a crowd while keeping meal prep on the day to a minimum, so you can enjoy yourself too.

	snack	main	salad	dessert
Option 1	Pork and caramelised apple sausage rolls (p. 54) Make ahead and freeze raw to cook on the day	Marinated lemon and oregano chicken skewers (p. 229)	Classic caesar salad (p. 198)	One-bowl chocolate sheet cake (p. 208) Make in advance, ice fresh
Option 2	Ham and sweetcorn tartlets (p. 64) Make ahead and freeze, then reheat before guests arrive	Pulled pork sliders with slaw (p. 90) Slow cook the day before	N/A see the slaw recipe (p. 90)	Rocky road ice-cream cake (p. 216) Make in advance
Option 3 – Vegetarian	Hummus and cheese crackers (p. 56) with veggie sticks Pre-make and chop in the morning	Vegetable and red lentil lasagne (p. 144)	Roast cauliflower and chickpea salad (p. 200)	Pavlova platter (p. 212) Make the day before, pre-prep the toppings

reduce waste

All of us would probably love to reduce our waste even more than we already do. The trick to reducing your waste is to have a plan at the beginning of the week and to try to stick to it as much as possible. You want to be left with an empty fridge ready to stock the following week. Try to use up all of the fresh food you bought and not pour away half a tin of this or that.

How we have tried to eliminate waste in this book:

- Where possible we have tried to include a full tin or jar of prepackaged ingredients. If we can't include it all we have offered suggestions for other recipes that use the same ingredient.
- We offer storage suggestions for each recipe so you can reheat leftovers or freeze them for another day.
- We recommend using reusable freezer-proof bags or containers with lids for the dump bags. These will not only hold the ingredients better than plastic bags but will also reduce waste as you begin to use them more often.
- We suggest flash freezing (p. 20) baked goods. That way you can then tip them into a baking box without the need for extra wrapping. The idea is to use up these baked goods within the month and constantly rotate them, avoiding the issue of freezer burn.
- We offer a downloadable meal planning template pack to help you keep track of what's in the freezer, reducing the need to throw out unused food.

- We recommend always taking stock of your freezer and pantry before creating your meal plan for the week, and using up any leftover food or ingredients that might be nearing their use-by date.

- We use simple and affordable everyday ingredients. This will limit the need to buy one-off ingredients that may be half used and wasted. Some exceptions to this are ingredients that may be required to cater to allergies or intolerances. We recommend choosing a wholefood shop where you can scoop the exact amount you need.

vegetarian

The benefits of including meat-free meals throughout the week are widely documented. Enjoying a broad range of plant-based foods such as grains, legumes and vegetables is vital to a balanced diet. Not only does going meat-free one day a week (or more) reduce your carbon footprint, it can also have a positive impact on your and your family's health. Not to mention it encourages a greater interest in and more experimentation with vegetables, legumes and nuts in a main meal.

It is recommended that toddlers enjoy around two and a half serves of vegetables daily, and for primary-school kids this increases to five serves. For some parents, this can be made more achievable by offering a small amount of raw or cooked vegetables at each snack time and mealtime and by boosting main meals with tinned lentils and grated or pureed vegetables. Enter the veggie grab box (p. 28)! Our Salads chapter (p. 185) also provides some wonderful tips and mealtime strategies to both incorporate more veggies into your weekly meal plan and have your children enjoy them too.

In our previous books we included a specific vegetarian chapter. For this book we wanted to include a vegetarian serving suggestion wherever possible. So look out for these suggestions, give them a try, and share with our online community what worked well for you.

How to plan for meat-free meals:

- Start by scheduling at least one vegetarian meal each week. Once you have this mastered, aim for two meals.
- Look at our vegetarian serving suggestions and try swapping half the meat for vegetables. For example, if you're making the beef skewers (p. 178), try halving the amount of beef and alternating with vegetable cubes as suggested.
- Plan in advance so you can think about ways to 'bulk up' meals with more veggies, or ways to serve veggies alongside your meat meals. You can reduce some of the meat in our homestyle Beef, sweet potato and kale casserole (p. 128), for instance, and add more carrot and sweet potato plus a tin of cannellini beans at the end. When bulking up your meals with vegetables, you might also find you have more leftovers, allowing you to freeze a second portion for another meal.

- Plan on making some extra veggie-based meals towards the end of the week. This will give you a chance to use up anything that is slowly wilting in the fridge. Recipes such as a Zucchini slice (p. 136), our Fast-prep pasta bake (p. 173), a stir-fry (p. 230) or a vegetable stock can quickly and effectively clear the fridge and stock your freezer. We have more tips to reduce fresh fruit and veggie wastage in our Salads chapter (p. 185).

considering meat

When selecting meat for our families we love to choose quality free-range poultry and pork products, MSA-grade beef, sustainable or locally caught seafood, preservative-free sausages and nitrate-free or minimal-nitrate ham and bacon from a deli or butcher. They might be a few dollars more expensive weight for weight, but if you are mindful of the quantity of your purchase and ensure none of it goes to waste, this may be a more economical, environmentally friendly and health-conscious way to shop.

baby *and* toddler serves

We've stepped up our game. We knew one chapter dedicated to meals the whole family can share wouldn't be enough, so this time around all our Winner dinners (p. 83) and Salads (p. 185) have baby and toddler serving suggestions to eliminate the guesswork. We have fussy eating tips for many of the recipes too, to help make offering new meals to reluctant eaters as relaxed, happy and pressure-free as possible.

Discovering the art of feeding the whole family the same meal really does open up a world of possibilities. It saves a huge amount of time and a lot of money, and research has shown that this mode of feeding can reduce fussy eating behaviours. If it is unrealistic for your family to sit down together to eat, offering leftovers from the family meal to your young children the next day for lunch or dinner, with a parent, carer or older sibling, can hugely improve their eating behaviours and increase the amount of variety they accept.

foods to avoid

Naturally there are certain foods that should not be offered to babies under the age of 12 months and should be limited for toddlers for various health and nutritional reasons. These include:

- **Honey:** avoid until 12 months due to the risk of infant botulism.
- **Cow's and goat's milk:** should not be your child's main drink before 12 months of age, as they have a high renal solute load, which places unwanted strain on the kidneys. They are also poor sources of iron and can contribute to iron-deficiency anaemia.
- **Soy, rice, oat and almond milk:** should not be your child's main drink before 2 years of age (unless recommended by a health professional) as they are nutritionally incomplete.
- **Skim and low-fat dairy:** avoid until 2 years of age, as the fat provided by full-fat dairy is an important source of energy for growing babies and toddlers.
- **Fruit juice and sweetened drinks:** avoid for as long as possible (or at least 12 months) – they reduce the appetite for whole fruits, more nutritious foods and milk, and can cause tooth decay.
- **Whole nuts, raw carrot, celery sticks and chunks of apple:** avoid until 3 years of age due to the risk of choking.
- **Raw or undercooked eggs:** avoid until 2 years of age due to the risk of salmonella poisoning.
- **Salt and high-salt foods:** avoid for as long as possible (or at least 12 months) – too much salt/sodium can place strain on your baby's developing kidneys and create a preference for salty foods.
- **Tea, coffee and caffeinated drinks:** avoid for as long as possible, as too much caffeine can overstimulate the nervous system and reduces the absorption of calcium.
- **Artificial sweeteners:** avoid for as long as possible due to the unknown safety and side effects of these products.

nutritional considerations

Eating the same foods as your children doesn't mean you have to sacrifice stronger flavours or the meals you love. It does however take a little extra thinking and planning time to adapt your meals for young children. The flavourful, nutritious recipes in this book are perfect for the whole family, but if you have some old favourites, here's what you need to consider:

- Use no-added-salt and salt-reduced products where possible and season adult portions separately (more on salt in Winner Dinners, p. 83).
- Omit alcohol and substitute with salt-reduced stock or water.
- Use herbs and spices to add flavour and adapt quantities if required. Most herbs and spices are appropriate – for example, our Butter chicken (p. 93) is a huge hit with many babies and toddlers we know. However, avoid or reduce quantities of fresh and dried chilli and spicy powders that may not be tolerated.

- Consider offering high-allergen foods on their own first to young babies.
- Check that ingredients are appropriate for young children.
- Serve meals in an age-appropriate way – refer to the baby and toddler serving suggestions below and at the bottom of each recipe in the Winner Dinners and Salads chapters.
- Include extra grated or pureed vegetables in your meals where possible.
- Avoid adding sugar (and honey for babies under 12 months).

baby serves

Generally speaking, most happy, healthy babies will accept a wide range of foods fairly easily and 'give anything a go'. As long as the food offered is a safe and age-appropriate size, they will smush and devour everything to their heart's content. We love offering babies over the age of 6 months a combination of spoon-fed meals and finger foods. Depending on your baby and their food and feeding preferences, you might offer more or less of one than the other. That's okay – tune in to their hunger and fullness cues and continue to offer them a variety of foods, flavours and textures as they progress in their learning-to-eat journey.

toddler serves

Older babies and toddlers are more inclined to use their hands (or kids' utensils) and prefer a bits-and-pieces approach so they can choose and be in control. Offering a toddler their food on a separate tasting plate (p. 221) in bite-sized portions keeps them interested. Older toddlers and preschoolers in particular also love to choose from a variety of foods during deconstructed mealtimes (p. 221). Smaller portions are encouraged as toddlers can often feel overwhelmed and may begin to throw the food around before they are actually full. Top up their plate as they go while tuning in to their hunger and fullness cues.

deconstructed mealtimes and tasting plates

These are both great tools to make mealtimes positive and happy. Deconstructed mealtimes are a wonderful way to accommodate a range of food preferences within a family. And combined with pressure-free mealtimes and the Division of Responsibility (p. 8), these are both excellent ways to encourage reluctant eaters who may have narrowed down their food choices to accept more variety. Using a range of serving styles is often a good way to start, as you might find that one technique suits you and your family over others, or that a combination allows you flexibility and convenience. Offering both deconstructed mealtimes and tasting plates when eating together as a family will give you the greatest results. The social connection, the focus on family rather than on food, and the ability to role model positive eating behaviours only enrich the process. We cover both tasting plates and deconstructed mealtimes in more detail in our Winner Dinners (p. 86) and Marinades (p. 221) chapters.

when *to* seek help

Healthy children vary widely in their growth and achievement of developmental milestones. However, if you do have any concerns regarding the growth, development, health and wellbeing of your child or the nutritional adequacy of their diet, please don't hesitate to seek the advice of a relevant healthcare professional. Doctors, child and family health nurses, paediatricians, Accredited Practising Dietitians (APDs), speech pathologists, occupational therapists, physiotherapists and psychologists are all qualified to assist in improving the quality of children's diets and/or eating behaviours. In some cases, treatment may involve more than one of these professionals. If your family doctor or child and family health nurse believe that areas of your child's health need addressing, they will alert you to their concerns.

food storage *and* safety basics

Keeping your food clean and safe is essential for preventing illnesses and maintaining good health within your family. While always unpleasant, food poisoning can be very serious and even life-threatening among babies and young children. Preparing, cooking, storing, freezing, defrosting and reheating food and meals appropriately and in a timely manner is important to keeping well and reduces food wastage. If you are at all in doubt, throw it out. Here's our go-to guide for safe food handling in your home.

safe-temperature guide

The bacteria responsible for food poisoning grow rapidly in the temperature 'danger zone' between 5°C and 60°C. To prevent and slow bacteria growth in your food to keep your family safe, remember to:

- **Keep chilled food at 5°C or colder.**
- **Keep frozen food frozen solid, ideally at -18°C.**
- **Keep hot food at 60°C or hotter.**

One of the best ways to prevent bacteria growth is to avoid leaving food that needs to be refrigerated or frozen at room temperature for too long.

safe food preparation

A clean kitchen bench along with clean, dry hands and foods that have been stored correctly is the best place to begin. You should also:

- Wash your hands before handling or preparing meals and snacks.
- Use different towels for drying your hands and washing dishes.
- Ensure your kitchen benches, chopping boards, cookware and utensils are kept clean and dry.
- Wash fruits and vegetables with water before preparing and eating them.

- Use food items that have been stored correctly and are within their use-by and best-before dates.
- Avoid cross-contamination by keeping raw food and cooked or ready-to-eat food separate.
- Use different chopping boards and utensils for raw food and cooked food.
- Avoid making food for others if you are ill, particularly if you have a gastro-intestinal illness.

safe food storage

Storing your food safely and appropriately will minimise the time it spends in the temperature 'danger zone' and slow the growth of any harmful bacteria. Any high-risk food or cooked meal that has spent 2–4 hours in the 'danger zone' cannot be put back in the fridge and must be eaten. Any longer than 4 hours and the food must be thrown out. To store food safely you can:

- Store it in clean, dry containers that are airtight, if possible. We prefer oven-proof glass containers for our casseroles and pasta bakes, and reusable silicone snap-lock bags for our dump bags, marinades and sauces.
- Choose to use separate shallow containers, rather than large deep containers, which will help your food cool down and/or freeze faster and help prevent bacteria growth.

- Ensure your fridge temperature is lower than 5°C and frozen food is kept below -18°C.
- Keep raw and cooked food separate and always try to store cooked food on shelves above raw food to prevent cross-contamination.

freezing your batch cook, dump bags and leftovers

Firstly, label your food with the meal name, the date it was frozen and the date it should be used by. There's nothing worse than forgetting what's in your freezer, leaving it for too long and having to throw it out. Because it's recommended we don't keep food frozen for longer than 2 months, we suggest keeping your dump bags and any cooked leftovers in the freezer for no longer than this. The freezing process does not actually kill harmful bacteria and other organisms that were present in the food before freezing. However, while frozen, bacteria populations do not continue to grow, although they will resume doing so once your food is thawed. So never refreeze raw meat once it has thawed.

freezing your sweet and savoury snack foods

Find some quality BPA-free plastic containers or lidded glass storage containers that fit the freezer well. Layer your muffins, biscuits, slices and bliss balls with baking paper or flash freeze them first (see below). Flash freezing rissoles, meatballs and nuggets etc. raw will help with flavour, texture and nutritional value. Remember to label your frozen items and avoid freezing raw and cooked foods together.

how to flash freeze

Place the food items on a small baking tray or baking-paper-lined plate that fits in your freezer. Cover with another layer of baking paper or foil and place the tray in the freezer. Leave for 1–2 hours, then transfer to a reusable freezer-proof storage bag or airtight container. Simply defrost and cook as required.

safely storing leftovers

In general, refreezing food once it has thawed is not recommended as it affects food quality. However, previously frozen food can be refrozen once it has been cooked. This means you can freeze the leftovers from your dump-bag meal once it has been fully defrosted and cooked according to instructions. We also recommend enjoying any leftovers kept in the fridge within 24–48 hours, and reheating them till they are piping hot.

defrosting and reheating foods safely

Defrosting foods safely is as important as safely preparing your foods.

- Remove your dump bag or leftovers from your freezer and place them in the fridge the day before you plan to cook them, at a temperature lower than 5°C.
- Ensure the contents have fully defrosted before cooking.
- Fruits and veggies can be prepared and cooked from a frozen state, while raw meat should always be thoroughly defrosted before cooking.
- Keep defrosted food in the fridge, for no longer than 24 hours, until you are ready to cook or reheat it.
- If you are reheating leftovers or defrosted frozen meals in the microwave or on the stovetop, stir intermittently to ensure they have been reheated appropriately and evenly.

- If you have cooked frozen pies, lasagnes or pasta bakes from the freezer, ensure the middle has cooked thoroughly and to an appropriate temperature – you may need to allow more cooking time than you would if cooking them fresh.
- Never leave food to defrost on the kitchen bench or sink or anywhere other than in your fridge. Outer layers of the food can warm up quickly and breed harmful bacteria.

For more information on safe food handling and storage visit the Australian Institute of Food Safety's website: www.foodsafety.com.au.

food storage guide

You will find conflicting advice on how long it is appropriate to keep food for. Below is our general guide, although many suggest that all food cooked for infants should be used within a month.

cooked food type	fridge	freezer
Egg	1 day	1–2 months
Meat	1 day	1–2 months
Meat/vegetable combination	1–2 days	1–2 months
Fruits and vegetables	2–3 days	1–3 months

allergies *and* intolerances

Given that food allergies and intolerances are extremely common in young babies and children, we cater to these as much as we can in each of our recipes. Focusing on the most common allergens – cow's milk protein; egg; peanuts, tree nuts and sesame; gluten and wheat; and fish and shellfish – we suggest alternative ingredients where possible.

Please note that the ingredient substitutions provided for allergies and intolerances are suggestions only and have not all been tested.

egg-replacer recipes

While commercial egg replacers are available for cooking, you can also use common pantry staples as replacers in a range of your favourite recipes. The following substitutes equal 1 egg:

Agar agar: combine 1 tablespoon agar agar with 1 tablespoon water. Use in sweet dishes and baked goods.

Apple sauce (unsweetened) or puree: use ¼ cup (75 g) apple sauce or puree in sweet dishes and baked goods.

'Chia egg': combine 1 tablespoon chia seeds with ⅓ cup (80 ml) water. Set aside for 5 minutes to soak, then stir and continue to soak for a further 5 minutes or until the mixture has a gel-like consistency.

'Linseed egg': combine 1 tablespoon ground linseed (flaxseed) with ¼ cup (60 ml) water. Set aside for 1 minute to soak, then stir until thick and creamy.

Nut butter: use 3 tablespoons pure smooth peanut butter or almond butter in sweet dishes and baked goods.

Banana: mash ½ ripe banana. Use in sweet dishes and baked goods.

key to recipe symbols

We use the following symbols for our recipes:

F	Freezable		**DF**	Dairy-free
GF	Gluten-free		**EF**	Egg-free
WF	Wheat-free		**V**	Vegetarian

Now you're fully equipped to optimise your time in the kitchen, cook more with minimal effort, fill your freezer and save money, all while having some fun with the family along the way. The benefits of offering thought-out, nutritious and varied food each week will likely reduce your mental load and increase the acceptance and enjoyment of food for everyone. We can't wait to hear what you get up to and which snacks and meals become family favourites for years to come. So let's get started.

sweet *and* savoury snacks

Meal planning and filling your freezer isn't always about dinners and large meals. We also love to bake and freeze bite-sized sweet and savoury snacks, and pre-prep fruits and veggies.

When you are organised with your snacks you will find that the whole family will consume more fruits and vegetables, you will save so much time and reduce your mental load, and the monotonous task of filling those lunchboxes will suddenly become not so hard. To streamline the snack process, we love to have a stash readily available right when we need it by using two simple meal-prepping hacks:

HACK 1   have accessible fruit and vegetable grab boxes full of washed and chopped fresh produce that you've put together straight after the weekly grocery shop or delivery.

HACK 2   create a fast-moving baking box in the freezer that you can consistently top up with homemade snacks, so that you'll always have something quick and nutritious on hand.

Not only will these two hacks make your life easier, they will also limit the amount of pre-packaged snacks you need to buy, saving you money too. Here's how we do them.

1. fruit *and* veggie grab boxes

If you're someone who likes to do one big shop at the beginning of the week you'll be all too familiar with the overwhelming task of packing it all away. This step can help make or break the organisation of your week so it's good to spend some time doing it properly. Fruit and veggie grab boxes are one simple step that can be added to this process that will change the way you and your family snack, and shred time off your meal prep for the week. If you are a busy family, we guarantee that this is one change you won't go back from.

Both fruit and veggie grab boxes are a game changer when it comes to snacking, filling up lunchboxes and adding quick sides to the kids' dinner plates or veggies to a stir-fry. The pre-peeled and chopped bite-sized pieces will also encourage more veggie consumption and interaction. If the kids are hungry before dinner, we love to whip out the veggie grab box as a simple and healthy option!

fruit grab box

Wash your fruit in a clean, empty sink with fresh running water. If needed use a clean vegetable brush to scrub any firm produce, then peel, trim or chop as required. Fruits that take up a lot of room in the fridge, such as melons and pineapples, take up far less room when chopped, and are more likely to be eaten. Arrange the chopped fruit in separate airtight containers within a single box or section of your fridge, or combine them, depending on the size of your containers and your preference. Most fruit should store well for at least 3 days, if not longer, depending on the quality of your containers.

Fruits that we find work well:

- watermelon
- rockmelon
- pineapple
- grapes

Strawberries should only be washed if you are going to eat them immediately. Don't wash strawberries in advance, as the added moisture will cause them to deteriorate faster.

veggie grab box

Wash your vegetables in a clean, empty sink with fresh running water. If needed use a clean vegetable brush to scrub any firm produce, then peel, trim or chop as required. Only prep the amount of vegetables you think will be used within half a week. Then simply wash and top up the containers in your veggie box once they are all gone.

Veggies that work well:

- green beans
- snow peas
- sugar snap peas
- capsicum
- celery
- cherry tomatoes

Carrots can be prepped in advance too, but they are better submerged in water in a small airtight container or glass jar. This will keep their colour vibrant and texture crunchy.

One of the most commonly asked questions about grab boxes is whether the fruit and vegetables store well when chopped up. It's important to note that these boxes are intended to be used up fast – ideally within 3–4 days. They are there for the family to enjoy! We use the pre-chopped veggies and fruit to fill lunchboxes, as simple sides for afternoon tea, snacks to beat the pre-dinner hungries, and quick and easy sides for dinner.

NOTE Fresh leafy green vegetables are best washed and dried right before use.

2. baking boxes

Baking boxes are a handy hack for busy families who have multiple lunchboxes to fill and what might seem like an endless number of snack times to cater for. Baking boxes are containers that live in the freezer and are consistently topped up with a variety of bite-sized baked goods. The baking box is intended to be fast moving and used daily. You only want the snacks in it to last a few weeks or up to a month, not long enough to get freezer burn. Simply bake once or twice a week to keep your boxes topped up and varied, and enjoy having all the snacks on hand. We love to add one or two pieces from the baking box to lunchboxes or snack boxes when we are out and about. Because the pieces are small they should thaw out in a few hours and be ready to eat by morning tea or lunchtime.

We find it useful to have one sweet box and one savoury box; however, depending on how many snacks you are making, you may only need one. Below are some of the things you can fill your box with – healthy lunchbox ideas that are achievable and that the kids will enjoy. But really you can use any of your favourite bite-sized recipes. We have also created a meal plan on p. 12 that includes some great ideas for filling the freezer fast.

TIP With full baking boxes in the freezer and fruit and veggie grab boxes ready to go, you can have a lunchbox or snack plate ready in moments.

sweet baking box

- Pick 'n' mix bulk biscuits (p. 34)
- No-bake 'snickers' slice (p. 40)
- Banana, apple and cinnamon loaf, cut into slices (p. 50)
- Lemon zucchini cake, cut into small squares (p. 42)
- Spelt and sunflower biscuits (p. 44)
- Chocolate and kidney bean cupcakes (p. 48)
- Rice Bubble and seed mini bars (p. 46)
- Avocado and ricotta pikelets (p. 45)
- Sultana oat pancakes (p. 75)
- Fruity lunchbox muffins (p. 76)
- Raspberry and white chocolate blondies (p. 80)
- Ginger and yoghurt cake, cut into squares (p. 215)
- Lemon curd shortbread slice (p. 210)
- One-bowl chocolate sheet cake, cut into small squares (p. 208)

savoury baking box

- Pick 'n' mix cheesy lunchbox rolls (p. 51)
- Pork and caramelised apple sausage rolls (p. 54)
- Spinach and cheese 'croissants' (p. 52)
- Tuna and pesto balls (p. 58)
- Veggie noodle muffins (p. 62)
- Ham and sweetcorn tartlets (p. 64)
- Cheesy turkey and sage patties (p. 65)
- Leftover vegetable curry puffs (p. 110)
- Zucchini slice (p. 136)
- Zucchini nuggets (p. 136)
- Tomato and chorizo frittata (p. 180)
- Homemade baked chicken nuggets (p. 179)

NOTE Baking boxes also work for baby and toddler snacks and meals. You can have a baking box in the freezer full of smaller-sized meals with no added sugar for your baby or toddler. Nuggets, frittata fingers, meatballs, homemade rusks and oat bars are all wonderful additions to your baby or toddler baking box.

build *a* healthy lunchbox

Having your weekly veggie and fruit boxes prepped and your baking boxes well stocked makes preparing nutritious lunchboxes a breeze, helps you to avoid that stuck-in-a-rut feeling and allows variety in the day to day. Another easy time-saving strategy to ensure a nutritious and varied lunchbox is to have a simple checklist in your head of the different food groups to try to offer in your child's lunchbox each day. This ensures they have key nutrients such as quality carbohydrates, protein, calcium, iron, zinc and omega-3 fatty acids to help them learn and play.

1 Choose quality carbohydrates
Wholegrain products (including breads, wraps, pasta, crispbreads and cereals), brown rice, quinoa and legumes are higher in fibre, B vitamins and folate than white and refined varieties. They also provide longer-lasting energy, helping children to concentrate in the classroom.

2 Include protein
Protein is important for satisfying hungry little appetites and helping kids to feel full. Lean red meat slices or meatballs, leftover roast chicken, lean ham, canned fish, eggs, hummus and cheese are great in sandwiches. Look to your savoury baking box for other nutritious and delicious bite-sized options to add variety if you feel your child is becoming bored with sandwiches. Cheese slices or sticks, yoghurt tubs, plain milk, nuts (depending on your child's age and your school's rules) and wholegrain muesli bars are also sources of protein and great for snacks.

3 Pack vegetables
They provide a variety of important nutrients and add fibre and bulk to children's diets. If your child is old enough to eat raw veggie sticks, pull out the veggie grab box (p. 28) and pop a veg or two in their lunchbox for both morning tea and lunch. Including a variety of veggies at as many mealtimes as you can throughout the day can take the pressure out of dinner, when children are often tired and are likely to refuse them. Try cherry tomatoes, carrot, capsicum or celery sticks, or even snow peas or green beans as snack options, and include salad fillings such as lettuce, grated carrot and cucumber in sandwiches. Some kids love homemade dips and deconstructed or leftover salads (p. 185), and these can help with enjoyment and acceptance of veggies.

4 Provide fresh fruit
Whole fruit is a more satisfying, nutritious and high-fibre option than juice or processed fruit snacks, plus it's lower in sugar and energy than dried fruit. Fruit that is local and in season is most likely to be cheapest, tastiest and most nutritious. Mix up the fruits you offer in lunchboxes by using sliced apples, whole bananas, mandarins, orange wedges, berries or whatever else is in season and in your fruit grab box.

5 Include water as a drink
Pack frozen water bottles or add ice cubes to their drink bottle if your child prefers colder water – especially on hot days. Try to avoid juices, cordials and soft drinks.

a note about 'sometimes foods'

Consistently providing healthy, varied foods at home and in lunchboxes means there is always room for 'sometimes foods'. These are things like popcorn, crackers, chips and other pantry staples that are eaten around more nutritious foods. They also include sweeter home-baked goods, such as those in the sweet baking box list on p. 30, flavoured yoghurts and milk, and mini chocolate bars. These offer another source of energy for active kids who are always hungry and growing fast. We like to buy these in larger packets to then distribute into containers or the smaller sections of bento-style lunchboxes. It reduces plastic waste and litter and supports the nude-food movement at schools. 'Sometimes foods' are an important part of normal eating and also help to prevent your children from feeling 'lunchbox envy'.

If this is new to you, or your child prefers the same food prepared in the same way every day, give yourself a little time to find your new groove and a balance between what they love, what they're learning to love and what you'd like them to love! You can transition slowly and stretch them sensitively.

incorporating lunch orders

If your school canteen offers lunch orders and your budget allows for them, they can be a fun part of the weekly, monthly or term lunchbox routine. We do love a Friday lunch order for an end-of-week break, but you may prefer a Monday or mid-week order and then use that day to get organised or catch up. Most schools have some nice nutritious options and it's a good opportunity for kids to try something new. Enjoying food they have chosen is a positive meal experience and we are all for that.

appetite for lunchboxes

How much food to pack in lunchboxes is a question we're asked often. Every child is different in terms of how much food they eat at school. Some love a little of many options, while others enjoy fewer options and some are in between. Referring to our simple 'Build a healthy lunchbox' checklist (p. 31), offering all the food groups across morning tea and lunch, and offering varied meals and snacks at home, will ensure you are doing everything you can to give your child an array of nutritious foods, regardless of how much or little gets eaten.

- If their lunchbox consistently comes back empty: check in with your child and see if they have enough to eat. It might be that you are packing just the right amount, or they may request an extra item or two. Growth spurts and developmental leaps also influence their appetite. We find rainy days, where they sit inside to eat, good days to pack a bit extra as they have time to eat without the rush to run out and play.
- If their lunchbox is half-eaten: are the same types of foods coming back uneaten? Are the sandwiches becoming soggy? Do the carrots take too long to chew? Is there too much food? Try varying how the veggies are offered – ensuring they are easy to eat – modifying the sandwich fillings and perhaps reducing the quantity just slightly for a few days.
- If their lunchbox is regularly untouched: too much food can be overwhelming for some children – or sometimes, after sitting down in the classroom for a while, they just want to run and play when the bell rings. Perhaps reduce the quantity and variety each day but still maintain variety throughout the week, allow them a say in which foods are packed, and prepare their food so it's easy to eat and enjoy. If they begin to eat more, slowly add more.

time-saving lunchbox hacks

Along with fruit, veggie and baking boxes, there are plenty of ways to reduce the time spent packing lunchboxes. Here are a few of our favourites:

- Pack lunchboxes the evening before, as you are preparing dinner. If you have many school-aged children or don't have the fridge space available, even just packing morning tea at night can save a heap of time in the morning.
- Invest in quality airtight, leak-proof containers or bento-style lunchboxes, and you can pack two days' worth of lunchboxes in advance. Crackers and even apples will stay crisp and fresh when prepared and stored correctly.

- Reheat leftovers until they are hot and pop them in a thermos for children's lunches. Ideas include Butter chicken and rice (p. 93), Melt-in-your-mouth meatballs and pasta (p. 146), Fast-prep pasta bake (p. 173), Hoisin and ginger beef meatballs with hokkien noodles (p. 160) and Cheat's lamb moussaka (p. 142).

lunchbox food safety

If you are out and about with your baby and toddler often, or sending older children off to preschool or school with a packed lunch, it can be natural to worry about food safety and food poisoning.

Bacteria responsible for causing food poisoning grow between 5–60°C. Keeping cold food cold and hot food hot will prevent the growth of harmful bacteria. By packing your child's lunchbox or snack box appropriately, you can continue to offer them all your home-cooked delights without the worry of food poisoning.

Our tips for packing a food-safe lunchbox:

- Make sure you have clean hands when handling food.
- Keep your child's lunchbox in the fridge until you need to leave the house.
- Invest in an insulated lunchbox or cooler bag to help maintain a safe temperature.
- Pack a small frozen bottle of water or ice pack in your child's lunchbox next to the food that needs to be kept cold.

- Include items that do not need to be kept cold or require reheating.
- Use a thermos or a lunchbox that has a section to keep foods hot.
- At the end of the day be sure to throw out any perishable food that doesn't get eaten.

Refer to our safe food preparation and storage tips on p. 19 for more information.

pick 'n' mix bulk biscuits

Everyone needs a bulk biscuits recipe that churns out perfect biscuits in record time. This recipe makes more than 80, so choose from a range of toppings to keep them interesting in the lunchbox rotation, or simply roll out logs of the dough for the freezer for impromptu playdates or unexpected guests.

makes **80+ biscuits**
prep time: **15 minutes**
cooking time: **12 minutes**

500 g unsalted butter, chopped
⅔ cup (150 g) caster sugar
395 g tin sweetened condensed milk
5 cups (750 g) self-raising flour
Toppings e.g. strawberry jam,
    chocolate chips, Smarties, rainbow
    sprinkles, sultanas

Preheat the oven to 160°C (140°C fan-forced) and line 2 or more baking trays with baking paper.

Using an electric mixer, beat together the butter and sugar for 5 minutes or until light and fluffy.

Add the condensed milk and beat for 1 minute or until well combined.

On a low speed add the flour ½ cup (75 g) at a time until combined into a soft dough.

Roll mixture into walnut-sized balls and flatten slightly. To make jam drops, press your thumb into the centre of each biscuit and fill with ½ teaspoon of jam. For all other toppings sprinkle on top and gently push into the biscuits. Excess dough can be shaped into logs (20 cm long × 4 cm wide), rolled in baking paper and placed in the freezer.

Bake for 12 minutes or until lightly golden. Allow to cool on the baking tray for 10 minutes before serving.

TIME-SAVING TIP: if you don't have time to make all the biscuits, roll some of the dough into logs and freeze in baking paper. Simply pull the logs out when you need them, slice into 1 cm rounds, top with your favourite toppings and bake.

NOTE: depending on how many biscuits you are cooking you may need to cook in two batches.

STORAGE: keep in an airtight container for up to 5 days. To freeze, place the cooled biscuits in a freezer-proof bag or your baking box (p. 28) for up to 2 months. Raw dough can be frozen for up to 3 months.

ALLERGIES/INTOLERANCES:
Gluten/wheat: use gluten-free flour.
Dairy: try coconut oil or a light-flavoured olive oil instead of the butter. Use condensed coconut milk.

overnight muesli banana muffins

A muffin mix you can make as much of as you want, whenever you want – for breakfast or afternoon tea, or perhaps as a snack before bed. The wonderful thing about this recipe is that the muffin mix can be made in advance and kept in the fridge for up to 4 days. Or you can bake all the muffins at once and stash them in the freezer for lunchboxes.

makes **24**

prep time: **15 minutes +**
    overnight soaking

cooking time: **25 minutes**

1¾ cups (190 g) untoasted muesli mix
    (or rolled oats)

1 cup (150 g) wholemeal
    self-raising flour

1 cup (150 g) self-raising flour

2 ripe bananas

⅓ cup (80 ml) honey or
    pure maple syrup

2 eggs

2¼ cups (560 ml) milk

3 teaspoons pure vanilla extract

¾ cup (180 ml) extra virgin olive oil
    (light-flavoured if preferred)

1 cup (150 g) frozen berries

Place the muesli and flours in a medium bowl and mix to combine.

Place the bananas in a medium bowl and mash with a fork. Add the honey, eggs, milk, vanilla and oil and mix well to combine.

Make a well in the centre of the dry ingredients, pour in the wet ingredients and berries and gently mix with a wooden spoon to combine. Cover and place in the fridge overnight, or for at least 2–3 hours, to allow the oats to soften and create a creamy consistency.

When ready to cook, preheat the oven to 200°C (180°C fan-forced) and line 2 × 12-hole regular muffin tins with paper cases. Fill the cases with ⅓ cup of the mixture, or ¼ cup of the mixture to make smaller, toddler-sized muffins.

Bake for 20–25 minutes or until the muffins are golden brown and the tops spring back when touched. Allow to cool slightly before transferring to a cooling rack. The muffins are best eaten while warm.

STORAGE: store the uncooked muffin mixture in an airtight container in the fridge for up to 4 days. Alternatively, simply cook all the mixture. Keep muffins in an airtight container at room temperature for up to 3 days, or in the freezer for up to 2 months.

NUTRITION NOTE: please use maple syrup if you are offering the muffins to babies under 12 months.

TIP: feel inspired and mix and match the recipe to your own flavour preferences with a combination of oats and dried or fresh fruits, or try out some different muesli flavours for variety.

ALLERGIES/INTOLERANCES:
Gluten/wheat: use a gluten-free muesli and gluten-free flour.
Egg: use 2 'chia eggs' (p. 21) or add an extra overripe banana in place of the eggs. Dairy: use your preferred dairy-free milk. Nuts: choose a nut-free muesli.

There is a formula to making a frozen smoothie bag that ensures a perfectly balanced fruit-to-veggie ratio while also guaranteeing that creamy texture. In other words, this filling and nutritious snack will give you the benefits of hidden veg with the sweet and creamy flavours of the fruit and yoghurt! These are our top three flavoured bags that can be adapted to include whatever you have available. Freezing any fruit that is starting to turn in the fruit bowl is a great way to keep your smoothie bags full.

frozen smoothie bags

makes **1½ cups (375 ml)**
prep time: **5 minutes**
blend time: **1 minute**

frozen smoothie formula

We have chosen our favourite smoothie combinations for you to try but you can also experiment with your own combinations.

Liquid: add this to your blender first to help with a smooth blend. Use around 1–1½ cups of milk or water to blend with your smoothie ingredients. Try mixing up your liquid choice with options such as coconut milk, almond milk or pure fruit juice. You can use more or less depending on the consistency you enjoy.

Fruit: choose 1 cup of chopped frozen fruit as the base flavour for your smoothie. We love using frozen banana as a base to create that classic, creamy smoothie consistency.

Vegetables: including veggies in your smoothie is a great idea for added nutrients. Use mild-flavoured green vegetables, which are often undetectable in smoothies. We love zucchini, baby spinach and kale.

Nutritious thickeners: we love a thick, creamy texture for our smoothies. You can add fillings that are nutritious without having an overpowering flavour. Ingredients such as pure peanut butter, seed butters, almond butter, chia seeds, flaxseeds, rolled oats or plain Greek-style yoghurt are all great options – just add 1 tablespoon.

Sweeteners: if you choose a sweet fruit base you often won't need sweeteners. If you do need to add a little sweetness we love to use pitted dates, honey, maple syrup, vanilla extract or cinnamon.

Texture: if you have a child who appreciates a little texture, you can top your smoothies with a complementary ingredient. We love topping our smoothies with coconut, toasted muesli premix (p. 73) or grated chocolate.

Continued →

choc-peanut

Combine the banana, avocado, cacao or cocoa, peanut butter and rolled oats in a freezer-proof bag. Freeze for up to 2 months.

To make the smoothie, pour the milk into the blender, add the dates and top with the frozen ingredients. Blend for 1 minute or until smooth and creamy.

½ frozen banana, chopped
¼ avocado, roughly cubed
2 teaspoons unsweetened cacao or cocoa powder
1 tablespoon pure peanut or seed butter
1 tablespoon rolled oats
2 pitted dates
1 cup (250 ml) your preferred milk, or more to taste

mango tango

Combine the banana, mango and zucchini in a freezer-proof bag. Freeze for up to 2 months.

To make the smoothie, pour the milk into the blender then add the yoghurt and honey. Top with the frozen ingredients. Blend for 1 minute or until smooth and creamy.

½ frozen banana
1 cup (170 g) frozen mango chunks
¼ zucchini, roughly chopped
1 cup (250 ml) your preferred milk, or more to taste
½ cup (125 g) plain Greek-style or vanilla yoghurt
1 tablespoon honey (omit for babies under 12 months)

mixed berry

Combine the banana, mixed berries, spinach and peanut butter in a freezer-proof bag. Freeze for up to 2 months.

To make the smoothie, pour the milk into the blender and top with the frozen ingredients. Blend for 1 minute or until smooth and creamy.

½ frozen banana
1 cup (150 g) frozen berries
½ cup (10 g) baby spinach
1 tablespoon pure peanut or seed butter
1 cup (250 ml) your preferred milk, or more to taste

BUSY FAMILIES TIP: while we love to advise sitting down and enjoying a mindful meal, this isn't always possible. Busy families are often rushing here, there and everywhere from dawn till dusk and it's important to fuel growing bodies with convenient, nutritious food. Smoothies are a great way to ensure that nutrition still stays on track.

ALLERGIES/INTOLERANCES: Gluten/wheat: omit the oats. Dairy: use your preferred dairy-free milk and yoghurt or water. Nuts: omit the peanut butter and try a seed butter instead.

no-bake 'snickers' slice

An energy-dense little snack packed full of seeds and nuts that tastes amazing straight from the freezer. We love any opportunity to pack our snacks full of whatever added goodness may be on hand. Keeping your fridge and freezer well stocked with homemade snacks means little hands will reach for more nutritious items.

makes **16–24**
prep time: **15 minutes**
chilling time: **10 minutes**

15 pitted dates
¼ cup (25 g) cacao or cocoa powder
½ teaspoon pure vanilla extract
¼ cup (60 ml) pure maple syrup
2 tablespoons pure peanut butter
1 cup (140 g) crushed peanuts,
    plus extra to sprinkle
¼ cup (20 g) shredded coconut,
    plus extra to sprinkle

optional
¼ cup (30 g) flaxseed meal
¼ cup (45 g) chocolate chips
pinch of salt
¼ cup (35 g) chocolate melts, melted

Line a 20 cm square cake tin with baking paper. Place the dates, cacao or cocoa, vanilla, maple syrup and peanut butter in a food processor and process until well combined. Add all of your chosen remaining ingredients (except the melts) and, using the pulse button, process until finely chopped and well combined, while leaving some texture.

Press the mixture into the prepared tin and sprinkle with extra crushed nuts and coconut. Drizzle with melted chocolate if desired. Alternatively, roll the mixture into walnut-sized balls.

Place in the freezer for 10 minutes or until firm. Cut into squares to serve.

NUTRITION NOTE: this grab-and-go snack is perfect for active kids. Serve alongside some veggie sticks, fruit, cheese and wholegrain crackers to make a nutritious snack platter if you're feeding a crowd. Our hummus (p. 56) would be a great addition too.

NOTE: if your kids love this slice you can always double the recipe and roll half the mixture into balls for a change of texture.

STORAGE: keep in an airtight container or a freezer-proof bag in the freezer for up to 2 months.

ALLERGIES/INTOLERANCES:
Dairy: omit the chocolate chips and melted chocolate. Nuts: try a mix of sunflower seeds or pepitas as a substitute for the crushed peanuts. Omit the nut butter or use seed butter or tahini as an alternative.

lemon zucchini cake

For morning tea from the lunchbox, or for afternoon tea when they are ravenous, many children love eating sweet loaves and cakes. The great news is that children are usually also very accommodating when it comes to healthy ingredient swaps, such as the addition of wholemeal flours and veggies. Packed with flavour and some hidden veggie goodness, this cake will keep little tummies fuller for longer.

Preheat the oven to 180°C (160°C fan-forced). Grease 2 × 21 cm × 10 cm loaf tins (base measurement) and line with baking paper.

In a large bowl, sift the flours, then add cinnamon, salt and brown sugar and mix to combine. Add the zucchini, sultanas and coconut. Mix well to combine.

In a separate medium bowl, whisk together the eggs, lemon zest, vanilla and oil.

Add the wet ingredients to the dry and stir to combine. Pour into prepared tins. Bake for 45–50 minutes, until golden brown and a skewer inserted into the centre comes out clean.

Allow to cool in the tins for 10 minutes before transferring to a wire rack to cool completely.

Meanwhile to make the icing, sift the icing sugar into a medium bowl and drizzle in enough lemon juice to reach your preferred consistency. Spread the icing over one of the cakes and allow to set. Sprinkle with extra coconut and lemon zest if desired. Leave to set, then slice and serve.

Wrap the remaining loaf in baking paper and/or foil and store in the freezer for up to 3 months.

makes **2 loaf cakes**
prep time: **20 minutes**
cooking time: **45–50 minutes**

1 cup (150 g) self-raising flour
1 cup (150 g) wholemeal
   self-raising flour
2 teaspoons ground cinnamon
pinch of salt
1 cup (200 g) brown sugar,
   lightly packed
3½ cups (500 g) coarsely grated
   zucchini, excess liquid squeezed out
   (about 4 zucchini)
1 cup (160 g) sultanas
1 cup (100 g) moist coconut flakes
4 eggs
1½ tablespoons finely grated lemon zest
2 teaspoons pure vanilla extract
1 cup (250 ml) light-flavoured
   extra virgin olive oil, or melted
   coconut oil

lemon icing (for one cake)
1 cup (160 g) icing sugar, sifted
1–1½ tablespoons lemon juice
extra coconut flakes or lemon zest,
   to garnish (optional)

FUSSY EATING TIP: peel all or some of the zucchini, and either omit the sultanas or replace them with grated pear or apple if sultanas aren't a favourite.

TIPS: you can substitute desiccated or shredded coconut for coconut flakes; however, reduce the quantity to ¾ cup (60 g).

When it's time to enjoy the frozen loaf cake, thaw in the fridge or on the kitchen bench and serve dusted with icing sugar as a simple alternative to preparing another batch of icing. Or serve simply as it is! You can use 19 × 9 cm tins if that is what you have. If you only have one tin, cook one loaf at a time, or try some muffins, baking for 20–25 minutes in muffin tins lined with paper cases.

ALLERGIES/INTOLERANCES:
Gluten/wheat: use gluten-free flour. Egg: substitute the eggs with commercial egg replacer, 4 'chia eggs' (p. 21) or 2 large overripe mashed bananas.

STORAGE: keep in an airtight container on the bench or in the fridge for up to 5 days, or in the freezer for up to 3 months.

spelt *and* sunflower biscuits

These are a simple butter biscuit with a few easy substitutions to add extra nutritional value to snack times and lunchboxes, while the Smarties, choc chips or sprinkles keep kids interested and engaged. If you have the time and ingredients, this is a great recipe to double or triple to make enough to store in the freezer.

F
V

makes **25**
prep time: **15 minutes**
cooking time: **18 minutes**

½ cup (75 g) sunflower seeds
125 g unsalted butter, softened
¾ cup (150 g) brown sugar,
    lightly packed
1 egg
1 cup (150 g) plain spelt,
    white or wholemeal flour
½ teaspoon baking powder
pinch of salt
100 g Smarties, choc chips or
    sprinkles

Preheat the oven to 180°C (160°C fan-forced) and line a baking tray with baking paper.

Place the sunflower seeds in the bowl of a food processor and process to a fine meal. Set aside until ready to use.

Place the butter and sugar in the bowl of an electric mixer and beat until light and creamy. Add the egg and mix until well combined.

Add the flour, sunflower seed meal, baking powder and salt and mix until just combined.

Roll level tablespoons of mixture into balls, place on the prepared baking tray and flatten slightly. Place a few Smarties or a pinch of choc chips or sprinkles on each biscuit. Bake for 18 minutes or until golden.

Allow to cool for a few minutes on the baking tray before transferring to a wire rack to cool completely.

NUTRITION NOTE: for younger toddlers who aren't yet interested in or don't care for Smarties or choc chips, add some extra seeds such as sunflower, sesame, chia and/or pepitas for colour and interest.

STORAGE: keep in an airtight container for up to 5 days or freeze in a freezer-proof bag for up to 3 months.

ALLERGIES/INTOLERANCES:
Gluten/wheat: use gluten-free flour.
Egg: substitute the egg for 1 'chia egg' (p. 21), ¼ cup (75 g) apple puree or 1 overripe banana. Dairy: try coconut oil or a light-flavoured olive oil instead of the butter.

Sweet and snacky, our avocado and ricotta pikelets are a nutrient-packed source of energy for active kids. Feel free to reduce or omit the sugar if topping the pikelets with sweet spreads such as maple syrup, honey or jam.

Place the avocado, ricotta, milk, egg and sugar in a food processor or blender and process until smooth. Transfer to a mixing bowl.

Sift in the flour and stir until just combined.

Heat a large frying pan over medium heat and add a little butter and olive oil. The olive oil will prevent the butter from burning.

Spoon heaped tablespoons of batter into the frying pan and cook the pikelets in batches, for 2–3 minutes on each side.

Enjoy warm or cold and spread with a little butter, extra ricotta, cream cheese, jam or nut butter.

avocado *and* ricotta pikelets

makes **10**
prep time: **10 minutes**
cooking time: **15 minutes**

1 small (200 g) ripe avocado, flesh chopped
½ cup (120 g) smooth ricotta
½ cup (125 ml) milk
1 egg
1 tablespoon sugar (optional)
1 cup (150 g) self-raising flour
1 tablespoon unsalted butter
1 tablespoon extra virgin olive oil
extra butter or ricotta, cream cheese, jam or nut butter, to serve

FUSSY EATING TIP: there's usually a reason why kids don't like a particular food. It could be the colour, the texture, the taste or the smell. Incorporating this food in recipes with other foods they do like can help a child to become more familiar with it. For example, chopped avocado in a banana or fruit smoothie adds to the cold creaminess they enjoy – especially if the banana or avocado has been frozen. A ripe avocado can also be used in place of butter or oil in your favourite banana bread or muffin recipe. Another winning tip is to spread a little avocado instead of butter on Vegemite toast or sandwiches.

WASTE-REDUCING TIP: if you have an overripe avocado or one that you know you won't eat, chop the flesh and freeze in an airtight container or small reusable freezer bag for up to 3 months. Defrost at room temperature for an hour and use for these pancakes, in smoothies, on sandwiches or mashed on toast.

STORAGE: keep in an airtight container in the fridge for up to 3 days. Alternatively, layer with baking paper and store in an airtight container in the freezer for up to 2 months.

ALLERGIES/INTOLERANCES:
Gluten/wheat: use gluten- or wheat-free flour. Egg: replace the eggs with 1 'chia egg' (p. 21) or a mashed overripe banana. Dairy: omit the ricotta; you might like to try replacing it with an overripe banana instead. Use a dairy-free milk, adding a little extra to replace the ricotta if you have simply omitted it.

rice bubble *and* seed mini bars

Satisfy appetites with this lunchbox-friendly slice that is easily frozen, adapted and enjoyed. Mix and match the seeds, sticking with just sunflower seeds and no dried fruit if your kids have a preference for white or more plain-coloured foods, and slowly incorporate new ingredients once they become more familiar with them.

makes **28**
prep time: **10 minutes**
cooking time: **20 minutes**

½ cup (125 ml) pure maple syrup
½ cup (140 g) tahini or
   sunflower seed butter
1 cup (35 g) Rice Bubbles
½ cup (45 g) rolled oats
¼ cup (20 g) desiccated coconut
¼ cup (35 g) sunflower seeds
⅓ cup (35 g) pepitas
½ cup (80 g) sultanas, or choc chips
   or chopped pitted dates (optional)

Preheat the oven to 180°C (160°C fan-forced). Line a 22 cm square cake tin with baking paper, extending up two sides.

Place the maple syrup and tahini or sunflower seed butter in a large mixing bowl and stir until well combined. Add the remaining ingredients, including any preferred optional extras, and mix until well combined.

Spoon the mixture into the prepared tin and press with the back of a spoon to evenly distribute. Bake for 20 minutes, or until golden. Allow to cool for 10 minutes in the tin before transferring to a wire rack to cool completely. Slice into small rectangles and serve.

MEAL PLANNING TIP: to reduce wastage of your seeds, and to use them more in your everyday cooking and baking, decant into small jars or airtight containers and keep them together in your pantry or cupboards. This allows you to easily take stock of what you have and to ensure you don't have multiple opened packets of the same seeds floating around your kitchen.

FUSSY EATING TIP: if tahini is a new flavour for the kids, try substituting half of the tahini for butter.

STORAGE: keep in an airtight container in the fridge for up to 5 days, or in the freezer for up to 3 months.

ALLERGIES/INTOLERANCES:
Gluten/wheat: use gluten-free Rice Bubbles and either additional Rice Bubbles or quinoa flakes instead of the rolled oats.
Sesame: use sunflower seed butter.

chocolate *and* kidney bean cupcakes

Highly nutritious red kidney beans add a wonderful texture to these muffins without compromising the taste. Plus who doesn't love a little extra nutrient boost in their child's lunchbox?

makes **12**
prep time: **15 minutes**
cooking time: **25 minutes**

400 g tin red kidney beans,
    drained and rinsed
¼ cup (60 ml) extra virgin olive oil,
    or melted coconut oil
2 eggs, lightly beaten
2 tablespoons natural or
    plain Greek-style yoghurt
⅓ cup (80 ml) pure maple syrup
1 teaspoon pure vanilla extract
½ cup (75 g) wholemeal plain flour or
    ⅔ cup (70 g) almond meal
¼ cup (25 g) cacao or cocoa powder
½ teaspoon baking powder
¼ teaspoon bicarbonate of soda
pinch of salt
natural or plain Greek-style yoghurt,
    to serve (optional)
fresh berries, to serve (optional)

Preheat the oven to 160°C (140°C fan-forced) and line a 12-hole cupcake tin with paper cases.

In a food processor, puree the kidney beans, olive oil, eggs and 2 teaspoons of water for approximately 5 minutes until smooth. This will also aerate the mixture.

Pour in the yoghurt, maple syrup and vanilla and process for about 30 seconds to combine. Scrape the sides of the bowl when necessary.

Add the flour or almond meal, cacao or cocoa powder, baking powder, bicarbonate of soda and salt. Process until just combined.

Spoon the mixture evenly among the cupcake cases. Bake for 25 minutes or until a toothpick inserted into the centre of a cupcake comes out clean.

Allow cupcakes to cool before turning out on a wire rack. Serve with your favourite yoghurt and fresh berries.

NUTRITION NOTE: legumes are delicious, versatile, economical and satisfying. High in slow-release carbohydrates, protein and fibre, they also offer a range of health-promoting nutrients, making these cupcakes a great addition to snack times and lunchboxes.

STORAGE: keep in an airtight container in the fridge for up to 3 days or wrap individually in plastic film and store in an airtight container in the freezer for up to 3 months.

ALLERGIES/INTOLERANCES:
Gluten/wheat: use gluten-free flour or almond meal. Use a gluten-free baking powder. **Egg:** replace the egg with 1 chia or linseed egg (p. 21) or ¼ cup (75 g) apple sauce or puree. **Dairy:** use coconut or dairy-free yoghurt.

banana, apple *and* cinnamon loaf

Everyone loves banana bread, but how about trying something a little different? Transform the popular flavour combination of apple and cinnamon into this tasty loaf. Perfect for morning tea with friends, or as a little treat in the lunchbox. Try spreading with some ricotta and honey for a wholesome morning snack.

makes 1 loaf
prep time: 15 minutes
cooking time: 1 hour

3 ripe bananas, mashed
   (1½ cups mashed)
¼ cup (60 ml) pure maple syrup
¼ cup (60 ml) milk
1 teaspoon apple cider vinegar
2 eggs
½ cup (125 ml) extra virgin olive oil
2 teaspoons pure vanilla extract
2 cups (300 g) wholemeal plain flour
½ cup (110 g) caster sugar
1 teaspoon baking powder
1 teaspoon ground cinnamon
pinch of salt
3 cooking apples, peeled, diced
   into 1 cm cubes (or grated for
   younger children)

topping (optional)
2 tablespoons rolled oats
1 tablespoon brown sugar
40 g unsalted butter, melted

Preheat the oven to 170°C (150°C fan-forced). Grease a 22 × 11 cm loaf tin (base measurement) and line with baking paper.

In a large bowl mix together the mashed banana, maple syrup, milk, apple cider vinegar, eggs, olive oil and vanilla extract.

Add the flour, sugar, baking powder, cinnamon and salt. Stir until just combined. Gently fold through the apple pieces. Pour the mixture into the loaf tin and sprinkle with the combined topping mixture, if using.

Bake for 1 hour, or until a skewer inserted into the centre comes out clean. Allow to cool for 10 minutes in the tin before transferring to a wire rack to cool completely. Slice and enjoy.

STORAGE: store the loaf in an airtight container in the fridge for up to 3 days. To freeze, we like to cut the loaf in half and wrap each half in baking paper and foil. Freeze for up to 2 months.

FOOD WASTAGE TIP: got a bunch of bananas turning brown? Never fear! This is the best time to use them in your baking treats. If you aren't quite ready to bake, simply peel and chop the banana and place in a freezer-proof bag. You can use the frozen banana pieces in smoothies, or when you're ready to make this wonderful slice just blitz the frozen banana in a blender.

ALLERGIES/INTOLERANCES:
Gluten/wheat: use a gluten-free plain flour. **Egg:** try 2 'chia eggs' (p. 21) as a substitute for the eggs or 2 additional overripe bananas. **Dairy:** use your preferred milk. Use coconut oil instead of the butter or omit the topping.

These irresistible cheesy lunchbox rolls are a true crowd-pleaser and so simple to make. There's no proving time to worry about, and with only two ingredients you'll find yourself coming back to this recipe time and time again. What's more, they can of course be frozen and popped into the lunchbox for a perfectly thawed snack come lunchtime. We have included three topping ideas to get you started, but the possibilities are endless.

Preheat the oven to 190°C (170°C fan-forced) and line a large baking tray with baking paper.

To make the dough, place the flour and yoghurt in a large bowl and mix until just combined. Gently knead on a floured surface until it forms a sticky dough. Roll into a ball and rest for 5 minutes.

Flour a clean surface and divide the dough evenly into 8 balls. Arrange the balls on the baking tray and flatten to 5-cm-wide rounds, spaced so they are just touching. Choose your pick 'n' mix topping and top the rolls starting with any sauce, then the cheese and finishing with meat or herbs. Bake for 20 minutes or until lightly golden. Transfer to a wire rack to cool slightly. Serve immediately.

pick 'n' mix cheesy lunchbox rolls

makes **8**
prep time: **15 minutes**
cooking time: **20 minutes**

1⅔ cups (250 g) self-raising flour
1 cup (250 g) plain Greek-style yoghurt
chosen topping ingredients
    (see below)

cheese and bacon
1½ cups (180 g) grated cheddar
    cheese
3 rashers short-cut bacon,
    finely chopped

barbecue salami
2 tablespoons salt-reduced
    barbecue sauce
1½ cups (180 g) grated cheddar
    cheese
4 slices (100 g) mild Danish salami,
    finely chopped

margherita
2 tablespoons no-added-salt
    pizza sauce
1½ cups (180 g) grated cheddar cheese
small handful of torn basil leaves,
    or 1 tablespoon dried basil

FUSSY EATING TIP: try adding some sliced baby spinach, chopped mushrooms, olive halves, fresh herbs, diced capsicum (pepper) or pineapple to any of the pick 'n' mix basics to encourage a bit of variety.

STORAGE: store rolls in an airtight container in the fridge for up to 2 days. To freeze, allow to cool completely, then wrap the rolls individually in plastic film and place in a freezer-proof bag for up to 2 months.

ALLERGIES/INTOLERANCES:
Gluten/wheat: use a gluten- or wheat-free flour as appropriate.
Dairy: use a dairy-free plain yoghurt and omit the cheese, or choose a dairy-free alternative. Make a regular, yeast-risen pizza dough.

spinach *and* cheese 'croissants'

Spinach and cheese pastries are a fan favourite and none more so than these, because they are so quick and easy to prepare. We highly recommend you make a double batch so you have a freezer stash up your sleeve.

makes **8**
prep time: **15 minutes**
cooking time: **30 minutes**

120 g baby spinach leaves
⅓ cup (80 g) smooth ricotta
½ cup (60 g) grated cheddar cheese
2 sheets (25 cm × 25 cm) frozen
     puff pastry, just thawed
1 egg, lightly beaten

Preheat the oven to 200°C (180°C fan-forced) and line a baking tray with baking paper.

Place the spinach in a heatproof bowl and pour over some boiling water. Stand for 20 seconds, to wilt. Drain the spinach, rinse under cold water and squeeze out the excess liquid. Finely chop.

Place the spinach in a small mixing bowl with the ricotta and cheddar and stir until well combined.

Halve each pastry sheet then cut each piece diagonally in half so you have 8 long triangular strips of pastry. Place a heaped tablespoon of filling at the widest end of each strip and roll up to enclose.

Place the pastries on the prepared tray and brush with the egg. Bake for 25 minutes, or until puffed and golden.

MEAL PLANNING TIP: try these little pastries with whatever you might have on hand, such as some roast pumpkin, baked beans or leftover bolognese. Alternatively, for a sweet snack, swap out the spinach for some chopped berries and the cheese for a sprinkle of cinnamon or drizzle of maple syrup.

STORAGE: keep leftovers in an airtight container in the fridge for up to 2 days. Cooked and uncooked croissants can be stored in an airtight container, layered with baking paper if required, in the freezer for up to 2 months.

ALLERGIES/INTOLERANCES:
Gluten/wheat: use gluten-free pastry or try the filling as a toasted sandwich using gluten- or wheat-free bread. Egg: brush the pastries with milk instead of the egg. Dairy: substitute the ricotta for medium tofu, drained and mashed, and substitute the cheddar cheese for a dairy-free alternative. For a cheesier flavour you might also like to add a teaspoon of nutritional yeast to any dairy-free version.

pork *and* caramelised apple sausage rolls

We've sealed the deal on these pork sausage rolls by adding a sweet apple mixture to bring them to life. The kids will enjoy these as a cold sandwich alternative in lunchboxes or as a hot weekend lunch. Plus we love to have them waiting in the freezer ready to be cooked for unexpected guests.

F

makes **18**
prep time: **20 minutes**
cooking time: **50 minutes**

1 tablespoon unsalted butter
1 brown onion, finely chopped
100 g streaky bacon, finely chopped
    (optional)
2 cooking apples, peeled and
    diced into small (1 cm) cubes
1 tablespoon brown sugar or
    maple syrup
½ teaspoon fennel seeds
500 g free-range pork mince
1 tablespoon chopped thyme
3 sheets (25 cm × 25 cm) frozen
    puff pastry, just thawed
1 egg, lightly beaten
1 tablespoon sesame seeds (optional)
salt and ground black pepper

Melt the butter in a small saucepan over medium–low heat. Add the onion, bacon (if using) and apple and cook for 3–4 minutes or until softened. Sprinkle over the brown sugar or maple syrup and 1 tablespoon of water and toss to coat. Add the fennel seeds and cover the pan. Cook, stirring often, for a further 10 minutes or until the apple is soft. Set aside to cool. Roughly mash with a potato masher to break up the apple.

Preheat the oven to 200°C (180°C fan-forced) and line a large baking tray with baking paper.

In a large bowl, combine the pork mince, thyme and apple mixture. Season with salt and pepper.

Cut each pastry sheet in half. Place ⅙ of the mixture running lengthways down one of the pastry strips, moulding it to form a long sausage shape. Brush the edges of pastry with water and fold over to enclose the filling. Cut into 3 pieces (or more, depending on your chosen portion sizes) and place on the lined tray, seam side down. Repeat with the remaining mixture and pastry. You can freeze the sausage rolls at this point.

Brush the egg over the tops of the sausage rolls, then sprinkle with the sesame seeds, if using. Bake for 35 minutes or until golden brown and cooked through.

TIP: cooked sausage rolls make a great addition to your savoury baking box.

STORAGE: keep in an airtight container in the fridge for up to 2 days. Alternatively, freeze cooked or uncooked sausage rolls in individual portions, wrapped in plastic film, for up to 2 months.

ALLERGIES/INTOLERANCES:
Gluten/wheat: use gluten-free pastry.
Egg: brush the pastry with your preferred milk instead of the egg.
Dairy: use olive oil instead of butter.
Sesame: simply omit or use poppy seeds as an alternative.

hummus
and **cheese crackers**

Many children love to dip! Homemade veggie- and legume-based dips are a nutritious option and a fabulous and non-confronting way to introduce a range of flavours and textures to kids. You can further boost your dips by serving them with veggie sticks or our homemade cheesy crackers, or as a spread on sandwiches.

makes **1½ cups (375 g)**
prep time: **10 minutes**

400 g tin chickpeas, drained,
    liquid reserved
1 clove garlic, finely chopped
1 tablespoon tahini
1 lemon, juiced
1 tablespoon olive oil
pinch of ground cumin (optional)
salt and ground black pepper, to
    taste (optional)

hummus

In a food processor, combine the chickpeas, garlic, tahini and lemon juice. Blend to combine and scrape down the sides. Continue to blend, slowly adding the olive oil until the mixture has a smooth and creamy consistency. If more liquid is required use a small amount of the reserved chickpea liquid. Season to taste, if desired.

NUTRITION NOTE: store-bought crackers are a convenient choice for snacks and lunchboxes. Try choosing wholegrain varieties and opt for those with a lower sodium content.

STORAGE: hummus can be stored in an airtight container in the fridge for up to 5 days. To freeze, store in individual airtight containers for up to 2 months. Thaw in the fridge overnight and blend to aerate before serving.

TIP: not sure what else to use tahini for? Try our delicious Roast cauliflower and chickpea salad (p. 200) or the Rice Bubble and seed mini bars (p. 46) to use up the rest of the jar.

ALLERGIES/INTOLERANCES: Sesame: omit the tahini and use a nut or seed butter.

cheese crackers

Preheat the oven to 180°C (160°C fan-forced) and line 2 large baking trays with baking paper.

In a food processor combine the flour, baking powder and butter. Using the pulse button, process in short bursts until the mixture has the consistency of breadcrumbs. Add the cheese, pulse a few times and then add the water if needed to form a soft dough. Add the seeds, if using, and pulse a few times until evenly combined.

Turn dough out onto a lightly floured bench and knead for a few minutes. Shape into a 30 cm long log, wrap in baking paper and refrigerate for 30 minutes.

Use a sharp knife to slice the dough into 5 mm thick rounds. Place 3 cm apart on the baking trays. Bake for 15 minutes or until lightly browned. Cool on the baking trays.

makes **50–60 crackers**
prep time: **15 minutes +**
    30 minutes chilling
cooking time: **15 minutes**

1 cup (150 g) plain flour
2 teaspoons baking powder
½ cup (125 g) unsalted butter, chopped
2 cups (240 g) grated cheddar cheese
½ cup (75 g) mixed seeds* (optional)
*We love using pepitas, sunflower seeds, sesame seeds and poppy seeds

dairy-free crackers

Preheat the oven to 180°C (160°C fan-forced) and line 2 large baking trays with baking paper. Combine the nutritional yeast, garlic powder, salt, wholemeal four and polenta in a food processor and process until well combined. Add the olive oil and pulse until fine crumbs form. Add the cold water slowly, pulsing until the mixture just forms a dough.

Turn dough out onto a lightly floured bench and form the dough into a disc. Use a rolling pin to roll the dough out to a large rectangle about 5 mm thick. Use a 3 cm cookie cutter to cut round pieces of dough. Place onto prepared trays and prick the centres with a fork. Bake for 15 minutes or until puffed and golden. Store in an airtight container for 2 days or freeze for up to 2 months.

makes **50–60 crackers**
prep time: **15 minutes +**
    30 minutes chilling
cooking time: **15 minutes**

3 tablespoons nutritional yeast
½ teaspoon garlic powder
½ teaspoon salt
1 cup (160 g) plain wholemeal flour
¼ cup (40 g) polenta
¼ cup (60 ml) olive oil
¼ cup (60 ml) cold water

STORAGE: store the biscuits in an airtight container for up to 5 days. Freeze flat in layers with baking paper in between in freezer-proof bags for up to 2 months.

ALLERGIES/INTOLERANCES:
Gluten/wheat: use a gluten-free flour.

tuna *and* pesto balls

A nutritious snack for young and old, these tuna balls can be added to any fruit and veg plate for busy kids alongside mayonnaise, aioli or a sweet chilli dipping sauce if they like to dip. Save some for the freezer too, and try them tossed through a simple tomato and basil pasta sauce (p. 173) with cooked pasta for an easy weeknight dinner.

F

makes **20**
prep time: **15 minutes**
cooking time: **10 minutes**

2 × 185 g tins tuna in oil, drained
1 cup (70 g) fresh breadcrumbs
¼ cup (65 g) homemade (see tip) or good-quality store-bought basil pesto
1 egg
¼ cup (60 ml) extra virgin olive oil
whole-egg mayonnaise, aioli or sweet chilli sauce to serve (optional)

Place the tuna, breadcrumbs, pesto and egg in the bowl of a food processor and pulse until combined. Roll level tablespoons of the mixture into balls.

Heat the oil in a frying pan over medium–high heat. Add the tuna balls in batches and cook, turning, for 3 minutes or until golden. Drain on paper towel and serve warm with your preferred condiment.

MEAL PLANNING TIP: to make your own basil pesto combine 1 cup (45 g) basil leaves, ½ cup (40 g) finely grated parmesan cheese, ⅓ cup (50 g) pine nuts, ½–1 clove garlic, crushed, and ½ cup (125 ml) extra virgin olive oil in a blender or food processor and process until smooth. Boost your own homemade version with some broccoli stems, spinach or kale leaves, if you like. Transfer to an airtight container or glass jar, cover with a little extra virgin olive oil and store in the fridge for up to 1 week. Alternatively, spoon the pesto into ice-cube trays, top each with a little extra olive oil, cover and freeze for up to 3 months. Pesto is a fabulous and tasty emergency ingredient to serve with pasta alongside scrambled eggs, tinned tuna or as an addition to a quick cheese and leftover lamb (p. 226) toasted sandwich.

NOTE: to bake the tuna and pesto balls, toss them in a tablespoon or two of olive oil, place on a baking tray lined with baking paper and bake in a preheated 180°C (160°C fan-forced) oven for 12–15 minutes, until golden brown.

STORAGE: keep cooked tuna balls in the fridge for up to 2 days or in the freezer for up to 2 months. Alternatively, flash freeze (p. 20) uncooked tuna balls and store in an airtight container in the freezer for up to 2 months.

ALLERGIES/INTOLERANCES:
Gluten/wheat: use gluten-free bread to make breadcrumbs. Egg: try 1 'chia egg' (p. 21) as a substitute for the egg. Nuts: use a nut-free pesto or make your own using sunflower seeds.

bright and colourful snack platters offer a fun and engaging way to share food

rainbow rice salad

The tanginess from the simple dressing and pops of sweetness from the currants will dispel any doubt you have about a brown-rice salad. We love prepping this salad in advance and adding it to lunchboxes for a sandwich alternative. Plus you can use any leftover veggies to create a veggie grab box (p. 28), and enjoy watching the household veggie consumption rise.

serves **8**
prep time: **15 minutes**
cooking time: **30 minutes**

1 cup (200 g) brown rice, rinsed
3 spring onions, finely chopped
½ cup (80 g) currants
1 small red capsicum (pepper), finely diced
1 carrot, finely diced or grated
2 celery stalks, finely chopped
½ cup (70 g) slivered almonds or chopped flaked almonds, lightly toasted (optional)
¼ cup (35 g) sunflower seeds, lightly toasted
¼ cup finely chopped flat-leaf parsley

dressing

1 tablespoon salt-reduced soy sauce
1 tablespoon lemon juice
1 teaspoon extra virgin olive oil
½ clove garlic, crushed

Cook the rice according to packet instructions.

Once the rice has cooled, toss through the remaining ingredients. Stop here to freeze in small portions.

For the dressing, place all ingredients in a small bowl and mix well to combine. Pour over the salad right before serving.

NUTRITION NOTE: given it has more vitamins and nutrients than white rice, and much more texture and flavour, there's a lot to love about brown rice. We love using it in our salads, but if your kids aren't convinced you can always try half brown rice and half white rice as you build up acceptance.

NOTE: if packing for work or school lunches, be sure to keep your salad fresh with a well-fitting ice pack for food safety.

SAFETY NOTE: consider your child's age and eating ability when offering this salad to your family. The diced carrot and celery and the nuts may pose a choking hazard. Please omit and adapt if necessary.

STORAGE: the salad can be kept in an airtight container in the fridge for up to 3 days. To freeze, assemble the salad (without the dressing) and freeze in airtight containers for up to 2 months.

ALLERGIES/INTOLERANCES:
Gluten/wheat: use a gluten-free soy sauce or tamari. Nuts: omit the almonds.

veggie noodle muffins

Want a lunchbox recipe that's guaranteed to be eaten? We bet that, when the lunch bell rings, sitting down and eating a time-consuming meal isn't your child's number-one priority. These irresistible little noodle muffins are a great way to satisfy hungry tummies, and easy enough to eat that kids can simply munch and go!

makes **18**
prep time: **15 minutes**
cooking time: **30 minutes**

2 × 85 g packets instant noodles
(omit flavouring sachets)
3 eggs
420 g tin corn kernels, drained
(or kernels cut from 2 corn cobs)
1 zucchini (courgette), grated
1 carrot, grated
3 spring onions, finely chopped
¼ cup flat-leaf parsley, finely
chopped
1½ cups (180 g) grated cheddar
cheese

Preheat the oven to 180°C (160°C fan-forced). Grease 2 × 12-hole regular muffin tins.

Break the instant noodle blocks into quarters and place in a large bowl. Cover with boiling water and let stand for about 5 minutes, until soft. Drain well and use kitchen scissors to cut noodles into smaller pieces.

Add the eggs, corn, zucchini, carrot, spring onion, parsley and 1 cup (120 g) of cheese. Stir to combine.

Divide the mixture evenly into the prepared tins and sprinkle with the remaining cheese.

Bake for 30 minutes or until golden and set. Remove from the oven and allow to cool slightly before serving warm, or transfer to a wire rack to cool completely.

TIP: if you don't have any instant noodles in the pantry you can try another affordable noodle such as dried rice vermicelli.

STORAGE: keep in an airtight container in the fridge for up to 2 days, or layer in an airtight container with baking paper and freeze for up to 3 months.

ALLERGIES/INTOLERANCES:
Gluten/wheat: substitute an equal amount of gluten-free noodles such as rice vermicelli. Egg: substitute the eggs for 100 g firm tofu, drained and mashed. Dairy: omit the cheese. For a cheesy flavour you might like to add a teaspoon of nutritional yeast.

ham *and* sweetcorn tartlets

To be enjoyed for lunch or as a satisfying snack, these delicious savoury tartlets are perfect to pop into a snack box for your outdoor adventures.

(F)

makes **24**
prep time: **20 minutes**
cooking time: **25 minutes**

420 g tin creamed corn
1 cup (120 g) grated cheddar cheese
150 g sliced ham, chopped
2 eggs, lightly beaten
½ cup (125 ml) milk or cream
2 tablespoons chopped chives
salt and ground black pepper,
    to taste (optional)
6 sheets (25 cm × 25 cm) frozen
    puff pastry, just thawed

Preheat the oven to 200°C (180°C fan-forced) and generously grease 2 × 12-hole regular muffin tins.

Place the creamed corn, cheese, half the ham, the eggs, milk or cream and chives in a medium bowl and mix until combined. Season to taste, if desired.

Use a 10 cm round pastry cutter to cut 24 rounds from the pastry. Place into the prepared muffin tins. Spoon filling evenly into the pastry cases and top with remaining ham.

Bake for 20–25 minutes, or until the pastry is golden brown and crisp and the filling has set. Remove from the oven and cool for 5 minutes before removing from the tins.

Serve warm (or at an appropriate temperature for your child) on a tasting plate with a serve of veggies and/or fruit.

NUTRITION TIP: when buying ham or bacon, it's always best to choose an Australian free-range and nitrate-free variety. Ask your butcher or local deli.

MEAL-PLANNING TIP: if your kids love these tartlets and love ham, try to transition them to other leftover sliced meats such as chicken or lamb when they're available. Or try a spinach and corn option as a more nutritious vegetarian alternative, including ham just sometimes.

STORAGE: keep in an airtight container in the fridge for up to 2 days, or layer in an airtight container with baking paper and freeze for up to 3 months.

ALLERGIES/INTOLERANCES:
Gluten/wheat: use gluten-free pastry. **Egg:** substitute the eggs with 200 g firm tofu, rinsed, wrapped in a tea towel and drained under a heavy plate or chopping board to remove excess liquid. Blend the tofu with the milk and process until smooth. **Dairy:** use a dairy-free milk in place of the milk or cream. **Vegetarian:** swap the ham for some chopped baby spinach or peas.

A quick and flavourful rissole for finger-food lovers, perfect for a midweek dinner or nutritious lunch. Prep smaller-sized patties for babies and toddlers and larger-sized ones to be included in burgers with some lettuce, tomato and cheese, and cranberry sauce for adults.

cheesy turkey *and* sage patties

makes **24**
prep time: **20 minutes**
cooking time: **15 minutes**

Pick the sage leaves, reserving the smaller ones to garnish the tops of the patties if you like. Finely chop the remaining leaves to get about 2½ tablespoons.

Place the turkey, eggs, onion, oats, cheese, Worcestershire sauce, carrot, zucchini and chopped sage in a large mixing bowl. Season and, using clean hands, mix well, until evenly combined.

Using a ¼ cup (60 ml) measure, scoop the mixture and roll into rounds. For smaller children, measure 1½ tablespoons of the mixture to create smaller patties. Place onto trays and flatten to 1–1.5 cm thick. Press the reserved small sage leaves on top of the patties if you like.

Set aside a portion for the freezer (see storage notes).

Heat the olive oil in a large frying pan over medium–high heat. Working in batches, add the patties and cook for 2–3 minutes on each side or until golden brown and cooked through.

Delicious served with cranberry sauce or chutney, steamed vegetables or wrapped inside a crunchy iceberg or cos lettuce leaf.

1 small bunch sage
1 kg turkey mince
2 eggs
1 small brown onion, coarsely grated
1 cup (90 g) rolled oats
1 cup (120 g) grated cheddar cheese
2 tablespoons Worcestershire sauce
1 small (70 g) carrot, coarsely grated
1 small (90 g) zucchini (courgette), coarsely grated
salt and ground black pepper, to taste
2 tablespoons olive oil
cranberry sauce or chutney, to serve (optional)

TIME-SAVING TIP: it takes a whole lot of stress out of the afternoon or night if you can spare 10 minutes to prepare the turkey mixture before work or during 'nap time'. All you need to do is roll the mixture into patties and drop them into a hot pan. If you are super short on time, and don't require a large quantity or need a freezer stash, halve the ingredients and prepare a smaller quantity.

STORAGE: keep any cooked patties in an airtight container in the fridge for up to 2 days. Flash freeze (p. 20) uncooked patties and store in the freezer for up to 2 months.

ALLERGIES/ INTOLERANCES:
Gluten/wheat: use gluten-free breadcrumbs instead of the oats and a gluten-free Worcestershire sauce. Egg: use an egg-replacer or 2 'chia eggs' (p. 21). Dairy: omit the cheese or use a dairy-free cheese if preferred.

crispy baked pork *and* prawn wontons

If you love crispy wontons and dumplings but don't want to fiddle around with deep-frying, these are for you. Satisfy your cravings quickly with this easy recipe.

makes **50**
prep time: **40 minutes**
cooking time: **10 minutes**

300 g free-range pork mince
100 g prawn meat
2 cloves garlic, finely chopped
1 carrot, coarsely grated
1 golden or red shallot, finely sliced
1 tablespoon oyster sauce
2 teaspoons soy sauce
½ teaspoon sesame oil
2 teaspoons cornflour
large pinch of white pepper
2 × 300 g packets wonton wrappers,
    or 2 × 275 g gow gee wrappers
spray oil or canola oil
sweet chilli sauce, mayonnaise or
    soy sauce, to dip

Preheat the oven to 200°C (180°C fan-forced). Line 2 large baking trays with baking paper.

Combine the pork mince, prawn meat, garlic, carrot, shallot, oyster and soy sauces, sesame oil, cornflour and pepper in a large bowl. Using clean hands, mix until evenly combined.

Lay out half of the wrappers on a clean bench and place a heaped teaspoon of filling into the centre of each. Slightly moisten the edges with water and fold them over to encase into triangles, then moisten one corner and fold the triangle corners together to form a wonton shape. Place the wontons onto the prepared trays in a single layer, leaving a little room between each. Repeat with the remaining filling and wrappers.

Generously spray wontons with oil (or gently toss in a drizzle) to coat. Bake for 10 minutes or until crispy and golden.

Serve with your preferred dipping sauce.

MEAL-PLANNING TIP: if you have time on your hands and a house full of dumpling lovers, we highly recommend preparing a double batch! Making the dumpling mixture in advance gives you a head start, and a few little helping hands *might* make the assembly line easier too.

STORAGE: keep leftovers in an airtight container in the fridge for up to 2 days. Alternatively, uncooked wontons can be stored in the freezer, layered with baking paper, for up to 2 months. Wrap and freeze any leftover wonton or gow gee wrappers for later use.

ALLERGIES/INTOLERANCES:
Gluten/wheat: gluten-free wrappers are difficult to find, so perhaps try your hand at making some homemade wrappers using gluten-free flour. Use gluten-free soy and oyster sauce. Egg: double-check the ingredient list on your wonton or gow-gee wrappers to see if they contain egg. Vegetarian: omit the pork mince and prawn meat and substitute with extra-firm tofu, pressed and drained. Use a vegetarian oyster sauce.

premixes

Preparing a premix is the perfect kitchen hack for the busy baker. It's a fantastic way to cut your baking prep time in half and reduce clean-up. No organised pantry is complete without a premix! You can make your own in next to no time with wholesome ingredients and none of the additives or preservatives.

So what exactly is a premix? It's a bulk combination of the dry ingredients that a recipe calls for. When you're ready to bake you simply measure out the required amount, add the wet ingredients and go. For example, if you've tripled a recipe's dry ingredients and mixed them well, you can then scoop out a third of the mixture when you want to make one serve. Premixes are perfect for simple recipes with high quantities of dry ingredients that you know you'll love and make over and over again.

Cooking with kids: we all know that cooking with kids is great for giving them hands-on exposure to foods in a fun environment, away from the pressure of the dinner table. But sometimes children's limited attention spans, along with their knack for making a huge mess, can make us cringe just thinking about this. Premixes are a fantastic way to involve children in the exciting parts of baking (mixing, cracking eggs, scooping into tins) while containing the chaos and keeping them engaged.

Storage: premixes last best when stored in a cool, dry space out of direct sunlight, such as in your pantry. Any airtight container will do – try using large glass canisters, pyrex containers, plastic Tupperware-style boxes or reusable ziplock bags, and see what works best for you. Just make sure there's enough space to give the premix a good shake prior to measuring. We recommend labelling the container with the name of the recipe, the date that you created the premix and the additional ingredients needed, plus the page number of the recipe so it's easy to locate. This will make your baking as quick and easy as possible when you're in a hurry.

Time-saving tip: when dealing with larger quantities of ingredients, such as flour and oats, we find it quicker to weigh them rather than to measure with cups. This also increases accuracy and reduces the amount of equipment needed (and therefore clean-up!).

Prep ahead tip: if you don't have the storage space for large quantities of premixes, next time you're baking, keep an airtight container to the side and measure a second set of the dry ingredients into it. It will be ready and waiting the next time you need a lunchbox or playdate snack in a pinch.

A note on measuring: these recipes have been triple-tested in our home kitchens with our families, but it's important to keep in mind that if you find the final batch of your premix has a little more or less of the quantity you need, don't worry! Our recipes are very forgiving and you will be able to make small adjustments, if needed, with the liquids that you add to ensure the batter has the right consistency.

breakfast oats four ways

Waking up to a nourishing breakfast premix is one of the quickest and healthiest ways to start the day. The beauty of this premix is its versatility – it can be used for a huge variety of breakfast options to suit all tastes and preferences, without compromising on flavour or nutrition.

makes **8 ⅔ cups (950 g) premix**
prep time: **5 minutes**

To prepare the premix, combine the ingredients in a large bowl and mix well. Store in a large airtight container in a cool, dry space in the pantry for up to 2 months.

oat premix
6 cups (540 g) rolled oats
1 cup (115 g) roughly chopped nuts, such as almonds, walnuts, pecans, macadamias
1 cup (160 g) mixed seeds, such as pepitas or sunflower seeds
½ cup (80 g) chia seeds or flaxseeds
1 tablespoon ground cinnamon
¼ cup (55 g) brown sugar (optional)

NUTRITION NOTE: packed with nuts and seeds, this delicious oaty mix is bursting with complex carbohydrates, fibre, omega-3 fatty acids and antioxidants. This is the kind of slow-release energy that will fuel busy little bodies.

SAFETY NOTE: for babies and toddlers, nuts can be a choking hazard, so please finely crush any nuts you may be using.

ALLERGIES/INTOLERANCES:
Gluten/wheat: use quinoa flakes in place of the oats.

stovetop porridge

serves 2–3
prep time: **5 minutes**
cooking time: **5 minutes**

Place the oat premix in a small saucepan and add the milk, along with 1 cup (250 ml) water.

Add the mashed banana and cook over medium heat, stirring, for 5 minutes or until the oats have softened and the milk is almost absorbed. Add a little more milk or water if the mixture is too thick.

Serve with your choice of toppings.

1 cup (110 g) oat premix,
    mixed well prior to measuring
1 cup (250 ml) milk
½ banana, mashed (optional)
fresh berries, stewed or pureed fruit,
    crushed nuts or seeds, drizzle of
    maple syrup or honey, and/or
    yoghurt, to serve (optional)

STORAGE: leftover porridge can be stored in an airtight container in the fridge for up to 2 days.

ALLERGIES/INTOLERANCES:
Gluten/wheat: use quinoa flakes in place of the oats. Dairy: use your preferred dairy-free milk alternative; either omit the yoghurt or use a coconut or soy variety. Nuts: omit the nuts and add extra seeds, if desired.

simple toasted muesli

makes **3 cups (375 g)** /
    approx. **10 serves**
prep time: **5 minutes**
cooking time: **20 minutes**

Preheat the oven to 160°C (140°C fan-forced) and line a large rimmed baking tray with baking paper.

In a large bowl, combine the oat premix, oil, vanilla and maple syrup. Mix well to evenly coat.

Place the mixture on the prepared tray and spread evenly. Bake for 10 minutes then give the tray a shake and bake for a further 5–10 minutes, checking at 3 minute intervals, until toasted to your liking.

Allow to cool and serve with milk or yoghurt.

3 cups (330 g) oat premix,
    mixed well prior to measuring
2 tablespoons macadamia oil or
    melted coconut oil
1 teaspoon pure vanilla extract
1 tablespoon pure maple syrup
milk or plain Greek-style yoghurt,
    to serve

STORAGE: keep muesli in an airtight container for up to 10 days.

ALLERGIES/INTOLERANCES:
Gluten/wheat: use quinoa flakes in place of the oats. Dairy: use your preferred dairy-free milk alternative; either omit the yoghurt or use a coconut or soy variety. Nuts: omit the nuts and add extra seeds, if desired.

Continued →

makes **9**
prep time: **10 minutes**
cooking time: **25 minutes**

2½ cups (275 g) oat premix,
mixed well prior to measuring
1 teaspoon baking powder
1 cup (250 ml) milk
¼ cup (60 ml) pure maple syrup
1 egg, lightly whisked
1 tablespoon olive oil or melted
coconut oil
1 teaspoon pure vanilla extract
¼ cup (40 g) sultanas, optional
½ cup (75 g) fresh or frozen
blueberries
¼ cup (40 g) chopped walnuts,
pecans or macadamias (optional)
1 teaspoon brown sugar (optional)
milk or plain Greek-style yoghurt,
to serve (optional)

baked porridge squares

Preheat the oven to 180°C (160°C fan-forced) and line a 23 cm (base measurement) square slice tin with baking paper.

Place the oat premix, baking powder, milk, maple syrup, egg, oil, vanilla and sultanas (if using) in a large bowl and mix well to combine.

Spread the mixture evenly into the prepared tin and top with blueberries and chopped nuts (if using). Gently press the mixture down with the back of a spoon or spatula. Sprinkle with the brown sugar, if desired.

Bake for 20–25 minutes or until the batter is golden brown and springs back to the touch. Allow to cool in the tin, then cut into squares. Serve with milk or yoghurt, or on their own for breakfast-on-the-run.

STORAGE: keep in an airtight container in the fridge for up to 3 days, or in the freezer for up to 3 months.

ALLERGIES/INTOLERANCES:
Egg: use ½ mashed banana or 1 'chia egg' (p. 21). **Dairy:** use your preferred dairy-free milk alternative; either omit the yoghurt or use a coconut or soy variety.

serves **2**
prep time: **5 minutes +**
overnight soaking

1½ cups (165 g) oat premix,
mixed well prior to measuring
½ cup (125 ml) milk
¼ cup (70 g) plain Greek-style
yoghurt
1 small apple or pear, peeled and
coarsely grated (optional)
1 teaspoon pure maple syrup
(optional)
extra milk and/or plain Greek-style
yoghurt, almond butter or peanut
butter, fresh berries or chopped
fruit, to serve (optional)

overnight oats

Place the oat premix, milk, yoghurt, grated apple or pear and maple syrup (if using) in a bowl and mix well to combine.

Cover and place in the fridge overnight.

Divide between serving bowls and top with extra milk or plain Greek-style yoghurt, almond or peanut butter, berries or chopped fruit.

STORAGE: leftovers can be stored in an airtight container in the fridge for up to 2 days.

ALLERGIES/INTOLERANCES:
Dairy: use your preferred dairy-free milk alternative; omit the yoghurt or use a coconut or soy variety.

All the nourishing goodness of porridge wrapped up in a pancake! Whether you serve these as breakfast finger food or as a satisfying afternoon tea, everyone from babies to big kids will enjoy these tasty little snacks.

To prepare the premix, combine the ingredients in a large bowl and mix well. Store in a large airtight container in a cool, dry space in the pantry for up to 2 months.

To make the pancakes, whisk the milk, egg and half the oil in a mixing bowl. Add the pancake premix and mix until just combined. Allow the mixture to stand for 5 minutes so that the oats absorb some of the moisture.

Heat a large frying pan over medium heat and add the remaining oil. Spoon heaped tablespoons of batter into the frying pan and cook the pancakes in batches for 2–3 minutes each side until golden brown and cooked through.

MEAL-PLANNING TIP: next time you're flipping pancakes for breakfast try making a double batch. Half can then be frozen and ready to grab for a portable and wholesome breakfast or snack-on-the-go.

STORAGE: keep leftover cooked pancakes in the fridge for up to 2 days. Alternatively, layer with baking paper in an airtight container and freeze for up to 3 months.

ALLERGIES/INTOLERANCES:
Gluten/wheat: use gluten- or wheat-free flour and choose quinoa flakes instead of the oats. **Egg:** use ½ mashed overripe banana or 1 'chia egg' (p. 21). **Dairy:** use your preferred dairy-free milk alternative.

sultana oat pancakes

makes **6 batches of premix (14 pancakes per batch)**
prep time: **10 minutes**
cooking time: **15 minutes**

pancake premix
6 cups (540 g) rolled oats
½ cup (110 g) brown sugar, firmly packed
3 cups (450 g) plain flour, or wholemeal plain flour
¼ cup (55 g) baking powder
1½ tablespoons ground cinnamon
1½ cups (240 g) sultanas
½ teaspoon salt (optional)

pancake ingredients
(makes 1 batch)
1 cup (250 ml) milk
1 egg, lightly beaten
2 tablespoons olive oil or melted coconut oil
1½ cups (240 g) pancake premix, mixed well prior to measuring

single batch ingredients
1 cup (90 g) rolled oats
½ cup (75 g) plain flour, or wholemeal plain flour
1 tablespoon brown sugar
2 teaspoons baking powder
1 teaspoon ground cinnamon
¼ cup (40 g) sultanas
pinch of salt
1 cup (250 ml) milk
1 egg, lightly beaten
1 tablespoon olive oil or melted coconut oil, plus extra for cooking

fruity lunchbox muffins

These muffins are the ultimate last-minute solution for empty lunchboxes and hungry tummies. Packed with fruity goodness and lots of mix-in options, they are a good way to encourage your kids to join in the cooking and get creative with flavour combinations to see what they enjoy most!

makes **4 batches of premix (12 muffins per batch)**
prep time: **10 minutes**
cooking time: **25 minutes**

muffin premix

4 cups (600 g) plain flour
4 cups (600 g) wholemeal plain flour
2 tablespoons baking powder
2 teaspoons bicarbonate of soda
2 cups (400 g) brown sugar, lightly packed
2 teaspoons ground cinnamon
½ teaspoon salt (optional)

muffin ingredients

(makes 1 batch)

1 cup (250 ml) milk
1 egg, lightly beaten
½ cup (125 ml) olive oil or melted coconut oil
¼ cup (60 ml) pure maple syrup (optional)
2½ cups (425 g) muffin premix, firmly packed, mixed well prior to measuring
1 cup (150 g) berries (fresh or frozen)
1 apple or pear, coarsely grated
¼ cup (40 g) chopped seeds, choc chips, nuts or dried fruit (optional)

To prepare the premix, combine the ingredients in a large bowl and mix well. Store in a large airtight container in a cool, dry space in the pantry for up to 2 months.

Preheat the oven to 170°C (150°C fan-forced) and line a 12-hole regular muffin tin with paper cases.

To make the muffins, place the milk, egg, olive or coconut oil and maple syrup (if using) in a large bowl and mix well to combine. Add the premix and mix until just combined. Fold through the berries, grated fruit and any additional mix-ins. Spoon the mixture into the paper cases.

Bake for 25 minutes, or until golden brown and the tops spring back when touched. Lift out onto a wire rack to cool.

single batch ingredients

1 cup (150 g) plain flour
1 cup (150 g) wholemeal plain flour
2 teaspoons baking powder
½ teaspoon bicarbonate of soda
½ cup (100 g) brown sugar, lightly
    packed
½ teaspoon ground cinnamon
pinch of salt (optional)
1 cup (250 ml) milk
1 egg, lightly beaten
½ cup (125 ml) olive oil or melted
    coconut oil
¼ cup (60 ml) pure maple syrup
    (optional)
1 cup (150 g) berries (fresh or frozen)
1 apple or pear, coarsely grated
¼ cup (40 g) chopped seeds, choc
    chips, nuts or dried fruit (optional)

NUTRITION NOTE: using wholemeal flour is an easy way to add some extra fibre and nutrients to your muffins.

STORAGE: keep leftover cooked muffins in the fridge for up to 3 days. Alternatively, layer with baking paper in an airtight container, or add to your baking box (p. 28), and freeze for up to 3 months.

ALLERGIES/INTOLERANCES:
Gluten/wheat: use gluten- or wheat-free flour. **Egg:** use ½ mashed overripe banana or 1 'chia egg' (p. 21). **Dairy:** use your preferred dairy-free milk alternative. **Nuts:** omit the nuts.

cake *in* a mug

Feel like cake but don't want to commit to a whole one? Enter the perfectly portioned cake in a mug. Perfect for a sweet afternoon tea or as a warming dessert, and cooked in around one minute flat, this will soon become a fun family favourite that even the kids can make!

makes **9 batches of premix (1 mug cake per batch)**
prep time: **5 minutes**
cooking time: **60–80 seconds**

cake-in-a-mug premix

1½ cups (225 g) plain flour
¾ cup (75 g) almond meal
2 teaspoons baking powder
½ cup (50 g) cacao or cocoa powder
¾ cup (150 g) brown sugar, lightly packed
¾ cup (140 g) chocolate chips, plus extra to top
½ teaspoon salt (optional)

cake-in-a-mug ingredients
(makes 1 large or 2 small mug cakes)

1 tablespoon coconut oil, melted
¼ cup (60 ml) milk
½ teaspoon pure vanilla extract
½ cup (about 80 g) cake-in-a-mug premix
vanilla ice-cream, cream or custard, to serve (optional)

single serve ingredients

2 tablespoons plain flour
1 tablespoon almond meal
¼ teaspoon baking powder
2 teaspoons cocoa powder
1 tablespoon brown sugar
1 tablespoon chocolate chips, plus extra to top
pinch of salt (optional)
1 tablespoon coconut oil, melted
¼ cup (60 ml) milk
½ teaspoon pure vanilla extract

To prepare the premix, combine the ingredients in a large bowl and mix well. Store in a large airtight container in a cool, dry space in the pantry for up to 2 months.

To make the cake in a mug, place the coconut oil, milk and vanilla in one 400 ml or two 200 ml microwave-proof ceramic mugs and whisk with a fork to combine. Add the cake-in-a-mug premix to the wet ingredients and mix well, scraping any batter from the sides. Sprinkle the batter with a few extra chocolate chips, if desired.

Place in the microwave and cook on high for 60–80 seconds for the large mug, or 40–50 seconds for each of the smaller mugs, or until the cake springs back to the touch. Allow to cool for a couple of minutes and then top with ice-cream, cream or custard and enjoy warm.

FUSSY EATING TIP: occasionally enjoying 'sometimes foods' such as desserts in a positive environment, without judgement or guilt or bribery, helps children to develop a balanced and mindful approach to eating. This mug pudding encourages children to get involved in the fun, and the individual serves are a clever way to model portion control.

STORAGE: this mug cake is best enjoyed immediately while still warm.

ALLERGIES/INTOLERANCES:
Gluten/wheat: use gluten- or wheat-free flour. **Dairy:** use your preferred dairy-free milk alternative; omit the chocolate chips or replace with cacao nibs. **Nuts:** replace almond meal with the same amount of plain flour.

raspberry *and* white chocolate blondies

Blondies, also known as butterscotch brownies, are a delicious addition to parties, playdates and lunchboxes. These ones have been given a fresh and healthy twist with the addition of wholemeal flour, quinoa flakes, grated carrot and raspberries.

To prepare the premix, combine the ingredients in a large bowl and mix well. Store in a large airtight container in a cool, dry space in the pantry for up to 2 months.

TIME-SAVING TIP: grated carrots are perfect to keep in the freezer to toss straight into your baking batter and cut down on prep time (and clean-up) when you're in a hurry. Just peel and grate, then transfer to a freezer-safe bag, pressing out any extra air before sealing. Label with the quantity and date frozen – they can be stored for up to 2 months.

NUTRITION NOTE: including veggies is a great way to bulk up baked goods, as well as adding moisture and colour. Kids will barely notice the vibrant orange in this blondie mix, and it will add an extra nutritional boost to snack time.

raspberry and white chocolate blondies

Preheat the oven to 180°C (160°C fan-forced). Line a 20 cm square baking tin with baking paper, extending up two sides.

Place the egg, butter, vanilla, carrot and blondies premix in a large bowl and mix until just combined. Gently fold in the raspberries, then press the mixture evenly into the prepared tin.

Bake for 25 minutes or until golden brown and firm to the touch. Cool in the tin, then lift out and cut into 16 squares.

STORAGE: keep leftover cooked blondies in the fridge for up to 2 days. Alternatively, layer with baking paper in an airtight container, or add to your baking box, and freeze for up to 3 months.

ALLERGIES/INTOLERANCES:
Gluten/wheat: use gluten- or wheat-free flour. Egg: use half a mashed overripe banana or 1 'chia egg' (p 21). Dairy: use your preferred dairy-free milk alternative, replace the butter with melted coconut oil, and omit the chocolate chips or replace with cacao nibs or sultanas.

makes **4 batches of premix (16 blondies per batch)**
prep time: **10 minutes**
cooking time: **25 minutes**

blondie premix
3 cups (450 g) wholemeal plain flour or plain flour
2 cups (160 g) desiccated coconut
1 cup (60 g) quinoa flakes
2 cups (400 g) brown sugar, lightly packed
1 cup (190 g) white chocolate chips
½ teaspoon salt (optional)

raspberry and white chocolate blondies ingredients
(makes 1 batch)
1 egg, lightly beaten
150 g unsalted butter, melted and cooled slightly
2 teaspoons pure vanilla extract
1 medium carrot, finely grated
2 cups (330 g) blondie premix
125 g fresh or frozen raspberries

single batch ingredients
¾ cup (115 g) wholemeal plain flour or plain flour
½ cup (40 g) desiccated coconut
¼ cup (15 g) quinoa flakes
½ cup (100 g) brown sugar, lightly packed
¼ cup (45 g) white chocolate chips
pinch of salt
1 egg, lightly beaten
150 g unsalted butter, melted and cooled sightly
2 teaspoons pure vanilla extract
1 medium carrot, finely grated
1 cup (135 g) fresh or frozen raspberries

winner dinners

When the family gathers around the table for dinner it's important to focus on the experience and enjoyment of eating together. Shifting your attention away from the food being consumed can reduce any worry around what and how much is being eaten, and you can instead rest assured that you've done your job in providing a nutritious meal that includes liked foods, so everyone will be satisfied no matter what they eat.

Happy and healthy family mealtimes are so important to the social, nutritional and developmental wellbeing of your family. They provide a meaningful shared experience that contributes to a child's learning in all sorts of ways. The dinner table is not just a place to learn about food and how to eat, but is also a place to build connections with other family members and share knowledge and information.

The recipes in this section are all about saving you time and making the most of your freezer so you can get food on the table and enjoy it together with as little stress as possible. So whether there's a freezer dump bag on the menu, leftovers from the night before, or 'something made from nothing' (p. 163), you can be confident that the week will be full of varied and nutritious meals.

what a family meal looks like

A family mealtime is unique to each and every family and depends on your routine. With work commitments and after-school activities, we understand that getting the whole family to sit down together can be a challenge. A family mealtime is having at least one parent or carer sitting down to eat the same meal at the same time as the kids (even if they are only eating a small portion). If the whole family can only manage to sit down together a few times per week, or mainly on the weekend, this still provides more benefits to your child than you may think.

Here are 10 reasons why family mealtimes are so important:

1 Parents are able to role model positive eating behaviours.

2 Children learn how to eat by watching their siblings and parents eat.

3 They stimulate conversation and encourage positive family interactions.

4 There are more opportunities for parents to talk to children about good food and nutrition.

5 Children are more likely to eat nutritious home-cooked meals with healthy, natural ingredients.

6 There are more opportunities to introduce and try new foods.

7 The TV, computers, iPhones and iPads are less likely to be used as distractions.

8 They encourage mindful eating and the ability to recognise hunger and fullness cues.

9 Parents can demonstrate and teach children good mealtime manners.

10 Children have more opportunities to be involved in food preparation and/or table set-up as part of a mealtime ritual.

If mealtimes are currently full of stress and anxiety, there are some simple adjustments you can make to start changing this. While it can feel overwhelming when you're in the thick of it, taking a step back to see where the challenges lie is always helpful. The information, tips and tricks in this chapter and throughout the whole book will give you ideas and inspiration to create calmer, more joyful mealtimes. Just like getting into the groove of meal planning, change a little at a time to keep it sustainable and positive. If your kids feel safe and secure at mealtimes, this may help to lessen any anxiety, improve behaviour and increase the variety of foods they will eat and enjoy.

establish daily structure and routine

Kids thrive on structure and routine. A daily structure of 3 main meals and 2–3 satisfying snacks as well as avoiding any grazing in between can really help ensure that kids have an appetite for the food on offer. Sometimes food refusal occurs at mealtimes because they're simply not hungry, so be conscious of any mindless grazing that may be happening at other times in the day. The veggie grab box (p. 28) is a go-to option for those 'I'm hungry' moments right before dinner.

look at the big picture

It's also helpful to look at your day or week of food and nutrition as a whole. While a dinner might be simple or incorporate leftovers, or your child might have eaten very little, don't discount a well-eaten meal earlier in the day or a hearty nutritious meal cooked from scratch the previous night.

consider pre-dinner activities

A child needs to be somewhat calm, yet alert, at mealtimes to successfully process all the sensory experiences that come from food and eating. Tuning in to your child and using the few minutes before mealtimes to assess how they might be feeling and better prepare them to sit down and enjoy the food can result in happier mealtimes. Beginning your mealtime routine with a warning that dinner is coming up in a few minutes is a good place to start. If kids have been doing a quiet activity they may like to spend a few minutes on something more active, such as yoga, jumping on the trampoline, swinging on a swing or doing star jumps, which will better prepare their body and its sense of awareness for mealtimes. If kids have been out riding bikes or dancing or have been overstimulated in fast and energetic play, something more calming might be in order. Pulling out the pencils for colouring, using playdough, blowing bubbles or doing some Lego can calm and prepare their bodies for the highly sensory activity that is eating.

develop a mealtime ritual

Mealtime rituals are often underestimated. They help kids feel safe and secure and can contribute to engagement with and enjoyment of new foods and challenging textures. It may start with hand-washing, setting the table and being seated correctly with proper posture. Allowing toddlers and preschoolers as well as older children an element of choice and control through tasting plates and/or deconstructed mealtimes, and ensuring at least one familiar and liked food is on offer, can keep them calm. Tune in to and respect their hunger and fullness cues, and when the mealtime is finished, clean hands and faces, if necessary, and clear the table.

manage reluctant eaters and food jags

Almost all children go through a period of food refusal. Toddlers in particular can sometimes experience 'neophobia', a fear of new foods, and this may last longer for some than for others. After the baby days of happy food acceptance, food choices may begin to narrow and this may take you by surprise. All of a sudden children are requesting the same foods offered in the same ways day in and day out. This is called a food jag and it can be incredibly frustrating. It's important to manage food jags and, better yet, prevent them. The last thing you want is for your child to 'burn out' on any of their few accepted foods and narrow down their preferences even further.

Here are a few tips to manage and prevent food jags:

- Avoid offering the same food prepared in the same way over two consecutive days. If your child loves cucumber, offer sticks one day and slices the next. Or if they love pasta or toast, try different shapes or offer it with different sauces or spreads. Changing things slowly and sensitively is important. Our Leftovers chapter (p. 103) also provides ideas about how to transform an enjoyed meal into something slightly different.
- Offer a variety of foods in a variety of ways. Use tasting plates and deconstructed mealtimes to offer their favourite foods served alongside new ones or regularly refused ones. Allow your child to choose the foods they want to eat from what's on offer, free of pressure. The consistency and positivity of the process will be rewarding.
- Try to sensitively stretch your child if you can, to help them progress from refusing food, to choosing to pick it up, to smelling it, to taking a bite, to finally eating and enjoying it. Check out the recipe notes on the Sausage ragu (p. 126), Green chicken curry and Green chicken nuggets (p. 139), and our Marinades (p. 219) and Salads (p. 185) chapters for more on this.

have deconstructed mealtimes

We love deconstructed mealtimes for big families and families with different food preferences, and to mix up mealtimes. Deconstructed mealtimes are particularly helpful in stretching and moving kids on from a food jag. For example, if they only like plain rice or plain pasta, try serving the pasta and sauce separately from the middle of the table to everyone's preference alongside some veggies and fruit, rather than putting everything into bowls in the kitchen. Perhaps it's Fish tacos (p. 122), with the fish, tortillas, salad elements and mayonnaise all served individually in the middle of the table, allowing everyone to choose what they would like from what's on offer, and how much. If this is a new way of serving meals for you, it may take a bit of time to get used to, and if your child is a reluctant eater you might notice they choose just the cheese and taco wrap or only bits of fish. That's okay. Over time, without pressure and perhaps after asking them a few times to 'please pass the avocado', you may get a nice surprise. Once again, practice, consistency, patience and positivity are key elements to making this work.

introduce learning bowls

These are handy to have up your sleeve from time to time. Learning bowls can sit alongside a child's tasting plate, or their main plate during a deconstructed mealtime. In it you can put a teeny portion of a food or texture that is new or regularly refused. For kids who might refuse it or have a meltdown when they see it on their plate, this takes away some of the anxiety and pressure they may feel and creates some positive interest in the food. For example, you could serve a little bit of pasta and some meatballs (p. 146) alongside a tasting plate, with the elements separate to one another. Or try offering a piece of Butter chicken (p. 93) on a toothpick with the sharp end snipped off, or a spoonful of the curry sauce alongside their tasting plate of rice, veggies and fruit.

Our previous books, *One Handed Cooks: How to raise a healthy, happy eater – from baby to school age*, and *Boosting Your Basics: Making the most of every family mealtime – from baby to school age*, expand on many of these principles in greater detail with more recipe examples, strategies and advice. We recommend taking a look if these concepts interest you further.

offer a tasting plate

The tasting plate has been the backbone of our feeding principles since our kids were babies. Young children love choice and control and the tasting plate caters to this perfectly. Presenting a tasty variety of foods at mealtimes, including at least one or two that are familiar and enjoyed, is a great way to introduce new foods and flavours to young children still learning to eat. It reduces the stress and anxiety around mealtimes and provides children with choice, independence and responsibility. As a child grows, they use the experience of a tasting plate to choose varied, nutritious items from a deconstructed mealtime, and that's wonderful to watch.

To prepare a balanced, varied tasting plate, start with wholegrains, add a protein such as chicken, fish, eggs, legumes, tofu or nuts, offer at least two different vegetables – mixing up the texture day to day (see Salads, p. 185) – include a serve of fruit (see Desserts, p. 203) and offer water as a drink.

If you are at all concerned about the nutritional adequacy of your child's diet, their growth, development or wellbeing, please seek the advice of a relevant healthcare professional. See 'When to seek help' (p. 18).

meal planning winner dinners

When it comes to meal planning for busy families we like to think there are four key ways of making a meal that maximises your precious time in the kitchen. Whether you have mere minutes to make dinner or the luxury of a couple of hours, there are some simple changes you can make that will significantly help your future self. We believe it's all about meals that are either quick to prep, or meals that allow you to make leftovers, a second batch or a frozen meal to enjoy later. There are six types of winner dinners, listed below, and once you've tried them we know you won't go back! Remember that incorporating these meals into your meal-plan formula (p. 12) will help reduce the amount of time you spend cooking each week.

winner dinners

Slow cooker + dump bag

Dinner + leftovers

Batch cooking

Meals 2 ways

Tray bakes

Fast meals

slow cooker + dump bag

ONE OF OUR FAVOURITE WAYS OF UTILISING OUR PRECIOUS TIME is to make a meal fresh and prep a freezer bag of uncooked ingredients at the same time. For example, while making Butter chicken (p. 93) for dinner, you can also make a bag of the uncooked curry ingredients and freeze it. So next week, when you know that you won't have time to cook, you can defrost and dump the freezer bag into the slow cooker with little to no other prep. These recipes are perfect for busy parents who want to keep the freezer stocked with nutritious and delicious ready-to-cook meals.

While slow cooking takes many hours, it requires only a small amount of preparation time earlier in the day. Plus, cooking meat, vegetables and sauce all in one pot significantly cuts down on the washing up.

If you don't have a slow cooker, these recipes can be adapted to be simmered on the stovetop. However, we do think a slow cooker or a multi-cooker (slow cooker and pressure cooker in one) is a brilliant investment for the busy family! These recipes have been tested in both 6-litre- and 7.6-litre-capacity slow cookers.

The nutritional benefits of slow cooking:

- It may add a depth of flavour to the meal, encouraging your child to accept and enjoy it.
- It can break down parts of some foods (such as dried and soaked legumes, tough cuts of meat, starchy vegetables) that are otherwise not digestible.

- Slow-cooked meats and vegetables are often easier for young children to chew, also making them easier to digest.
- Slow cooking some vegetables, rather than eating them raw, can increase the bioavailability of some nutrients, antioxidants and natural plant chemicals, which are good for our health and wellbeing.

sweet shredded pork

We love using this pork to make pulled-pork sliders but it's also delicious in quesadillas and pastry triangles, and sprinkled over pizza bases. Check out our feed-the-masses entertainer's meal plan on p. 14 to see what other recipes work well for simple, fuss-free entertaining.

To cook the pork, combine all ingredients (excluding the pork) in the bowl of a slow cooker along with 1 cup (250 ml) water. Add the pork skin side up and submerge it as much as you can in the sauce. Cover and cook on LOW for 8 hours or until it falls apart when you begin to shred it with two forks. Check on the pork intermittently and continue moving it around to keep it submerged in the liquid.

To make the coleslaw, use a mandolin to finely slice the cabbage. Mix with the grated carrot and parsley until well combined. In a separate bowl combine the mayonnaise, apple cider vinegar, Dijon mustard and horseradish cream (if using). Season to taste. Toss the salad in the dressing until well combined. This can be made in advance and kept in the fridge for up to 2 days.

Remove the pork from the slow cooker and shred the tender meat by pulling it apart with two forks. Discard the skin and any fat. Meanwhile, set your slow cooker to reduce and allow the sauce to bubble away and thicken for 10 minutes (if your slow cooker doesn't have this setting, simmer in a saucepan to thicken). Return the pork to the sauce and toss to combine. Halve the rolls and fill with pork, coleslaw and coriander (if using).

makes **6 cups (1.4 kg) (plus a dump bag for the freezer)**
prep time: **20 minutes**
cooking time: **8 hours 10 minutes**

3 cloves garlic, chopped
½ brown onion, finely sliced
2 cinnamon sticks
1–2 star anise
½ teaspoon Chinese five spice
1 cm piece ginger, sliced
½ cup (125 ml) Chinese rice wine
2 tablespoons brown sugar
1 tablespoon pure maple syrup
¼ cup (60 ml) dark soy sauce
1 tablespoon rice wine vinegar or
    apple cider vinegar
½ lime, juiced
½ orange, zest finely grated, juiced
1 kg boneless pork shoulder, skin on
brioche bread rolls, to serve
coriander, to garnish (optional)

+dump bag ingredients
3 cloves garlic, chopped
½ brown onion, finely sliced
2 cinnamon sticks
1–2 star anise
½ teaspoon Chinese five spice
1 cm piece ginger, sliced
½ cup (125 ml) Chinese rice wine
2 tablespoons brown sugar
1 tablespoon pure maple syrup
¼ cup (60 ml) dark soy sauce
1 tablespoon rice wine vinegar or
    apple cider vinegar
½ lime, juiced
½ orange, zest finely grated, juiced
1 kg boneless pork shoulder, cut in
    half to reduce thawing time

Continued →

simple coleslaw

½ white cabbage
½ red cabbage
1 carrot, grated
handful of parsley, chopped
½ cup (125 g) whole-egg mayonnaise
1 teaspoon apple cider vinegar or
    lemon juice
1 tablespoon Dijon mustard
1 teaspoon horseradish cream
    (optional)
salt and ground black pepper, to taste

baby serve: chop 2–3 slices (25 g) of pork and combine with a smooth puree such as pumpkin or sweet potato. Using a stick blender, pulse until it reaches your desired consistency, adding a few tablespoons of water or your baby's usual milk if required. Always be very careful to serve a consistent mixture, checking for large chunks of meat within the puree.

toddler serve: serve a small amount (30 g) of chopped pork with some cooked rice, either in a small bowl or as a tasting plate alongside some steamed vegetables and fruit.

FRUGAL TIP: 2 kg pork shoulder is often on sale at major supermarkets. Purchase the meat on sale, and cut it in half to make this meal and an accompanying dump bag for the freezer.

DUMP BAG PREPARATION: place the dump bag ingredients in an airtight container or freezer bag with air expelled. Freeze for up to 2 months.

TIP: you can freeze this without the pork, to add fresh when ready to cook your prepared dump bag.

TO THAW: place the dump bag in the fridge for 24 hours, ensuring the contents have fully thawed before adding to the slow cooker. Large cuts of meat need longer to completely thaw.

TO COOK: add the entire dump bag contents into the bowl of the slow cooker and follow the method from step 1.

STORAGE: keep shredded pork in an airtight container in the fridge for up to 2 days. Alternatively, freeze flat in a resealable freezer bag for up to 2 months. Simply snap off amounts of the shredded pork to use as desired.

ALLERGIES/INTOLERANCES:
Gluten/wheat: choose gluten- or wheat-free rice wine and tamari instead of dark soy sauce. Use gluten-free rolls or serve with rice. **Dairy:** choose a dairy-free mayonnaise and omit the horseradish cream. **Vegetarian:** replace the pork with Asian-style mushrooms, Asian greens, sweet potato or tofu.

A popular curry for families, butter chicken can be introduced to your baby from 6–7 months of age, once they are established on first tastes. It includes a variety of mild spices and is very flavourful but does not have the heat to deter young children. Regular exposure, along with familiar foods in a pressure-free mealtime environment, will help encourage more reluctant eaters.

butter chicken

For the onion and spice mix, melt the ghee in a heavy-based saucepan over medium–low heat. Add the onion and sauté for 5 minutes or until softened, being careful not to brown too much. Add the garlic and ginger and sauté for a further minute.

Add all the spices, and salt, if using, along with ½ cup (125 ml) water to the saucepan and stir for 3–5 minutes until fragrant and the mixture resembles a paste. Lower the heat and add a touch more water if the spices start to burn or stick to the bottom of the pan. Turn off the heat and allow the mixture to cool slightly.

Transfer half the mixture (approximately a heaped ½ cup) into a slow cooker. Set the remaining onion and spice mixture aside to prepare the dump bag.

Add the tomato paste, passata, coconut milk or cream and chicken to the slow cooker and mix well. Cover and cook on LOW for 4 hours, or on HIGH for 2 hours.

Turn off the heat, stir through the lemon or lime juice (if using) and serve with basmati rice, naan bread or roti, yoghurt and some steamed greens.

serves 6–8 (plus a dump bag for the freezer)
prep time: 25 minutes
cooking time: 2 or 4 hours 10 minutes (depending on slow-cooker setting)

1 tablespoon no-added-salt tomato paste
¾ cup (200 g) passata
270 ml tin coconut milk or cream
1 kg chicken thigh fillets, cut into 2.5 cm pieces

onion and spice mixture

(halve the ingredients if preparing only the fresh version and not the dump bag)
⅓ cup (80 g) ghee
2 small brown onions, finely chopped
8 cloves garlic, crushed
5 cm piece ginger, finely grated
1½ tablespoons garam masala
1 tablespoon ground cumin
1 tablespoon ground turmeric
3 teaspoons paprika
3 teaspoons ground coriander
1 teaspoon ground cinnamon
1 teaspoon kashmiri chilli powder (or a mild chilli powder), to taste (optional)
1 teaspoon salt (optional)

Continued →

+dump bag ingredients

1 tablespoon no-added-salt tomato paste

¾ cup (200 g) passata

270 ml tin coconut milk or cream

1 kg chicken thigh fillets, cut into 2.5 cm pieces

to serve

2 tablespoons lemon or lime juice (optional)

basmati rice, naan bread or roti

Greek-style yoghurt (optional)

steamed green vegetables

baby serve: chop, mash or blend the curry, stir through some rice and spoon feed to your baby. Mash through some additional vegetables if you wish, such as pumpkin, sweet potato, broccoli or carrot. Offer some finger-food fruit and vegetables.

toddler serve: serve the curry with some rice in a bowl. Alternatively, deconstruct it by keeping the rice and curry separate if your toddler prefers.

MEAL-PLANNING TIP: freeze portions of the leftover butter chicken and try dividing the dump bag into two smaller ones for an even larger freezer stash. Depending on the size of your slow cooker you may need to cook the half-size dump bags, once thawed, in a medium saucepan on the stovetop. Check the stovetop cooking method opposite. And if you'd like to take your meal planning to the next level, prepare a second jar of just the dry spices to make the meal and dump bag even more of a breeze next time around. Simply label 'Butter chicken spice mix' and store in your pantry.

DUMP BAG PREPARATION: place the reserved onion and spice mixture and the dump bag ingredients in an airtight container or freezer bag with air expelled. Freeze for up to 2 months.

TIP: you can freeze this without the chicken, to add fresh when ready to cook your prepared dump bag.

TO THAW: place the dump bag in the fridge overnight, ensuring the contents have fully thawed before adding to the slow cooker.

TO COOK: add the entire dump bag contents into the bowl of the slow cooker, cover and cook on LOW for 4 hours, or HIGH for 2 hours.

STOVETOP OPTION: choose a larger heavy-based saucepan to prepare the spice mixture. At step 3, remove half the onion and spice mixture to set aside for the dump bag. Add the tomato paste, passata, coconut milk and chicken to the saucepan. Bring to the boil over medium–high heat, then reduce the heat and simmer gently, partially covered and stirring occasionally, for 20 minutes or until the chicken is cooked through.

STORAGE: keep leftover cooked curry in an airtight container in the fridge for up to 2 days, or freeze for up to 2 months.

ALLERGIES/INTOLERANCES:

Dairy: in many cases ghee is compatible with a dairy-free diet, depending on tolerance, as the milk proteins and lactose have been removed. Alternatively, use coconut oil or a light-flavoured olive oil. Omit the Greek-style yoghurt.

Vegetarian: instead of the chicken use 1 head of cauliflower, chopped into florets, and a 400 g tin of chickpeas, rinsed and drained, each for both the cook fresh and dump bag portions.

mongolian lamb

Many of us know the takeaway classic Chinese-Australian 'Mongolian lamb', but do you also know how easy it can be to replicate at home? Once you've tried the irresistible sauce, you can experiment with chicken and even beef to keep this meal varied in the family favourites rotation.

serves 4 (plus a dump bag for the freezer)
prep time: 10 minutes
cooking time: 3½ hours

500 g lamb shank meat, cut into 2 cm strips
2 tablespoons cornflour
¼ teaspoon Chinese five spice
1 brown onion, finely sliced
2 cloves garlic, crushed
3 spring onions, finely chopped, plus extra to serve
2 tablespoons salt-reduced soy sauce
¼ cup (60 ml) hoisin sauce (see note)
2 tablespoons Shaoxing rice wine or mirin
1 tablespoon brown sugar
½ teaspoon sesame oil (optional)
steamed brown rice (or rice of your choice), to serve
steamed Asian greens, to serve
toasted sesame seeds, to serve (optional)

Place the sliced lamb in the bowl of a slow cooker. Sprinkle over the cornflour and Chinese five spice and toss to coat. Add all other ingredients except the sesame oil. Pour over ¾ cup (180 ml) water and stir to combine the ingredients and submerge the meat.

Cover and cook on LOW for 3½ hours. Check the meat is tender and the sauce has thickened, and cook for a further 30 minutes if required. Stir through the sesame oil if desired.

Serve with rice and steamed vegetables, and sprinkle with sliced spring onions and toasted sesame seeds if desired.

baby serve: best avoided for young babies, and only offered occasionally to young toddlers, due to the salt and sugar content of the sauce. Mash or blend a few pieces of cooked meat and stir through some rice. Spoon feed to your baby.

toddler serve: serve the lamb with some rice in a bowl. Alternatively, deconstruct it by keeping the rice and lamb separate if your toddler prefers, or even offer some of the lamb and vegetables as finger food alongside some other vegetables and fruit.

+dump bag ingredients

500 g lamb shank meat,
    cut into 2 cm strips
2 tablespoons cornflour
¼ teaspoon Chinese five spice
1 brown onion, finely sliced
2 cloves garlic, crushed
3 spring onions, finely chopped
2 tablespoons salt-reduced soy sauce
¼ cup (60 ml) hoisin sauce (see note)
2 tablespoons Shaoxing rice wine
    or mirin
1 tablespoon brown sugar

to add when cooking

½ teaspoon sesame oil (optional)

to serve

steamed brown rice (or rice
    of your choice)
steamed Asian greens
sliced spring onions, to garnish
toasted sesame seeds (optional)

MONEY-SAVING TIP: we suggest using more affordable lamb shank meat when it is readily available. As this meal is gently slow cooked you can try different meats with equally good results: chicken thighs, beef rump or sirloin, or even pumpkin for a vegetarian option.

NOTE: use a deep-coloured hoisin sauce rather than one with a lighter, more caramel colour.

DUMP BAG PREPARATION: place the dump bag ingredients in an airtight container or freezer bag with air expelled. Freeze for up to 2 months.

TIP: write any of the extra ingredients required for cooking on the dump bag.

TO THAW: place the dump bag in the fridge overnight, ensuring the contents have fully thawed before adding to the slow cooker.

TO COOK: follow the method from step 1.

STORAGE: keep leftover Mongolian lamb in the fridge for up to 2 days. Alternatively, freeze individual portions in airtight containers for up to 2 months.

ALLERGIES/INTOLERANCES: Gluten/wheat: choose gluten-free sauces. Vegetarian: try cubed pumpkin or sweet potato instead of the lamb and stir through a frozen bag of mixed Asian vegetables for the last 30 minutes of the cooking time.

coconut beef curry *with* vegetables

This is a super versatile, time-saving curry you can set in the morning and forget about until later in the day. You can serve it with your favourite veggies and use a curry paste of choice – we love korma and yellow curry paste in this one.

serves 6–8 (plus a dump bag for the freezer)
prep time: 25 minutes
cooking time: 6–8 hours

1 kg chuck or blade steak, diced
1 brown onion, diced
3 cloves garlic, finely chopped
1 tablespoon grated ginger
1 carrot, sliced
2 tablespoons mild korma or yellow curry paste
400 ml tin coconut milk
1 cup (250 ml) salt-reduced beef stock
1 tablespoon fish sauce
1 tablespoon light soy sauce
2 tablespoons brown sugar
1 large red capsicum (pepper), sliced
100 g green beans, trimmed and halved
425 g tin baby corn spears, drained and cut in half
steamed rice, to serve
coriander sprigs and chopped peanuts, to serve (optional)
sliced red chilli and lemon or lime wedges, to serve (optional)

Place the beef, onion, garlic, ginger, carrot, curry paste, coconut milk, stock, fish sauce, soy sauce and brown sugar in the bowl of a slow cooker and mix well to combine. Cover and cook on LOW for 6–8 hours, adding the red capsicum, green beans and corn spears in the last 1–2 hours of the cooking time.

Serve with steamed rice and garnish with coriander and some chopped peanuts for older children, if you like. Sprinkle with chilli and add lemon or lime wedges for adults, if desired.

baby serve: mash or blend the curry, stir through some rice and spoon feed to your baby. Omit the nuts for babies, or crush and blend to an appropriate size.

toddler serve: serve the curry with some rice in a bowl. Alternatively, deconstruct it by keeping the rice and curry separate if your toddler prefers, or even choosing some beef and vegetables to serve as finger food alongside some vegetables and fruit. Omit the nuts for young toddlers, or crush to an appropriate size.

freezer ready

+dump bag ingredients

1 kg chuck or blade steak, diced
1 brown onion, diced
3 cloves garlic, finely chopped
1 tablespoon grated ginger
1 carrot, sliced
2 tablespoons mild korma or
    yellow curry paste
400 ml tin coconut milk
1 cup (250 ml) salt-reduced beef stock
1 tablespoon fish sauce
1 tablespoon light soy sauce
2 tablespoons brown sugar

to add when cooking

1 large red capsicum (pepper), sliced
100 g green beans, trimmed and
    halved
425 g tin baby corn spears,
    drained and cut in half

to serve

steamed rice
coriander sprigs and chopped
    peanuts (optional)
sliced red chilli and lemon or lime
    wedges (optional)

MONEY-SAVING TIP: buying a lot of meat at once can be expensive. A more economical way to prepare a dump bag would be to freeze the sauces and vegetables and then buy the meat when you plan to cook and enjoy it.

DUMP BAG PREPARATION: place the dump bag ingredients in an airtight container or freezer bag with the air expelled. Freeze for up to 2 months.

TIP: write any of the extra ingredients required for cooking on the dump bag.

TO THAW: place the dump bag in the fridge overnight, ensuring that the contents have fully thawed before adding to the slow cooker.

TO COOK: follow the method from step 1.

STORAGE: keep leftover curry in the fridge for up to 2 days. Alternatively, freeze individual portions in airtight containers for up to 2 months.

ALLERGIES/INTOLERANCES:
Gluten/wheat: choose a gluten-free stock and a gluten-free soy sauce, or tamari. Check the ingredients of the curry paste for any allergens.
Nuts: omit the peanuts.

creamy garlic chicken

This irresistible creamy garlic sauce will work well with chicken, pork or veal, or for a vegetarian option use root vegetables. You can enjoy this recipe with pasta as we have suggested, or omit and serve with some steamed rice. This meal is also lovely in a thermos for keeping hungry tummies warm and full on those wintery school days.

serves **4 (plus a dump bag for the freezer)**
prep time: **20 minutes**
cook time: **2 hours 45 minutes or 5 hours (depending on slow-cooker setting)**

500 g free-range chicken breast fillets, halved
2 cloves garlic, finely chopped
2 tablespoons unsalted butter
½ leek, white part only, finely sliced
2 sprigs thyme
¼ cup (35 g) drained sun-dried tomatoes
2 cups (500 ml) salt-reduced chicken stock
1 tablespoon apple cider vinegar
2 cups (160 g) fusilli pasta
¾ cup (180 ml) cooking cream
2 cups (90 g) baby spinach leaves
½ cup (40 g) grated parmesan, to serve (optional)
crusty bread, to serve (optional)

Place the chicken, garlic, butter, leek, thyme, sun-dried tomatoes, chicken stock and apple cider vinegar in the bowl of a slow cooker.

Cover and cook on HIGH for 2½ hours or LOW for 4½ hours, or until the chicken is very tender.

Uncover briefly to stir in the pasta and cream. Cook for a further 15 minutes on HIGH or 30 minutes on LOW, or until the pasta has absorbed most of the liquid and is al dente. Stir through the spinach and turn off the slow cooker as the pasta will continue to absorb the liquid as it rests.

Serve with grated parmesan and crusty bread if desired.

baby serve: chop, mash or blend the chicken mixture, stir through a few pieces of chopped pasta and spoon feed to your baby. Mash through some additional vegetables if you wish such as pumpkin, sweet potato broccoli or carrot. Serve some pieces of soft chicken and pasta alongside as finger foods.

toddler serve: serve the chicken pasta in a small bowl alongside some steamed vegetables, bread and fruit. If you have a reluctant eater, cook some plain pasta and offer it deconstructed alongside the creamy sauce.

Continued →

+dump bag ingredients

500 g free-range chicken breast fillets, halved

2 cloves garlic, finely chopped

2 tablespoons unsalted butter

½ leek, white part only, finely chopped

2 sprigs thyme

¼ cup (35 g) drained sun-dried tomatoes

2 cups (500 ml) salt-reduced chicken stock

1 tablespoon apple cider vinegar

to add when cooking

2 cups (160 g) fusilli pasta

¾ cup (180 ml) cooking cream

2 cups (90 g) baby spinach leaves

½ cup (40 g) grated parmesan, to serve (optional)

crusty bread, to serve (optional)

WASTE-REDUCING TIP: whenever you need to open a can or jar to use just a bit of the ingredient, try to work the leftovers into the meal plan that week. We love to use the leftover sun-dried tomatoes as toppings on a lunchbox pizza.

NOTE: when cooking fresh, if time allows, you can increase the flavour by sautéing the garlic and leek in the butter for 5 minutes over a low heat.

DUMP BAG PREPARATION: place the dump bag ingredients in an airtight container or freezer bag with air expelled. Freeze for up to 2 months.

TO THAW: place the dump bag in the fridge overnight, ensuring the contents have fully thawed before adding to the slow cooker.

TO COOK: add the entire dump bag contents into the bowl of the slow cooker and continue at step 2.

STOVETOP OPTION: place the chicken, garlic, butter, leek, thyme, sun-dried tomatoes, chicken stock and apple cider vinegar in a large heavy-based saucepan. Bring to the boil then reduce the heat to low, cover and cook for 20 minutes or until the chicken is tender. Stir through the pasta and cream and additional ½ cup (125 ml) water, then cover and cook for a further 20 minutes or until the pasta has absorbed most of the liquid. Stir through the spinach and remove from the heat as the pasta will continue to absorb the liquid as it rests. Serve with grated parmesan and crusty bread if desired.

ALLERGIES/INTOLERANCES:
Gluten/wheat: use a gluten-free pasta. **Dairy:** use extra virgin olive oil instead of the butter and omit the parmesan. Instead of the cooking cream, try coconut cream. **Vegetarian:** try root vegetables such as sweet potato, and chickpeas instead of the chicken.

dinner + leftovers

OFTEN TERMED CONTINUAL COOKING, dinner + leftovers is simply making a meal and using the leftovers later in the week for a different meal. For example, you can make a Mexican-inspired beef and bean mix (p. 104) to enjoy with baked dumplings and use the remaining cooked meat a day or two later to create simple nachos (p. 106). When we use leftover meals for kids we like to create a completely different meal in either taste or texture to the one before. This means that while we are using the same base component, we are offering variety and preventing kids from becoming caught in a food jag (p. 86). By continually changing the way we offer our meals, we can stretch children's food preferences and enjoyment of food while still being able to utilise leftovers. It also means we can more easily stretch them on to less preferred foods. For example, if they love the Mexican-inspired beef as nachos, perhaps try a version using only beans or with shredded chicken. If you find they like the chicken or beans you can take it further with, say, enchiladas, or by trying the same meat with a slightly different sauce or on its own; for example, by offering some shredded Butterflied roast chicken (p. 114). Of course there are a lot of ways this can work. The trick is to start with a food you know your child enjoys and slowly vary the way you offer it to them, little by little, by changing the shape, the texture and the taste.

All of the recipes we have chosen for dinner + leftovers aim to showcase the leftovers in a new and varied way. Here are some other ideas for simple meals you can make in a busy week:

- Roast vegetable or basil pesto (p. 58) for a pasta bake, then used as a pizza sauce
- Tray-baked salmon (p. 154) for fish and chips, then stirred through a salmon pasta
- Hidden veggie sauce for meatballs and spaghetti, then used as the base for a ratatouille
- Roast or slow-cooked meats enjoyed with mashed potato, then served in a pie

mexican beef *with* dumplings + leftover nachos

Packed full of flavourful veggies and legumes, this Mexican beef will soon become a staple in your meal plan rotation. Enjoying the meal with dumplings one night and then as hearty nachos the next keeps leftovers varied and exciting.

F
DF
V
EF
GF
WF

makes ½ cup (50 g)
prep time: **5 minutes**

¼ cup (30 g) ground cumin
1 tablespoon garlic powder
1 tablespoon onion powder
1 teaspoon dried oregano
1 teaspoon smoked paprika
1 teaspoon ground coriander
½ teaspoon chilli powder (optional)
pinch of salt and ground black
    pepper

homemade mexican spice mix

Combine all of the ingredients in an airtight jar. Shake for a few seconds or until well combined. Store in the pantry for up to 3 months.

mexican beef with dumplings

Preheat the oven to 180°C (160°C fan-forced).

Heat the oil in a large frying pan over medium heat. Add the onion, garlic, celery and carrot and cook for 5 minutes or until fragrant. Add the beef and cook until brown all over, breaking it apart with a wooden spoon as you go. Sprinkle over the Mexican spice mix and stir through the beef. Stir in the corn kernels, red kidney beans, tomatoes, beef stock and tomato paste. Allow to simmer for 10 minutes or until the sauce thickens. Remove from the heat.

Meanwhile, to make the dumplings, place the flour in a bowl and rub in the butter using your fingertips until the mixture resembles fine breadcrumbs. Stir in the egg, milk, parsley, mustard and parmesan.

Remove at least 1½ cups (375 g) of beef mixture to use in the nachos.

Pour the remaining beef mixture into a 4-cup (1 litre) casserole dish. Dollop level tablespoons of the dumpling mixture onto the beef mixture. Cook for 25 minutes or until the dumplings are cooked and starting to turn golden brown.

Serve the Mexican beef with dumplings with a dollop of yoghurt, garnished with coriander if desired.

baby serve: combine ¼ cup cooked mince mixture with 1 tablespoon avocado and 1 tablespoon grated cheese, and mash or puree until you reach your desired consistency. Combine with some yoghurt or your baby's preferred milk as desired. For older babies serve with some chunks of avocado and broken up dumpling as finger food.

toddler serve: some toddlers will be perfectly happy enjoying their meal just as you enjoy yours, all together on one plate. Others may like it deconstructed with the mince, dumpling and yoghurt separate on their tasting plate with a separate bowl to mix themselves.

serves **4**

prep time: **25 minutes**
cooking time: **40 minutes**

F

1 tablespoon olive oil
1 brown onion, finely chopped
2 cloves garlic, finely chopped
2 celery stalks, finely chopped
2 carrots, coarsely grated
500 g premium beef mince
1 tablespoon Mexican spice mix
    (purchased or homemade;
    see opposite)
400 g tin corn kernels, drained, or
    2 fresh corn cobs, kernels removed
400 g tin red kidney beans, drained,
    rinsed
2 × 400 g tins no-added-salt
    chopped tomatoes
1 cup (250 ml) salt-reduced beef stock
2 tablespoons no-added-salt
    tomato paste
plain Greek-style yoghurt, to serve
    (optional)
coriander, to garnish (optional)

dumplings

2 cups (300 g) self-raising flour
100 g salted butter, roughly chopped
2 eggs, lightly beaten
½ cup (125 ml) your preferred milk
small handful flat-leaf parsley, finely
    chopped
2 teaspoons Dijon mustard
⅓ cup (25 g) finely grated parmesan

NUTRITION NOTE: making your own spice mix without additives and preservatives is as simple as shaking some spices together.

STORAGE: keep reserved mince mixture in an airtight container in the fridge for up to 2 days, or freeze for up to 2 months.

ALLERGIES/INTOLERANCES:
Gluten/wheat: use gluten-free flour.
Egg: try egg replacer or 2 'chia eggs' (p. 21) in place of the eggs.

Dairy: use a dairy-free yoghurt. Omit the parmesan and use nutritional yeast or 2 tablespoons of creamed corn. Try ¼ cup of olive oil instead of the butter. **Vegetarian:** we love using two 400 g tins of drained, rinsed brown lentils instead of the beef mince.

serves **4**
prep time: **10 minutes**
cooking time: **10 minutes**

230 g corn chips, plus extra corn chips to dip
1½ cups (375 g) leftover cooked Mexican beef (p. 104)
1 cup (120 g) grated cheddar cheese
guacamole (p. 106), to serve
sour cream, to serve (optional)

leftover nachos

Preheat the oven to 180°C (160°C fan-forced). Line a rimmed baking tray with baking paper.

Spread the corn chips over the baking tray. Spoon over the Mexican beef and sprinkle with grated cheese. Bake for 10 minutes, or until the cheese has melted and the beef is piping hot.

Serve with extra corn chips and guacamole, and sour cream if desired.

baby serve: combine ¼ cup cooked mince mixture with 1 tablespoon guacamole and mash or puree until you reach your desired consistency. Combine with some plain Greek-style yoghurt or your baby's preferred milk as desired.

toddler serve: on the tasting plate, serve the nachos separate to the guacamole and serve fresh chopped fruit on the side.

makes **1 cup (240 g)**
prep time: **5 minutes**

2 ripe avocados, diced
½ lime, juiced
pinch of salt
¼ red onion, finely diced
1 tomato, seeds removed, diced
1 tablespoon chopped coriander leaves

simple guacamole

Place the avocado, lime juice and salt in a bowl and roughly mash (alternatively, use a blender if you prefer a smooth consistency).

Stir in the onion, tomato and coriander until just combined.

GUACAMOLE STORAGE: place the avocado seed in the centre of the guacamole, cover with plastic film and keep in the fridge for up to 2 hours.

STORAGE: the nachos are best eaten straight away and any leftovers should be discarded if using leftover Mexican beef from the previous night.

ALLERGIES/INTOLERANCES:
Gluten/wheat: use gluten-free corn chips. **Dairy:** omit the sour cream or use a dairy-free version; omit the cheese.

pan-fried lemon fish ✚ creamy fish pies

serves **4**
prep time: **15 minutes**
cooking time: **30 minutes**

4 brushed potatoes, peeled and chopped into 1 cm thick chips
2 tablespoons olive oil
salt and pepper, to taste
½ cup (75 g) plain flour
600 g skinless boneless firm white fish fillets (such as flathead, snapper or barramundi)
2 tablespoons salted butter
½ cup (125 ml) cooking cream
1 lemon, halved (keep half for leftovers)
green salad, to serve

pan-fried lemon fish

Preheat the oven to 220°C (200°C fan-forced).

Toss the potato in the olive oil and spread on a baking tray, evenly spaced. Roast for 15 minutes. Turn chips and return to the oven for a further 15 minutes or until golden brown.

When the chips are almost cooked to your liking you can begin the fish. Place the flour in a shallow bowl. Cut the fish into 10 cm strips and dredge through the flour, lightly coating all over, Shake the excess flour off.

Heat 1 tablespoon of the butter in a large frying pan over medium heat. Cook the fish in batches for a few minutes each side, adding a little more butter as needed, until golden brown and cooked through. Remove from the pan.

Add the remaining butter to the pan, then pour in the cream and swirl around. Cook until bubbling and thickened slightly. Season with salt and pepper, and remove from the heat. Stir through a squeeze of lemon juice to taste. Reserve half the cooked fish fillets to use in the pies.

Serve the fish drizzled with the lemon butter sauce alongside the chips, and a green salad.

baby serve: remove some of the cooked fish and cooked potato. Mash or puree until you have your desired consistency, adding a little water or your baby's preferred milk if you require a thinner puree. Offer some whole pieces of the fish, or unsalted chips as finger food.

toddler serve: serve the unsalted chips and fish on a tasting plate with finger-food salad vegetables and fruit. Offer the sauce on the side as a 'dip'.

MONEY-SAVING TIP: choose an ethical, affordable, seasonal firm white fish that isn't too strong in flavour. This will help reduce the cost and is a good choice suitable for leftovers.

NOTE: if you aren't making this meal to allow for leftovers, simply reduce the quantity of fish to 300 g, or an amount suitable for your family.

STORAGE: this meal is best served fresh. Keep the reserved cooked fish in the fridge to use the next day.

ALLERGIES/INTOLERANCES:
Gluten/wheat: use gluten-free flour, such as rice flour, or omit. **Dairy:** omit the sauce and serve with fresh lemon juice.

Fish for leftovers? Yes, it's absolutely doable, with the right two recipes and the right kind of fish. We love to mix up this meal by choosing salmon instead of white fish, or swapping some of the fish for a few hundred grams of raw prawns. You can simply cook them the same way as the fish.

creamy fish pies

serves **4**
prep time: **15 minutes**
cooking time: **30 minutes**

Preheat the oven to 200°C (180°C fan-forced) and have 4 × 1-cup (250 ml) capacity ramekins ready.

Melt the butter in a large saucepan over medium heat. Add the leek and sauté, stirring occasionally, for a few minutes or until softened. Add the flour and cook, stirring, for 1 minute. Stir in the milk and lemon juice. Add the cream and cook, stirring occasionally, until the sauce begins to thicken. Stir through the parsley and parmesan, season with salt and pepper and remove from the heat.

To prepare the pies, create the pastry lids by lightly pressing a ramekin rim into the pastry. Cut pastry rounds 1 cm larger than the ramekin rim, to create the correct size. Divide the fish and peas among the ramekins. Pour over the sauce and then top with the pastry lids, pressing around the edges to secure.

Place the ramekins on a baking tray and bake for 20 minutes or until the pastry is golden. Serve the pies with leftover lemon wedges and a side salad.

baby serve: scoop out some of the cooked pie and mash or puree until you have your desired consistency, adding a little water or your baby's preferred milk if you require a thinner puree. Offer some whole pieces of the fish or peas as finger food.

toddler serve: serve the pie (after allowing the ramekin to cool until safe for your toddler) on their tasting plate with some finger-food salad and fruit.

2 tablespoons unsalted butter
1 leek, white part only, finely sliced
2 tablespoons plain flour
2 tablespoons milk
½ lemon, juiced
1 cup (250 ml) thickened cream
    or milk
2 tablespoons finely chopped
    flat-leaf parsley
¼ cup (20 g) finely grated parmesan
salt and ground black pepper, to taste
2 sheets (25 cm × 25 cm) frozen puff
    pastry, just thawed
300 g leftover cooked fish pieces
    (see opposite), roughly chopped
1 cup (120 g) frozen baby peas
leftover lemon wedges and salad,
    to serve

NOTE: if you are using fresh fish for this recipe simply cut into 2 cm cubes and increase the cooking time by 5 minutes or more until the fish is cooked through.

STORAGE: best served fresh when the pastry is golden and crispy. Discard any leftovers, as fish should not be reheated again. To freeze unbaked pies, wrap assembled pies in several layers of plastic film and freeze for up to 2 months.

ALLERGIES/INTOLERANCES:
Gluten/wheat: use gluten-free flour and pastry. Dairy: use olive oil instead of butter and try coconut cream or fish stock as an alternative to the milk and cream.

tray-roasted vegetable curry + leftover vegetable curry puffs

This is a tasty, child-friendly curry made all the sweeter by roasting the vegetables in this flavourful sauce. For added protein, toss through a tin of drained chickpeas at the end or serve alongside some grilled fish or halved hard-boiled eggs. Use the leftover roasted vegetables to make curry puffs. Add any leftover steamed rice to the filling for the more veggie-averse child.

serves **4–6**

prep time: **20 minutes**

cooking time: **25 minutes**

tray-roasted vegetable curry

Preheat the oven to 220°C (200 °C fan-forced). Line 2 large baking trays with baking paper.

Evenly divide the pumpkin, cauliflower, carrot, zucchini and onion between the 2 trays. Drizzle each tray with 2 tablespoons of olive oil, 1–2 teaspoons of curry powder (depending on taste preferences) and 2 teaspoons of honey or maple syrup. Toss well to combine, then spread to a single layer and bake for 20–25 minutes, turning the vegetables halfway through the cooking time.

Meanwhile, place ½ cup (125 ml) coconut milk, the garlic, ginger, extra curry powder (if using) and extra honey or maple syrup in a saucepan over medium heat. Cook, stirring, for 1–2 minutes or until fragrant. Add the soy sauce and remaining coconut milk. Simmer for 3 minutes, or until the sauce has thickened and reduced.

When the roasted vegetables are ready, set aside for a few minutes to cool slightly. Divide the spinach leaves between the trays and drizzle with the curry sauce. Toss gently to combine.

Serve one of the trays of the roasted vegetables with steamed rice and garnish with coriander. Cool the remaining tray of vegetables to use in the vegetable curry puffs.

500 g butternut pumpkin, cut into 2 cm cubes

½ cauliflower, cut into florets

2 carrots, cut in half lengthways, sliced

2 zucchini (courgettes), cut in half lengthways, sliced

1 large red onion, cut into thin wedges

⅓ cup (80 ml) olive oil

1–2 teaspoons extra mild curry powder, plus 1 teaspoon extra (optional)

1 tablespoon honey (or maple syrup for babies under 12 months), plus 2 teaspoons extra

400 ml tin coconut milk

2 cloves garlic, finely chopped

2 teaspoons grated ginger

2 teaspoons light soy sauce

60 g baby spinach leaves

steamed rice, to serve

coriander, to garnish

baby serve: mash or puree a few spoonfuls of the vegetable curry and combine with the rice for a textured spoon-fed meal, alongside some of the roasted vegetables offered as finger food and some fruit.

toddler serve: serve the curry, chopping some vegetables if needed, on top or to the side of some rice. Be sure to offer one or two foods you know your child enjoys, if they are still learning to like curry.

FUSSY EATING TIP: for children still learning to like curry, roast a portion of their preferred vegetables in only olive oil and honey, without the curry powder. Serve the veggies with rice and offer the curry sauce as a side dipping sauce. Enjoy eating together as a family, with others eating the roasted vegetable curry an opportunity for exposure. The quantity of curry powder can be easily adapted to your family's taste preferences.

STORAGE: keep reserved or leftover vegetable curry in an airtight container in the fridge for up to 3 days, or in the freezer for up to 3 months.

ALLERGIES/INTOLERANCES:
Gluten/wheat: use a gluten-free soy sauce or tamari.

makes **12**
prep time: **15 minutes**
cooking time: **20 minutes**

3 sheets (25 cm × 25 cm) frozen puff
    pastry, just thawed
leftover tray-roasted vegetable curry
    (p. 111)
1 egg, lightly beaten
2 teaspoons sesame seeds (optional)
green salad, to serve

cucumber raita
½ cup (125 g) plain Greek-style
    yoghurt
1 clove garlic, finely chopped
1 tablespoon lemon juice
1 Lebanese cucumber, coarsely
    grated, excess moisture
    squeezed out

leftover vegetable curry puffs

Preheat the oven to 220°C (200°C fan-forced) and line 2 large baking trays with baking paper.

Cut each pastry sheet into 4 even squares and fork-mash or chop some of the larger vegetables from the leftover curry into smaller pieces.

Place heaped tablespoons of the vegetable curry in the centre of each pastry square. Fold to make a triangle, then crimp the edges to seal. Brush the pastry with the egg and sprinkle with sesame seeds if using.

Arrange on the baking trays and bake for 20 minutes, or until the pastry has puffed and is golden brown.

Meanwhile, make the raita by combining the yoghurt, garlic, lemon juice and cucumber together in a small bowl.

Serve the curry puffs with the cucumber raita and a green leafy salad.

baby serve: serve leftover reheated vegetables mashed or as finger food to your baby. The mashed vegetables can be spread on toast fingers as an alternative finger-food option.

toddler serve: offer a curry puff alongside a serving of finger-food vegetables and fruit. Offer with their preferred sauce, if you like.

FUSSY EATING TIP: rally the kids and have them help you prepare this meal in the kitchen. Almost all of the tasks are age appropriate, whether it's mashing the vegetables, crimping the pastry, brushing it with the egg, sprinkling it with seeds or preparing the raita – all of these will help your child to progress towards eating this particular meal and to feel more secure when it comes to mealtime.

Food prep in the kitchen is a fabulous way to engage and communicate with your child. They may offer hints about why they do and don't like different tastes and textures, which will help you better adapt meals in the future.

STORAGE: cooked curry puffs must be eaten after cooking and can't be reheated. Uncooked curry puffs may be layered with baking paper in an airtight container and frozen for up to 3 months.

ALLERGIES/INTOLERANCES:
Gluten/wheat: choose gluten-free pastry. **Egg:** brush the pastry with your preferred milk. **Dairy:** avoid serving with the cucumber raita or choose a dairy-free plain yoghurt.

soy roast chicken leftover chicken fried rice

Cut down on roasting time with a butterflied roast chicken, and save even more time the following night by making a deliciously easy fried rice.

 DF
EF

serves **6**

prep time: **10 minutes**

cooking time: **40 minutes**

1.6 kg whole free-range chicken, butterflied (see p. 115)

¼ cup (60 ml) oyster sauce

2 tablespoons salt-reduced soy sauce

1½ tablespoons brown sugar

2 cloves garlic, crushed

3 cups (600 g) jasmine or brown rice

steamed green vegetables and corn cobs, to serve

extra soy sauce and sliced red chilli, to serve (optional)

soy roast chicken

Preheat the oven to 220°C (200°C fan-forced).

Rinse the chicken under cold water and pat dry with a paper towel.

Place the oyster sauce, soy sauce, brown sugar and garlic in a small bowl and mix to combine. Reserve 1 tablespoon of the marinade and coat the chicken with the rest. Place the chicken skin side up in a roasting pan. If time allows, place the chicken in the fridge to marinate for at least 1 hour, or up to 4 hours.

Roast the chicken for 20 minutes, then brush with the reserved marinade. Roast the chicken for a further 20 minutes, or until it has cooked through and the juices run clear. Remove from the oven and allow it to rest, loosely covered with foil, for 10 minutes.

While the chicken is roasting, cook the rice according to packet instructions. Drain well and set aside 3 cups (525 g) of cooked rice for the leftover chicken fried rice.

Carve the chicken into pieces and set some aside (160 g) for the leftover fried rice. Serve the chicken with the rice, steamed green vegetables and corn, with extra soy sauce and chilli, if desired.

baby serve: finely chop or mash some of the chicken, rice and vegetables to a vegetable puree and/or shred some of the chicken, being careful to remove any small bones, and serve as finger food alongside some of the steamed green vegetables and corn, and some fruit.

toddler serve: shred some of the chicken, being careful to remove any small bones, and serve alongside some rice and vegetables and some fruit. Alternatively, serve the chicken, rice and vegetables in the middle of the table and allow your toddler to choose, using small tongs with supervision, what they would like to eat from what's on offer and how much.

MONEY-SAVING TIP: save time and money by repurposing leftovers into a new and just as nutritious meal. Use the scraps of vegetables that might have been destined for the compost in the fried rice. The loose mushroom or two, the half-used carrots, the limp celery stalk and the last clump of peas are perfect here!

TIME-SAVING TIP: when buying your meat from your butcher, ask them to do all the chopping and trimming you need. Whether it's butterflying chickens, chopping meat for a curry, mincing meats, frenching shanks, or anything else you might require, it's always a huge time-saver, and also reduces your kitchen tidy-up.

MEAL PREP TIP: almost all of our 'Make-in-a-minute marinades' (p. 219) will suit this roast chicken recipe too, so please try a few out and let us know which is your favourite!

HOW TO BUTTERFLY A CHICKEN: pat the chicken dry with a paper towel to remove any excess moisture. Turn your chicken breast-side down on the cutting board, then, using a good pair of kitchen shears, if you have some, or a heavy cook's knife, cut along each side of the backbone and remove it. Turn the chicken breast-side up, then press the middle of the breastbone down with the palm of your hand until it cracks, and allow the chicken to splay flat. Freeze the backbone for a future batch of homemade chicken stock.

STORAGE: keep leftover chicken and rice in an airtight container in the fridge for up to 2 days.

ALLERGIES/INTOLERANCES: Gluten/wheat: use a gluten-free soy sauce or use tamari instead. Look for a gluten-free oyster sauce.

serves 4–6

prep time: 15 minutes

cooking time: 10 minutes

1 tablespoon olive oil

½ red onion, finely chopped or sliced

1 carrot, finely diced

½ cup (60 g) frozen peas

1 corn cob, kernels removed

2 broccolini stems, chopped

small handful of sugar snap peas

1 teaspoon sugar

1 tablespoon Shaoxing rice wine or mirin

3 eggs, lightly beaten

3 cups (525 g) leftover cold cooked rice

1 cup (160 g) shredded leftover roast chicken

¼ cup (60 ml) salt-reduced soy sauce

sliced spring onion, to serve

sliced red chilli, to serve (optional)

leftover chicken fried rice

Heat the olive oil in a wok over medium–high heat. Add the onion and cook, stirring, for 2 minutes. Add the vegetables and cook for 2–3 minutes, until vibrant and tender.

Add the sugar, stir for 30 seconds, then add the Shaoxing wine. Stir for a further minute.

Make a well in the middle and pour in the egg, waiting around 20 seconds before you start to scramble and break it up with a wooden spoon, ensuring the egg is cooked though.

Add the rice, chicken and soy sauce, toss together with the egg and vegetables and cook for a further 1–2 minutes until heated through.

Serve with sliced spring onion, and chilli, if desired.

baby serve: serve a small bowl of fried rice to your baby, offering some of the elements, such as the shredded chicken, egg and peas, as finger food.

toddler serve: serve the fried rice in a small bowl. If this is overwhelming you may like to reheat and serve some of the plain rice and chicken and some finger-food fruit and vegetables, alongside a small bowl of the mixed fried rice.

TIME-SAVING TIP: prep some of the veggies for the fried rice the night before, while the chicken is roasting in the oven and the rice is cooking. All of a sudden this will be a 5-minute meal! If you don't have any leftover chicken, try bacon, ham or prawns, or simply omit altogether and enjoy a simple egg and vegetable fried rice.

STORAGE: the fried rice must be enjoyed fresh and any leftovers discarded if using leftover chicken and rice from the previous night.

ALLERGIES/INTOLERANCES: Gluten/wheat: use gluten-free soy sauce or tamari. **Egg:** omit the egg, or cook the egg in a separate pan, mixing it through portions of fried rice for those who can tolerate egg. **Vegetarian:** omit the chicken.

barbecue mince *and* cheese-loaded baked potatoes

baked gnocchi

Beef mince doesn't always have to mean bolognese! You can enjoy this mince loaded onto a delicious baked potato or as a simple yet mouth-watering baked gnocchi. We love how leftovers can be transformed and combined with fresh ingredients in such a way as to keep meals varied and limit the risk of children developing food jags.

serves **4**

prep time: **15 minutes**

cooking time: **35 minutes**

4 even-sized brushed potatoes
   (180 g–200 g each), scrubbed

¼ cup (60 ml) olive oil

salt and ground pepper

1 brown onion, finely diced

2 carrots, coarsely grated

2 cloves garlic, crushed

500 g premium beef mince

½ cup (125 ml) smoky barbecue sauce

½ cup (125 ml) salt-reduced beef
   stock or water

½ cup (60g) grated cheddar cheese,
   to serve

2 spring onions, sliced, to serve

½ cup (140 g) plain Greek-style
   yoghurt or sour cream, to serve

mixed tossed salad or slaw, to serve

barbecue mince and cheese-loaded baked potatoes

Preheat the oven to 200°C (180°C fan-forced). Line a large baking tray with baking paper.

Cut the potatoes in half lengthways. Drizzle with 1 tablespoon olive oil, season with salt and pepper and toss to coat. Place the potatoes cut-side down on the tray and bake for 30–35 minutes or until golden brown, crisp and tender.

While the potatoes are cooking, heat 1 tablespoon of olive oil in a large frying pan over medium–high heat. Cook the onion and carrot for 4–5 minutes or until tender. Add the garlic and cook for a further 1 minute or until fragrant. Remove from the heat, transfer to a bowl and set aside.

Reheat the remaining oil in the pan, add the beef mince and cook, stirring often and breaking the meat apart with a wooden spoon, for 4–5 minutes until well browned.

Return the onion mixture to the pan with the barbecue sauce and stock. Cook over medium heat, stirring, for 2 minutes or until the mixture thickens and becomes glazed. Set aside 1–1½ cups of the meat mixture for the baked gnocchi.

Top the potato halves with remaining mince, then sprinkle with cheese and spring onion, along with a dollop of yoghurt. Serve with a tossed green salad or slaw. Optional extra step: place the potato halves topped with mince and cheese under a hot grill to melt the cheese before adding the spring onion and yoghurt.

baby serve: mash together some of the potato and a small spoonful of the cooked mince mixture, and top with a little yoghurt, if desired. Offer alongside some finger-food vegetables and a serve of fruit.

toddler serve: choose a small potato, top with the mince and cheese and serve on a tasting plate alongside some finger-food vegetables and a side of fruit. Alternatively, serve on a tasting plate with the potato, mince and cheese deconstructed.

STORAGE: keep leftover potatoes and mince in the fridge for up to 2 days. Use leftover mince mixture for the Baked gnocchi (p. 120), and any leftover potato can be used for Gado gado (p. 192). Alternatively, leftover cooked mince mixture can be frozen in an airtight container for up to 2 months.

ALLERGIES/INTOLERANCES:
Gluten/wheat: choose a gluten-free stock. **Dairy:** omit the cheese and yoghurt or sour cream. **Vegetarian:** substitute the beef mince for a 400 g tin of drained and rinsed brown lentils. Alternatively, try a tuna, corn and mayonnaise filling.

serves **6**

prep time: **10 minutes**

cooking time: **25 minutes**

150 g bacon rashers or shortcut bacon, trimmed and sliced

2 × 500 g packets potato gnocchi

¼ cup (60 ml) olive oil

300 ml thickened cream

½ cup (130 g) homemade or good-quality store-bought pesto (p. 58)

40 g unsalted butter, roughly chopped

1–1½ cups (235–350 g) leftover mince (p. 118)

60g baby spinach leaves

½ cup (120 g) chargrilled capsicum strips or halved cherry tomatoes (optional)

1 cup (120 g) grated cheddar cheese

salad, to serve

baked gnocchi

Preheat the oven to 220°C (200°C fan-forced).

Place the bacon and gnocchi in a large roasting pan. Drizzle with the olive oil and toss to coat. Bake for 12 minutes, or until they begin to turn golden around the edges.

Add the cream, ¼ cup (60 ml) water, the pesto, butter, leftover mince, spinach and capsicum or tomatoes (if using). Toss to combine. Sprinkle with cheese and bake for a further 10 minutes, or until golden.

Serve with salad.

baby serve: mash a portion of the baked gnocchi, avoiding any bacon, and spoon feed to your baby alongside a few gnocchi and some finger-food vegetables and fruit.

toddler serve: offer a portion in a bowl, or some gnocchi as finger food, alongside some vegetables and fruit.

TIP: instead of the gnocchi, substitute 400 g of cooked penne, fusilli pasta or fresh ravioli, added in at step 3.

STORAGE: best enjoyed fresh and discard any leftovers to avoid reheating the mince again.

ALLERGIES/INTOLERANCES:

Gluten/wheat: use gluten-free gnocchi, or 400 g cooked gluten-free pasta. **Dairy:** swap the cream and pesto for a 400 g jar of passata, omit the butter and choose a dairy-free cheese. Alternatively, cook the bacon in a large frying pan or saucepan and at step 3 add some passata, the mince and spinach and stir to reheat and serve, baking only the gnocchi. **Vegetarian:** omit the bacon and mince, substitute with some chickpeas or lentils and reduce the sauces, if necessary.

batch cooking

BATCH COOKING IS WHAT MOST MIGHT ASSUME to be typical or classic meal planning. This is where we take a little more time and double the quantity to cook two complete meals – one for now and one for the freezer. You are making the most of the same ingredients, only going through the process once, and saving precious time.

getting the most out of batch cooking

Batch cooking can be really useful for those who work during the week and use the weekend to get ahead on weekly meal prepping. Or you might find that making two meals at the same time is achievable for you once or twice a week if it means you don't have to cook at all on busier nights. Here are a few tips to save you even more time and money when you choose to batch cook:

- Look for weekly specials on meats that you like to cook with. When they're on sale, buy them in bulk and add them to your meal plan.
- Invest in some quality reusable containers that fit your freezer perfectly. Many people can only batch cook a few meals at a time, otherwise their freezer becomes too full.
- Start a batch-cooking group with a few close friends or neighbours. If you each make 1 batch meal a week to share, you will reduce your time in the kitchen even further.

- Recipes we love to batch cook are those that can be cooked together and that store well in the freezer. Lasagne, pies, cannelloni, pasta bakes and soups are all hearty meals that store really well.
- Always keep an inventory list of the meals you are adding to the freezer. Often we forget what's actually in there and the meal may end up wasted.
- We love to batch cook for new mums or friends in need. Invest in some disposable foil trays and make food for others – it is a feel-good gesture that anyone will appreciate.

fish tacos *with* corn salsa *and* lime mayonnaise

Crispy parmesan-crumbed fish will take your next 'Taco Tuesday' to another level. Serve this meal family-style, enjoy it all together, and take the stress out of mealtimes by making sure you have something on offer to suit all taste preferences.

makes about 30 fish pieces
prep time: 25 minutes
cooking time: 10 minutes

1 kg fresh boneless firm white fish fillets (such as hoki, snapper or flathead)
½ cup (75 g) plain flour
salt and ground black pepper
3 eggs
3 cups (185 g) panko breadcrumbs
1 cup (80 g) shredded parmesan
extra virgin olive oil, to shallow-fry

to make tacos (serves 4)
2 corn cobs, steamed, kernels removed, or 300 g tin corn kernels, drained
60 g baby spinach leaves, roughly chopped
250 g cherry tomatoes, halved or quartered
2 teaspoons extra virgin olive oil
2 teaspoons white wine vinegar
¼ cup (60 g) whole-egg mayonnaise
1 lime, cut into wedges
10 mini flour tortillas

Cut the fish fillets into 2–3 cm thick slices, measuring about 8–10 cm in length.

Place the flour on a large plate and season with a little salt and pepper. Whisk the eggs in a shallow bowl and combine the panko and parmesan in a large shallow bowl.

Working with a few pieces at a time, toss the fish in the flour and shake off excess. Roll in the egg, then press into the panko mixture, turning to coat. Place onto a lined baking tray and repeat with the remaining fish. Set aside in the fridge until you are ready to cook (this can be done up to 1 day ahead).

Reserve half the crumbed fish for the freezer, layering between sheets of baking paper in airtight containers. Only freeze fish which hasn't previously been frozen.

To cook the fish, add enough oil to cover the base of a large frying pan and heat over medium heat. Working in batches, cook the fillets for 2–3 minutes each side, depending on thickness, until the fish is golden brown, crispy and cooked through when tested with a fork. Remove from the pan and place on a plate or small tray lined with paper towel to drain excess oil.

Make a salsa by combining the corn, spinach and cherry tomatoes in a bowl. Drizzle with olive oil and vinegar and toss to coat. Mix the mayonnaise with a squeeze of lime juice to taste.

Heat the tortillas in the microwave or gently toast them in a dry frying pan over medium–high heat for 30 seconds each side.

To assemble the tacos, top each tortilla with crispy fish, followed by the salsa. Drizzle with the lime mayonnaise and serve with lime wedges.

baby serve: flake the fish and serve as finger food and/or mash or finely chop some fish through a vegetable puree.

toddler serve: serve the fish, salsa and tortilla deconstructed on a tasting plate with a serve of fruit. Alternatively, prepare a taco with some of the ingredients, wrapping tightly to make it easy for your toddler to hold.

TIME-SAVING TIP: your future self will always thank you when you take a little extra time to batch cook the more labour-intensive elements of a recipe. Having a stash of nutritious and tasty crumbed fish in the freezer gives you versatile options for quick and easy midweek meals – try serving the fish with roasted or mashed potatoes and steamed veggies or salad for a classic yet nutritious option, or even flaked and tossed through a simple pesto pasta.

STORAGE: keep leftover cooked fish in an airtight container in the fridge for up to 2 days. Freeze reserved crumbed, uncooked fish layered with baking paper in airtight containers for up to 3 months. To thaw, place in the fridge to defrost overnight. Keep refrigerated until you are ready to cook, and use within 24 hours of defrosting.

ALLERGIES/INTOLERANCES: Gluten/wheat: use gluten-free breadcrumbs and tortillas. **Egg:** try coating the fish in natural or plain Greek-style yoghurt, or equal parts olive oil and milk (dairy-free if required), before crumbing. Choose an egg-free mayonnaise. **Dairy:** omit the parmesan. **Vegetarian:** try sautéing some chickpeas in a Mexican spice, or scrambling an egg or two with some parmesan and a touch of milk.

chicken *and* leek pie *with* cauliflower potato mash

Cauliflower adds a lighter texture and flavour to the potato mash that tops this delicious chicken and leek pie. It's also a stepping stone for kids who might like potato mash but don't yet like cauliflower. Begin to serve some steamed cauliflower florets on the side to further boost exposure and interest.

makes **2 pies**
prep time: **20 minutes**
cooking time: **1 hour**

1 small cauliflower (1 kg), cut into florets
800 g potatoes, peeled, diced
140 g unsalted butter
460 ml milk
⅓ cup (80 ml) olive oil
2 leeks, white part only, finely sliced
2 carrots, cut in half lengthways, finely sliced
4 cloves garlic, finely chopped
1.3 kg free-range chicken thigh fillets, cut into 2 cm pieces
½ cup (75 g) plain flour
¼ cup (70 g) wholegrain mustard, or 1 tablespoon Dijon mustard
1½ cups (375 ml) salt-reduced chicken stock
1 cup (120 g) grated cheddar cheese
steamed vegetables or green salad, to serve

Preheat the oven to 180°C (160°C fan-forced). Lightly grease 2 x 6-cup (1.5 litre) capacity ovenproof dishes, including one that is freezer-proof and has a tight-fitting lid.

Place the cauliflower and potatoes in a large saucepan, cover with water, bring to the boil and cook for 15 minutes, or until tender. Drain well and return to the saucepan. Add 80 g of the butter and ⅓ cup (80 ml) milk and mash until smooth. Set aside and clean the saucepan.

Heat 2 tablespoons of the olive oil in the saucepan over medium–low heat. Cook the leek and carrot for 10 minutes or until soft and lightly golden. Add the garlic and cook, stirring, for 1 minute, or until fragrant. Transfer the vegetables to a plate and set aside.

Increase the heat to medium–high, add the remaining oil and cook the chicken in batches for 5 minutes, or until browned. Return the vegetables to the pan and scrape any brown bits from the bottom of the pan to add flavour.

Reduce the heat to medium, then add the remaining butter, stirring to melt. Sprinkle over the flour and stir to coat, then stir in the mustard. Gradually add the chicken stock and remaining milk, stirring constantly. Bring to the boil then reduce heat and simmer for 5 minutes or until the chicken is cooked through and the sauce has thickened.

Divide the filling between the prepared dishes, top with the mash and sprinkle with cheese. Set one pie aside to cool slightly, then cover with a tight-fitting lid and store in the freezer.

Place the remaining pie in the oven and cook for 30 minutes or until the filling is hot and the mash is cheesy and golden. Alternatively, you can grill the pie under medium–high heat for 10 minutes or until golden brown. Serve with steamed vegetables or green salad.

baby serve: chop or mash the pie to your baby's preferred consistency and spoon feed to your baby. Offer some chicken pieces as finger food alongside some vegetables and/or fruit.

toddler serve: serve a portion of the pie on a tasting plate alongside some vegetables and fruit.

TIME-SAVING TIP: divide half of the filling evenly between ovenproof pie dishes, small bowls or large ramekins, then top with puff pastry and brush with egg. Bake in an oven preheated to 200°C (180°C fan-forced) for 25–30 minutes, or until the pastry is golden. Freeze the other half in a reusable freezer bag or an ovenproof dish, and prepare half the cauliflower potato mash when you are next ready to bake and enjoy it.

TIP: for extra veggies and a colourful addition, add 1 cup (120 g) of frozen green peas at the end of step 5.

STORAGE: keep any leftover cooked pie in an airtight container in the fridge for up to 2 days. Store the uncooked pie in the freezer for up to 2 months. Thaw in the fridge overnight prior to cooking.

ALLERGIES/INTOLERANCES: Gluten/wheat: use cornflour or gluten-free flour. Dairy: omit the cheese, use dairy-free milk and use additional olive oil instead of butter.

sausage ragu

If you're bored of bolognese but would still like to enjoy a hearty, warming pasta dish for winter, our sausage ragu is for you. It makes a big batch, so reserve some for the freezer or use leftovers in mini pies, in a small cheat's lasagne using ricotta as the 'bechamel', on top of roast potatoes, or in a simple toasted sandwich.

Heat half the olive oil in a large, heavy-based saucepan over medium heat. Squeeze the sausage meat from the casings and cook, breaking it up with a wooden spoon, for 10 minutes or until browned. Remove the sausage from the frying pan and place on a plate lined with paper towel to drain off excess oil.

Add the remaining olive oil to the saucepan with the onion and celery. Reduce the heat to low and sauté for 10 minutes, or until soft but not browned. Add the garlic and rosemary and cook, stirring, for 1 minute.

Increase the heat to medium, add the tomatoes, sugar and sausage meat and bring to the boil. Reduce the heat to medium–low and simmer uncovered for 25 minutes. Add the milk and lemon zest and simmer for a further 10–15 minutes, or until the sauce has thickened to your liking.

Set aside a portion of the ragu for the freezer. Cool completely then spoon into an airtight container to freeze.

Serve the remaining ragu with cooked pasta, grated parmesan and a green salad or steamed vegetables.

baby serve: best enjoyed by older babies or toddlers, due to the higher salt content of the sausages. Serve a little mixed and mashed through pasta or as finger food alongside some finger-food vegetables and a serve of fruit.

toddler serve: serve some ragu with the pasta and a serve of vegetables and fruit. Choose to serve with your child's preferred type of pasta if this is a new meal for them, or deconstruct on a tasting plate. See the fussy eating note for more tips.

makes **about 8 cups (1.6 kg)**
prep time: **15 minutes**
cooking time: **55–60 minutes**

¼ cup (60 ml) extra virgin olive oil
12 free-range pork sausages
    (at least 1 kg)
1 brown onion, finely chopped
2 celery stalks, finely chopped
3 cloves garlic, crushed
1–2 small rosemary sprigs, leaves
    finely chopped
3 × 400 g tins no-added-salt chopped
    tomatoes
1 tablespoon brown sugar
200 ml milk
1 lemon, zest finely grated

to serve (optional)
cooked pasta
grated parmesan
green salad or steamed green
    vegetables

FUSSY EATING TIP: serving new pasta sauces to little kids can be a 'hold your breath' moment. Serving them with their favourite pasta can help, as can serving 3 little bowls, one with just pasta, one with just sauce and one with the pasta and sauce together. This is less threatening and less scary if your child is unsure about new foods. They may go gung-ho straight to the mixed portion and that's wonderful, but offering the deconstructed version too means there's a back-up and the family mealtime can remain relaxed and enjoyable.

STORAGE: keep leftover ragu in an airtight container in the fridge for up to 2 days, or in the freezer for up to 3 months.

ALLERGIES/INTOLERANCES:
Gluten/wheat: choose gluten-free pork sausages and gluten-free pasta. Dairy: omit the milk and use beef or vegetable stock. Vegetarian: to make an Italian mushroom and lentil ragu, skip step 1 and omit the sausages. At step 2, sauté 200 g chopped Swiss brown mushrooms along with the onion and celery, and at step 3 add a 400 g tin drained and rinsed brown lentils with the milk and lemon zest.

beef, sweet potato *and* kale casserole

Nothing will make you feel quite as smug as prepping this nourishing and warming casserole on a wet and cold winter weekend. The tender beef and veggies will offer a nutritional boost to keep any sniffles at bay. We've used chicken stock for a slightly lighter flavour that may suit younger children, and the leftovers can be frozen, transformed into pies or enjoyed to your liking.

makes 10 cups (2.2 L or 2.6 kg)
prep time: 15 minutes
cook time: 3 hours 45 minutes

¼ cup (60 ml) extra virgin oil
1.5 kg chuck steak, cut into 3 cm cubes
2 brown onions, diced
3 celery stalks, diced
2 cloves garlic, crushed
2 tablespoons Worcestershire sauce
salt and ground black pepper
¼ cup (35 g) plain flour
4 cups (1 litre) salt-reduced chicken stock
400 g passata
3 bay leaves
1 tablespoon soy sauce
3 carrots, halved lengthways, cut into 1 cm slices
1 sweet potato, cut into 1 cm chunks
2 cups chopped kale, spinach or silverbeet
crusty bread, cooked pasta, mashed potato or cannellini beans, to serve

Preheat the oven to 160°C (140°C fan-forced).

Heat 1 tablespoon of the oil in a large heavy-based flameproof casserole over medium–high heat.

Cook beef in small batches for 3–4 minutes, turning to brown all over. Add a little extra oil in between each batch. Transfer beef to a plate.

Reduce the heat to medium–low, add another tablespoon of oil and add the onion and celery. Cook for about 10 minutes, or until soft and translucent. Add in the garlic and stir for a further minute.

Add 1 tablespoon of Worcestershire sauce and a pinch of salt and stir to combine. Sprinkle the flour over the vegetables and stir continuously until the flour has dissolved and the veggies appear mushy.

Increase the heat to medium–high, add 1 cup (250 ml) of the chicken stock and stir through the veggies, scraping along the bottom of the dish, until the liquid has mostly evaporated and dissolved.

Return the beef to the dish and add the remaining stock, passata, bay leaves, soy sauce and remaining Worcestershire sauce. Bring to a simmer, then cover and cook in the oven for 1½ hours.

Remove from the oven and stir in the carrot and sweet potato. Cover and return to the oven for another 1½ hours or until the meat is very tender. To thicken the sauce a little, transfer to the stovetop and simmer uncovered over low heat for 15 minutes.

Stir through the kale, spinach or silverbeet and season with pepper. Cover and set aside for 10 minutes, to wilt the greens. Set aside half (or quantity not being consumed at this meal). Cool completely then spoon into an airtight container to freeze.

Serve with crusty bread, pasta, mashed potato or cannellini beans.

baby serve: chop or mash some beef with a few veggies and any pasta or beans and spoon feed to your baby. Offer some chopped beef, carrot or sweet potato as finger food too.

toddler serve: deconstruct and chop some beef and serve alongside a few of the veggies and any additional sides your toddler enjoys.

NUTRITION NOTE: this is an iron- and zinc-rich, veggie-packed meal to keep the immune system strong during the winter months.

STORAGE: keep leftovers in an airtight container in the fridge for up to 2 days. Freeze in one or two portions in airtight containers for up to 2 months.

CASSEROLE COOKING TIPS: sear the beef well at step 3. It's important not to rush this step and to make sure the beef pieces have been browned well for the best flavour and texture.

SLOW COOKER TIP: prepare to the end of step 6, then place everything (except carrot, sweet potato and kale) into a slow cooker. Cover and cook for 7–8 hours on LOW. Add the carrot and sweet potato about halfway through the cooking time (or at the beginning if you are out for the day). Stir through the kale and continue to cook for a further 30 minutes. Serve.

ALLERGIES/INTOLERANCES: **Gluten/wheat:** use gluten-free stock, Worcestershire and soy sauces and flour. **Vegetarian:** for a satisfying vegetable casserole, omit the meat, use a good-quality vegetable stock and add in an additional sweet potato and some potato. Reduce the cooking time to 1 hour, and you may like to reduce the liquid slightly too. Stir through some cannellini beans with the kale.

lemony chicken *and* risoni soup

Jess was gifted this as a new mum and we now gift this soup to you. It's a favourite winter batch cook, the ultimate nourishing soup to freeze in small portions or to gift to new parents, sick friends or a family that simply needs a nutritious meal. This soup cooks beautifully in a slow cooker or pressure cooker, if you have one – refer to the how-to instructions at the end of this recipe.

makes **10 cups (2.2 L or 2.3 kg)**
prep time: **25 minutes**
cooking time: **2 hours**

1.6 kg whole free-range chicken
3 tomatoes
1 brown onion, roughly chopped
2 celery stalks, roughly chopped
2 carrots, roughly chopped
2 teaspoons black peppercorns
4 cloves garlic, halved
1 bay leaf
¾ cup (165 g) risoni
large handful flat-leaf parsley,
    chopped
1 lemon, juiced
ground black pepper, to taste

Rinse the chicken well under cold water, then place it in a large heavy-based saucepan with 1 tomato, roughly chopped, the onion, celery, carrot, peppercorns, garlic, bay leaf and 8 cups (2 litres) of water. Finely chop the remaining tomatoes and set aside.

Cover with the lid and bring to a gentle simmer over medium heat. Adjust the heat to keep simmering gently with the lid on. Simmer for 1½ hours, or until the chicken is tender and comes off the bone easily. Check every 30 minutes to ensure it stays at a gentle simmer, and skim any scum off the surface of the broth.

Turn off the heat and carefully transfer the chicken to a plate. When it is cool enough to handle, remove the chicken meat from the bones and shred finely or coarsely, depending on your preference. There is plenty of chicken, so set aside some as finger food for your baby or toddler, or to toss through pasta or make a delicious sandwich filling (see note).

While the chicken is cooling, strain the liquid through a fine mesh strainer, lined with a muslin cloth or a light, cotton tea towel if you wish, for a clearer broth. Reserve some or all of the carrot and celery and discard the rest of the vegetables.

Return the strained broth to the saucepan and bring to the boil over medium heat. Add the risoni and cook for 10 minutes or until al dente.

Return the chicken, carrot and celery to the soup and stir in the parsley and reserved chopped tomatoes. Add the lemon juice a little at a time until you reach your desired taste. Season with pepper to taste. Cool leftover soup and portion into airtight containers.

Continued →

baby serve: mash or blend the soup and spoon feed to your baby. For a more textured meal, serve the soup with mostly the chicken, risoni and vegetables and just a spoonful or two of the broth. Serve some of the chicken and a portion of fruit as finger food alongside the spoon-fed meal.

toddler serve: serve the soup in a small bowl with bread or cheesy toast fingers for dipping, alongside some of their preferred vegetables and fruit. Alternatively, strain off most of the liquid for a spoon-fed or deconstructed meal.

FUSSY EATING TIP: you can easily adapt this soup to your child's and family's taste preferences by, for example, leaving the cooked carrot and celery out of the soup and serving a few on the side if they don't like everything mixed together. Leave out the finely chopped tomatoes if you need to, and add the parsley at the table for whoever would like some. Remember to add the lemon juice only a little at a time, to suit all tastebuds, and serve extra lemon juice at the table if anyone would like more.

STORAGE: keep leftover soup in an airtight container in the fridge for up to 2 days or freeze in airtight containers for up to 2 months.

A DELICIOUS SANDWICH FILLING: combine 1 cup of shredded chicken with 1 finely chopped celery stalk and 1–2 tablespoons of mayonnaise. Mix well, season with pepper and store in the fridge for up to 2 days to serve in wraps or sandwiches or on crackers.

HOW TO SLOW COOK: at step 1, place the ingredients in the bowl of a slow cooker, cover and cook for 8 hours on LOW, or for 4 hours on HIGH. Remove the scum off the surface and continue with steps 3 and 4. Return the strained broth to the slow cooker. To cook the risoni, add to the slow cooker and cook for 30 minutes on HIGH or until the risoni is tender. Return the chicken and vegetables to the soup with the parsley and lemon juice. Cook for a further 5 minutes on HIGH.

HOW TO PRESSURE COOK: at step 1, place the ingredients in the bowl of a pressure cooker, secure the lid and cook on HIGH pressure for 25 minutes. Allow the pressure to release naturally for 10 minutes before releasing the pressure valve. Remove the scum off the surface and continue with steps 3 and 4. Return the strained broth to the pressure cooker. After adding the risoni, secure the lid and set to HIGH pressure for 4 minutes. Allow the pressure to release naturally for 10 minutes before releasing the pressure valve. Continue with step 6.

ALLERGIES/INTOLERANCES: **Gluten/wheat:** choose gluten-free stock and pasta, or use rice and quinoa instead and cook according to packet instructions. Alternatively, you could add a 400 g tin of rinsed and drained chickpeas or cannellini beans at step 6. **Vegetarian:** make a simple veggie soup. Sauté some finely chopped onion, garlic and celery, add 6 cups (1.5 litres) of good-quality, light-flavoured vegetable stock (or a combination of stock and water) and bring to the boil. Add a 400 g tin of rinsed and drained chickpeas or cannellini beans, 1–2 finely chopped tomatoes, a handful of parsley and some lemon juice, and seasoned cracked pepper to taste.

meals 2 ways

BUSY PARENTS ARE KNOWN TO MULTITASK and there's no better place to do this than in the kitchen. This chapter demonstrates the art of meal coupling, or using similar base ingredients to create two separate meals. We believe that if you are making the time to be in the kitchen cooking a meal, there's probably another meal or part of a meal you can cook or prep at the same time.

For example, because Zucchini nuggets (p. 138) have all the same ingredients as a Zucchini slice (p. 136), you can make them both in almost the same time it would take to make one. With a little bit of foresight you can easily incorporate meal couples into your weekly plan and reduce the time spent in the kitchen considerably.

Meals 2 ways can also help to extend the palate of a child who is used to simpler flavours. For example, maybe you enjoy a green curry but you aren't sure that your kids will. If they enjoy plain rice you could offer green chicken curry (p. 139) alongside the rice for them to explore. Preparing the nuggets (p. 139) at the same time also offers the opportunity to explore the new flavour of the curry in a texture and shape they may be more familiar with, whether this is at the same mealtime or a later one. Offering some of the curry sauce as a dip for the nuggets is also a fabulous way to bridge the gap between the nuggets and the mixed-texture curry. All of a sudden you are expanding the textures and meals your family are beginning to accept and enjoy together.

power preps

Meals 2 ways are wonderful at keeping you on task and fully utilising your precious time in the kitchen. But what about when you only have a few minutes to spare? There are many ways to make the most of a toddler day nap, an episode of their favourite show, or those 20 minutes before school pick-up.

Choose one of these power preps to set yourself up for the better:

- **Similar ingredient bake-up:** find two recipes with similar ingredients and have a power prep session to maximise your time. Use the one bowl to quickly and efficiently prep ingredients. Think banana bread and banana muffins, or oat biscuits and toasted muesli.
- **Make a pesto:** blitzing some herbs together with a few other ingredients can create a wonderful pesto in seconds (p. 58). We love to freeze homemade pesto in small portions and stir it through some pasta for a fast meal on busy nights.
- **Mix some biscuit dough:** you can use the bulk biscuit recipe (p. 34) to prep biscuit dough and shape it into logs to freeze. We love having these in our freezer to whip up a batch of cookies in record time.
- **Create a premix:** having a premix in the pantry is an absolute game changer. Choose your favourite from our list (p. 69) and take a few minutes to mix it together for a convenient pantry staple.

- **Blitz some bread crusts:** homemade breadcrumbs are as simple as blitzing some stale bread in the food processor and putting it in the freezer to use as needed. We love boosting our breadcrumbs with quinoa flakes, rolled oats, almond meal and seeds such as sesame, poppy or chia!
- **Make some baby food:** if you have a baby in the house it's always nice to keep some pre-made purees or mashes in the freezer to mix with those textured family meals. Take a few moments to steam or roast chopped fruits and vegetables so you are always prepared and have something on hand.
- **Roast some veggies:** roasting vegetables brings out their natural flavour and roast veggies are a delicious addition to many meals or snacks. You can use up any leftover veggies by chopping them, tossing them in olive oil and roasting them until tender. Use them in salads, as finger foods for young babies and toddlers, in sandwiches, or to bulk up other leftover meals.
- **Marinate some meat:** many recipes call for pre-marinating meat. This can be done a few hours or up to 24 hours before cooking. Meat is often more tender and flavoursome if it has spent time marinating. Check out our beef skewers (p. 178), chicken drumsticks (p. 152) and marinades (p. 219) for inspiration.
- **Put on a stock:** use up any leftover veggies and herbs to create a flavoursome stock. Simply combining all the ingredients with some water in a slow cooker allows the flavours to infuse. Once it's finished cooking you can remove the veggies and place 1-cup (250 ml) quantities of the stock in the freezer to use as you need.
- **Boil some eggs:** we love using eggs as a quick and filling meal – and kids often love them too! Having a few boiled eggs in the fridge is a great idea – they can be used for salads and snacks or mixed with some mayonnaise and enjoyed in sandwiches.
- **Make a dip:** a homemade dip in the fridge with pre-chopped veggie sticks is a very appealing afternoon snack for the whole family.

other recipes that can be coupled together

Meals 2 ways aren't limited to dinner and main meals. You can also couple together anything that has similar ingredients. Here are a few more recipes from this book to get you started:

Banana, apple and cinnamon loaf (p. 50) . . . . Frozen smoothie bags (p. 37)

Pork and caramelised apple sausage rolls (p. 54) . . . . Fennel and rosemary marinade (p. 226)

Lemon zucchini cake (p. 42) . . . . Zucchini slice (p. 136)

Mexican bean burrito bowl (p. 182) . . . . Chocolate and kidney bean cupcakes (p. 48)

Sultana oat pancake premix (p. 75) . . . . Avocado and ricotta pikelets (p. 45)

Roast cauliflower and chickpea salad (p. 200) . . . . Hummus (p. 56)

Butter chicken (p. 93) . . . . Mexican spice mix (p. 104)

zucchini slice + zucchini nuggets

Grab your grater or attach the grating disc to your food processor! These recipes use similar ingredients to save your precious time. Arrange two bowls and simply add the ingredients simultaneously. Make 32 bite-sized snacks to fill your freezer and pat yourself on the back for weeks to come.

makes **16 squares**
prep time: **10 minutes**
cooking time: **40 minutes each**

5 eggs
1 cup (150 g) self-raising flour
3 zucchini (courgettes) (360 g),
    coarsely grated, liquid
    squeezed out
1 brown onion, finely chopped
4 rashers rindless bacon,
    finely diced
1 cup (120 g) grated cheddar cheese
¼ cup (60 ml) olive oil

zucchini slice

Preheat the oven to 180°C (160°C fan-forced). Line a 30 cm × 20 cm slice tin and a baking tray with baking paper.

To make the zucchini slice, beat the eggs in a large bowl until combined. Add the flour and mix until smooth, then add the zucchini, onion, bacon, cheese and oil and stir to combine. Pour into the prepared slice tin and bake for 40 minutes or until cooked through. Allow to cool in the tin, then cut into squares to serve.

makes **16 nuggets**

prep time: **10 minutes**

cooking time: **40 minutes each**

2 zucchini (courgettes) (240 g),
    coarsely grated

1 potato (200 g), peeled,
    coarsely grated

1 egg, lightly beaten

1 tablespoon self-raising flour

1 cup (70 g) fresh multigrain
    breadcrumbs

½ cup (60 g) finely grated
    cheddar cheese

olive oil, for drizzling

zucchini nuggets

To make the zucchini nuggets, squeeze the grated zucchini and potato to remove excess liquid. Place in a large mixing bowl and add the egg and flour. Mix with your hands until evenly combined. Place the breadcrumbs and cheese on a large plate and mix to combine. Shape teaspoons of the zucchini mixture into small nuggets, then coat the nuggets in the cheesy breadcrumbs. Place on the prepared tray. Drizzle the nuggets with olive oil and cook for 40 minutes, turning halfway through cooking, until golden brown and cooked through.

baby serve: omit the bacon from the zucchini slice when making for young babies. The nuggets and zucchini slice can be served as finger food from 6 months of age. Portions of the nuggets and zucchini slice can be chopped and mashed through other mashed vegetables for those that prefer to be spoon fed.

toddler serve: the nuggets and slice can be served on a tasting plate with other nutritious foods for snacks or mealtimes.

MONEY-SAVING TIP: buying imperfect picks can save you money when the fruits or vegetables are going to be chopped, diced or grated. You don't need beautiful-looking zucchini for these delicious and affordable recipes.

NOTE: bread going stale? Blitz it in the food processor and freeze it flat in a resealable freezer-proof bag. Snap off as needed.

STORAGE: keep the slice and nuggets in an airtight container in the fridge for up to 2 days. Alternatively, flash freeze (p. 20), then place in a freezer-proof container or in your baking box (p. 28) and freeze for up to 2 months.

ALLERGIES/INTOLERANCES:
Gluten/wheat: use gluten-free flour and gluten-free breadcrumbs. Egg: skip the slice and use 1 tablespoon plain Greek-style yoghurt in the nuggets instead of the egg. Dairy: omit the cheese and try adding a tablespoon of nutritional yeast for a cheesy flavour. Vegetarian: omit the bacon and add grated sweet potato.

thai green chicken curry ✚ thai green chicken nuggets

Just as our Butter chicken (p. 93) and Tandoori (p. 224) marinades are a mild entry into Indian flavours for little kids with sensitive palates, this green chicken curry is an introduction to the more fragrant flavours of Thai food.

thai green chicken curry

For the curry, place the curry paste and ½ cup (125 ml) of the coconut cream in a wok or large frying pan over medium–high heat and cook, stirring, for 3 minutes. Add the palm sugar and fish sauce and cook for a further 3 minutes, adding a little more coconut cream to loosen the sauce if necessary. Add the chicken and remaining coconut cream. Bring to the boil, then reduce the heat to low and simmer for 10 minutes, or until the chicken is tender and cooked through. Add the green beans or peas and baby corn and cook for a further 2 minutes. Stir through the basil leaves and serve with steamed rice.

baby serve: finely chop and mash some chicken and vegetables with rice and sauce and spoon feed to your baby. Offer some small portions of chicken and vegetables as finger food.

toddler serve: serve a small bowl of rice with curry to your toddler and/or deconstruct a portion if they prefer on a tasting plate, with the curry separate to the rice alongside some of their favourite vegetables and fruit.

thai green chicken nuggets

To prepare the chicken nuggets, place the curry paste, chicken, fish sauce, palm sugar and lime leaves or zest in a food processor and process until well combined. Shape heaped tablespoons of the mixture into nuggets 1–1.5 cm thick and place on a tray. Cover and refrigerate for at least 30 minutes or until you are ready to cook them.

To cook the nuggets, heat enough olive oil for shallow-frying in a large frying pan over medium–high heat. Add the nuggets and cook for 3–4 minutes each side, until golden brown and cooked through. Serve with veggies, and rice, if desired.

Continued →

serves **4**
prep time: **25 minutes**
cooking time: **22 minutes**

2–3 tablespoons Thai green
   curry paste (p. 140)
400 ml tin coconut cream
1 tablespoon finely grated palm sugar
   or brown sugar
1 tablespoon fish sauce
500 g chicken thigh or breast fillets,
   cut into 2 cm pieces
100 g green beans, snow peas or sugar
   snap peas, trimmed and halved
400 g tin baby corn spears, drained,
   spears cut in half
handful basil leaves
steamed rice, to serve

thai green chicken nuggets

makes **15 nuggets**
prep time: **25 minutes**
cooking time: **10 minutes**

1½ tablespoons Thai green
   curry paste (p. 140)
500 g chicken breast fillets,
   roughly chopped
1 tablespoon fish sauce
1 tablespoon finely grated palm sugar
   or brown sugar
2 very finely shredded makrut lime leaves
   or ½ teaspoon finely grated lime zest
olive oil, to shallow-fry
steamed green beans, sugar snap
   peas, baby corn, to serve
steamed rice, to serve (optional)

baby serve: mash a nugget with some of their favourite veggie puree and cooked rice and spoon feed to your baby. Slice nuggets into strips or cubes for your baby to enjoy as finger food with steamed green beans and a portion of fruit.

toddler serve: serve Thai green chicken nuggets on a tasting plate with some rice, green beans and a portion of fruit.

makes ½ cup (110 g)
prep time: **15 minutes**
cooking time: **5 minutes**

1 teaspoon white peppercorns
1 teaspoon cumin seeds
2 teaspoon coriander seeds
2 cloves garlic
4 spring onions, trimmed
1 bunch coriander, roots included,
    washed and dried
handful Thai or regular basil leaves
1 tablespoon fish sauce
1 lime, juiced
1–2 green chillies (optional,
    if heat is tolerated)

thai green curry paste

Dry-roast the peppercorns, cumin and coriander seeds in a small frying pan over medium–low heat for 4–5 minutes or until fragrant. Transfer to a food processor with the remaining ingredients and process until you reach a paste consistency. Stop the food processor 2–3 times and use a spatula to scrape down the sides. Place the paste in a small airtight container and keep in the fridge for up to 3 days, or freeze in small portions for up to 3 months.

FUSSY EATING TIP: it is easy to prepare the nuggets at the same time as the ingredients for the chicken curry, and you might like to fry a few to have on offer to enjoy with the curry, for kids who may still be learning to like saucy meals, as well as saving a batch for the freezer.

TIP: for a vegetarian option choose tofu instead of chicken for the curry or simply bulk up with extra veggies.

STORAGE: uncooked chicken nuggets can be stored in the fridge, covered, for up to 24 hours. To freeze, layer with baking paper in an airtight container and freeze for up to 3 months. Leftover cooked nuggets can be stored in an airtight container in the fridge for up to 2 days, or in the freezer for up to 3 months. Leftover curry can be kept in the fridge for up to 2 days.

ALLERGIES/INTOLERANCES:
Vegetarian: use 400 g firm tofu, sliced and pan-fried, and/or additional veggies instead of chicken for the curry, adding it with the green beans and baby corn. Try pressed and drained tofu instead of chicken when preparing the nuggets. Omit the fish sauce if seafood is not tolerated.

cheat's lamb moussaka spiced lamb pastry pockets

Lamb mince is an affordable and underutilised meat to get creative with. Our cheat's moussaka smells amazing bubbling away in the oven and it takes no time at all to make some flavoursome little pastries to fill the freezer and cook when needed.

(F)

serves **6–8**
prep time: **10 minutes**
cooking time: **50 minutes**

1 tablespoon olive oil
1 brown onion, finely chopped
1 carrot, coarsely grated
1 clove garlic, finely chopped
500 g lamb mince
1 teaspoon ground cinnamon
2 × 400 g tins no-added-salt
  chopped tomatoes
ground black pepper
1 small eggplant (aubergine),
  cut into 5 mm thick discs
½ cup (60 g) grated cheddar cheese

bechamel sauce
2 tablespoons unsalted butter
1 tablespoon plain flour
2 cups (500 ml) milk
1½ cups (180 g) grated
  cheddar cheese

cheat's lamb moussaka

Preheat the oven to 190°C (170°C fan-forced). Line 2 baking trays with baking paper. Lightly grease an 8-cup (2 litre) 33 × 23 cm ovenproof dish with olive oil.

To make the moussaka, heat the oil in a large, deep non-stick frying pan over medium heat. Sauté the onion and carrot for 2 minutes, then add the garlic and continue to cook for a further 1 minute. Add the lamb mince and cinnamon and cook, breaking up with a wooden spoon, for 5 minutes or until the meat is brown. Add the tinned tomatoes and season with a pinch of pepper. Simmer, stirring occasionally, for 20 minutes or until thick.

To make the bechamel sauce, melt the butter in a small saucepan over medium–high heat until foaming. Add the flour and cook, stirring, for 1 minute or until bubbling. Remove from the heat. Add the milk a little at a time, stirring until smooth between each addition. Return to the heat. Cook, stirring with a whisk, for 5 minutes or until the sauce comes to the boil and thickens. Remove from the heat and stir through the cheese until melted.

Scoop ½ cup lamb mixture into the prepared ovenproof dish and arrange half the eggplant slices on top in a single layer. Spoon over half the bechamel sauce. Top with the remaining meat, eggplant and bechamel, then sprinkle with cheese. Bake for 25 minutes or until the cheese is golden and the eggplant is tender. Allow to rest for 10 minutes before serving.

baby serve: combine ¼ cup (70 g) of the cooked moussaka with your baby's preferred milk and mash to create a textured meal for your baby. Serve alongside some steamed vegetables and fruit.

toddler serve: serve the moussaka or a halved pastry pocket alongside some steamed vegetables or salad and some fruit.

spiced lamb pastry pockets

Heat the oil in a large, deep non-stick frying pan over medium heat. Cook the onion, stirring, for 2 minutes until starting to soften. Add the mince, spices and sugar (if using) and cook, breaking up with a wooden spoon, for 5 minutes or until the meat is brown. Add the tomatoes and lentils and cook for 5 minutes or until the sauce has thickened. Transfer to a large bowl to cool completely.

Cut each sheet of pastry into four squares and arrange on baking trays lined with baking paper. Divide the lamb mixture evenly among the pastry squares and sprinkle each with some feta, if using. Fold over to form triangles and press the edges together to seal. Flash freeze (p. 20) any triangles you don't want to cook straight away. To cook, brush all over with egg (if using) and bake for 20 minutes or until golden brown.

makes **12**

prep time: **10 minutes**

cooking time: **25 minutes**

F

1 tablespoon olive oil

1 brown onion, finely chopped

200 g lamb mince

400 g tin brown lentils, drained and rinsed

½ teaspoon ground cinnamon

½ teaspoon ground cumin

1 teaspoon white sugar (optional)

400 g tin no-added-salt chopped tomatoes

3 sheets (25 cm × 25 cm) frozen puff pastry, just thawed

100 g feta, crumbled (optional)

1 egg, lightly beaten, to brush (optional)

FUSSY EATING TIP: is someone in the family learning to love eggplant? Try removing the cooked eggplant from the main meal and serving it on the side for them to explore. Still can't get them over the line? You can simply sub it with a similar-textured vegetable such as finely sliced zucchini or even fresh pasta sheets to mimic a traditional lasagne.

TIP: no time to make the bechamel? We love to layer the moussaka with some ricotta and top with grated cheese.

STORAGE: keep the moussaka in an airtight container in the fridge for up to 2 days. Freeze for up to 2 months. Flash freeze any triangles you don't need before cooking and keep in freezer-proof bags for up to 2 months.

ALLERGIES/INTOLERANCES:
Gluten/wheat: use gluten-free flour and pastry. Egg: brush the pastry with your preferred milk instead of the egg. Dairy: use dairy-free milk and cheese. Vegetarian: try two 400 g tins brown lentils, drained and rinsed, and some diced mushrooms instead of the lamb mince.

vegetable red lentil lasagne with spinach vegetable *and* red lentil soup

F
V
EF

serves **6–8**
prep time: **30 minutes**
cooking time: **1 hour 15 minutes**

2 tablespoons extra virgin olive oil
1 brown onion, diced
2 large carrots, diced
1 large red capsicum (pepper), diced
2 large zucchini (courgettes), diced
4 cloves garlic, finely chopped
2 tablespoons no-added-salt
    tomato paste
2 × 400 g tins no-added-salt
    chopped tomatoes
3 cups (750 ml) salt-reduced
    vegetable stock
1 cup (200 g) split red lentils
375 g instant lasagne sheets
40 g baby spinach leaves

bechamel sauce
60 g butter
⅓ cup (50 g) plain flour
4 cups (1 litre) milk
1 cup (120 g) grated cheddar cheese
salt and ground black pepper

vegetable red lentil lasagne with spinach

To make the lasagne, preheat the oven to 190°C (170°C fan-forced). Grease a 3.5–4 litre capacity ovenproof dish. Heat the oil in a large saucepan over medium heat. Cook the onion for 5 minutes, or until lightly golden. Add the remaining vegetables and cook for a further 5 minutes. Stir in the garlic and tomato paste and cook for a further minute, or until fragrant.

Add the tomatoes, stock and lentils. Cook for 15–20 minutes, or until the lentils are tender and the sauce has thickened.

Meanwhile, to make the bechamel sauce, melt the butter in a saucepan over medium heat. Add the flour and cook, stirring, for 1 minute. Remove from the heat. Add the milk a little at a time, stirring until smooth between each addition. Return to the heat and bring to a simmer. Reduce heat to medium–low and simmer for 2 minutes, then stir in ¼ cup (40 g) of the cheese. Season to taste.

Spread 1 cup of the lentil mixture over the base of the prepared dish. Arrange a layer of lasagne sheets on top, breaking to fit neatly if necessary. Spread with about 2 cups lentil mixture and some of the spinach leaves. Repeat to make about 4 layers, finishing with lasagne sheets.

Top with the bechamel sauce, sprinkle with remaining cheese and bake for 40–50 minutes or until golden brown. Stand lasagne for 10 minutes before cutting.

baby serve: mash or blend the lasagne to your baby's preferred consistency. Alternatively, slice into fingers or small squares and serve as finger food.

toddler serve: offer lasagne fingers or squares alongside a tasting plate of finger-food vegetables and a serve of fruit.

TIME-SAVING TIP: it's always assumed that lasagne is time-consuming to cook, but the sauces for this lasagne can be made in advance. Simply assemble the next day and bake as per instructions.

MEAL PLANNING TIP: this makes a generous lasagne, so if you'd prefer to prep one for the freezer, try assembling in 2 smaller baking dishes, rather than 1 larger one.

MEAL PREP TIP: to prepare both recipes at the same time, chop up all the carrots, capsicum and zucchini, toss together in a large bowl, and use half for each recipe. Roast the soup vegetables while the lasagne cooks on the lower shelf of the oven.

Soft, warm and comforting, this meat-free lasagne will appeal to the masses. The cheesy sauce and red lentils will offer the familiar texture and flavour that everyone loves. Enjoy the simplicity of making the red lentil soup alongside the lasagne, and stash it in the freezer for another day. We love to serve the soup with crusty bread and a fruit platter to encourage uncertain kids to give it a try.

vegetable and red lentil soup

For the soup, preheat the oven to 190°C (170°C fan-forced) and line 2 baking trays with baking paper. Divide the carrot, capsicum, zucchini and garlic between the trays, drizzle with 2 tablespoons of oil, sprinkle with cumin and toss to coat.

Bake for 20 minutes or until the veggies are golden and tender. When cool enough to handle, remove the skin from the garlic.

In a large saucepan, heat the remaining oil over medium–high heat and cook the onion for 4 minutes or until lightly golden. Add the tomato paste, cook for 1 minute, then add the roasted vegetables and garlic, tomatoes, lentils and stock. Bring to the boil, then reduce to a simmer and cook for 20 minutes or until lentils are tender and the soup has thickened.

Serve as is, or if you prefer a smoother soup, blend until you reach your preferred consistency.

While the soup is cooking, place the bread onto a baking tray, drizzle with olive oil and toss to coat. Sprinkle with cheese, and bake for 10 minutes or until crispy and golden.

Serve the soup topped with yoghurt, spinach and croutons.

baby serve: serve the soup as a spoon-fed meal to your baby, offering the croutons or toast fingers as a 'dipper' if they enjoy self-feeding and finger foods.

toddler serve: serve in small bowls with the croutons or toast fingers as a 'dipper' to encourage engagement. As an alternative serving option, the soup can be used as a pasta sauce too.

serves **4–6**
prep time: **20 minutes**
cooking time: **40 minutes**

2 large carrots, diced
1 large red capsicum (pepper), diced
2 large zucchini (courgettes), diced
4 cloves garlic, unpeeled
3 tablespoons olive oil
2 teaspoons ground cumin
1 brown onion, diced
2 tablespoons no-added-salt tomato paste
400g tin no-added-salt chopped tomatoes
1 cup (200 g) split red lentils
8 cups (2 litres) salt-reduced vegetable stock
plain Greek-style yoghurt, to dollop
20 g baby spinach leaves, roughly chopped, to garnish

cheesy croutons

6 slices wholemeal bread, roughly torn
olive oil, for drizzling
1 cup (120 g) grated cheddar cheese

STORAGE: keep leftover lasagne or soup in an airtight container in the fridge for up to 3 days, or freeze for up to 3 months. Uncooked lasagne can be stored, covered, in the freezer for up to 3 months. The lentil sauce can be frozen for up to 3 months.

ALLERGIES/INTOLERANCES: Gluten/wheat: use gluten-free lasagne sheets, flour, stock and bread. **Dairy:** use dairy-free milk and cheese to prepare the bechamel sauce. Alternatively, omit it and serve the lentil sauce stirred through some cooked pasta, rather than assembling into a lasagne. Omit cheese and yoghurt from soup recipe.

melt-in-your-mouth meatballs best-ever cheeseburgers

makes **30 meatballs**
prep time: **30 minutes +**
    30 minutes chilling
cooking time: **35 minutes**

½ cup (35 g) fresh or panko
    breadcrumbs
½ cup (125 ml) milk
500 g minced chuck steak (see note
    on p. 148)
1 brown onion, very finely chopped
1 egg yolk
½ cup (40 g) finely grated parmesan,
    plus extra to serve
2 tablespoons olive oil
1 brown onion, chopped
2 × 400 g tins no-added-salt
    chopped tomatoes
½ teaspoon sugar
cooked pasta, to serve

We've upped the ante by choosing flavourful chuck steak for our ever-popular melt-in-your-mouth meatballs and the best-ever cheeseburger that is loved by our community of kids. Ask your butcher to mince your chuck steak for you, or if you have a mincer you can do it yourself. Cook one to enjoy for dinner, and the other for the next night or for the freezer!

melt-in-your-mouth meatballs

Line a baking tray with baking paper.

Place the breadcrumbs and milk in a large mixing bowl and set aside to soak for 10 minutes.

Add the mince to the soaked breadcrumbs along with half the onion, the egg yolk and parmesan. Use clean hands to mix thoroughly. Shape level tablespoons of mixture into balls and place onto the other baking tray. Refrigerate for at least 30 minutes. Meanwhile, preheat the oven to 190°C (170°C fan-forced).

Remove the meatballs from the fridge and drizzle with 1 tablespoon olive oil, turning gently to coat. Bake for 12 minutes, or until browned but not yet cooked though.

In a large heavy-based saucepan or frying pan, heat remaining olive oil over medium heat. Add remaining onion and sauté for 3–4 minutes, until just soft. Add the tomatoes and sugar and stir to combine. Add the meatballs to the pan and simmer gently for 20 minutes until the sauce has reduced a little and the meatballs are cooked through.

Serve the meatballs and sauce over pasta, sprinkled with parmesan and seasoned with pepper, if desired.

baby serve: mash or chop some meatballs with the pasta and spoon feed to your baby, and/or halve or chop the meatballs into an appropriate shape and offer as finger food alongside some vegetables and some fruit.

toddler serve: serve the meatballs whole, halved or chopped on top of or alongside some pasta. Offer some vegetables and a serve of fruit too.

Continued →

makes **8 burgers**
prep time: **30 minutes +**
30 minutes chilling
cooking time: **10 minutes**

1 kg minced chuck steak (see note)
8 round rolls or burger buns, sliced
in half
8 cheese slices
sliced onion, pickles, tomatoes,
or lettuce to serve, as desired
tomato or barbecue sauce,
to serve (optional)

best-ever cheeseburgers

Divide the mince into 8 equal portions. Shape into burger patties about 1.5 cm thick and place on a lined baking tray. For young babies and toddlers, divide a few into even smaller portions (about 60–80 g each). Cover and place in the fridge for 30 minutes, to firm up.

To cook the burgers, preheat a chargrill pan or barbecue over medium–high heat. Cook the burgers for 3–4 minutes each side or until browned and cooked through. If you are using freshly minced chuck steak, you may like to cook your burgers to 'medium' rather than well-done for older children and adults, if they prefer.

Lightly toast the burger buns on the barbecue or under a preheated grill for 30 seconds.

Place a slice of cheese on each bun base, or on top of the hot burgers to melt. Serve the burgers in the buns, with any of your preferred extras.

baby serve: finely chop and mash ¼ –½ burger patty and combine with some cooked and mashed or pureed vegetables. Offer some sliced or chopped burger patty as finger food too, if desired.

toddler serve: choose a small burger patty and place in a small bread roll or sandwich to eat. Alternatively, serve the burger deconstructed and allow your child to enjoy all the elements separate to one another or give them the opportunity to 'build their own burger' from what's on offer.

TIP: we love to cook these meatballs in the slow cooker, and sometimes the pressure cooker. Cook in the slow cooker on LOW for 4–5 hours or in the pressure cooker on HIGH for 5 minutes. Allow the pressure to release naturally for 10 minutes and then use manual release to fully release the pressure.

NOTE: ask your butcher to mince the chuck steak. Alternatively, use premium beef mince, or pork and veal mince.

STORAGE: keep leftover cooked meatballs in an airtight container in the fridge for up to 2 days or in the freezer for up to 2 months. Uncooked meatballs can be flash frozen (p. 20) and stored in the freezer for up to 2 months. Leftover cooked burger patties can be stored in the fridge for up to 2 days. Uncooked burger patties can be layered with baking paper in an airtight container and frozen for up to 2 months.

ALLERGIES/INTOLERANCES:
Gluten/wheat: choose gluten-free rolls for the burgers and gluten-free breadcrumbs and pasta for the meatballs. **Egg:** omit the egg yolk from the meatballs or replace with 1 tablespoon chia seeds. **Dairy:** omit the cheese from the meatballs and when assembling the burgers.

tray bakes

EASY, NUTRITIOUS MEALS that can be made all on the one tray with very little clean-up sound pretty good to us. Tray bakes are the perfect meals for people who want to simplify dinner time by using just a baking tray and oven to create a delicious meal for the whole family. Tray bakes are often varied, colourful and bursting with flavour, and we are sure they will become regular favourites in your home too.

Tray bakes are an absolute time-saver and require just a few minutes' prep before going straight in the oven. They are perfect for those who need to get dinner on the table and have their hands free too. While you're planning your tray bakes you can also take the time to think about what else could be prepared or cooked for future meals, such as roast vegetable cubes for salads or mashed for baby food.

Incorporating some of these tray bake recipes into your weekly rotation will save you time and effort during those busy evenings.

Here are some extra time-saving tips:

- Collect all of the pantry ingredients in advance and have them ready on the bench.

- Pre-mix any sauces, marinades or mixed spices to reduce pre-cooking time.

- Chop any vegetables you can in advance and place them in the fridge – especially aromatics like onion, garlic and ginger, and hardy vegetables like celery, carrot and zucchini.

- Organise any extras you need, such as baking paper, measuring cups and utensils.

- For crispy, perfectly cooked tray bakes, we suggest investing in a quality heavy-based cast-iron baking tray.

- Chop any unused veggies hanging around in the fridge and bake them with your meal. You can use them for baby food, or mashed and enjoyed in sandwich press fold-ups (p. 170), or in salads for lunch the next day.

chicken drumsticks *and* roast veggie couscous

Tray-baked meals are designed to be as simple and versatile as possible. Our chicken drumstick tray bake is no exception. To make life even easier you can pre-chop many of the veggies the night before and create a prep box of ingredients to pull out and assemble at dinner time.

To make the spice rub, combine all the ingredients in a small bowl. Paste over the chicken drumsticks, focusing on the skin.

Preheat the oven to 200°C (180°C fan-forced). Place the capsicum, garlic, onion, lemon half and sweet potato in a large non-stick roasting pan. Drizzle with the olive oil and toss to coat. Arrange the spiced chicken drumsticks between the vegetables.

Bake for 45 minutes or until the chicken is cooked through and golden brown and the vegetables are tender. Transfer the chicken to a plate and set aside to rest. Add the couscous, hot chicken stock and olives (if using) to the pan and toss through the vegetables. Cover with foil and place in the oven for 5 minutes. Remove and fluff with a fork.

To serve, place the vegetable couscous in bowls topped with a chicken drumstick, and sprinkle over the pine nuts and feta (if using) and parsley.

baby serve: mash the vegetables with the couscous, or blend with some chicken meat to create a puree and spoon feed to your baby. Alternatively, offer your baby strips of chicken as finger food to chew on, served with either mashed or finger-food veggies. Be mindful of any bones or cartilage in the chicken, which can pose a choking risk.

toddler serve: serve the roast vegetable couscous and a chicken drumstick as finger food alongside some of their preferred vegetables and fruit. Be mindful of any bones or cartilage in the chicken, which can pose a choking risk.

serves **4**
prep time: **30 minutes**
cooking time: **50 minutes**

EF

800 g free-range chicken drumsticks, skin on
1 red capsicum (pepper), sliced into 3 cm thick strips
1 yellow capsicum (pepper), sliced into 3 cm thick strips
4 cloves garlic, unpeeled
1 red onion, sliced into wedges
½ lemon
1 sweet potato, peeled, cut into 2 cm cubes
2 tablespoons olive oil
1 cup (200 g) couscous
1 cup (250 ml) chicken stock, heated
¼ cup (40 g) green olives, pitted (optional)
¼ cup (40 g) pine nuts, toasted (optional)
¼ cup (50 g) feta (optional)
small handful flat-leaf parsley, finely chopped, to garnish

barbecue spice rub
1 teaspoon dried thyme
1 teaspoon garlic salt
¼ teaspoon smoked paprika
1 tablespoon melted butter or olive oil

MEAL-PLANNING TIP: chicken drumsticks are an affordable option that most kids enjoy. You can mix up the marinade in this recipe by using any of our marinades (p. 219).

NOTE: this tray bake is delicious served with the creamy feta sauce on p. 154.

STORAGE: allow to cool slightly and keep any leftovers in the fridge for up to 2 days. We love to have leftover chopped chicken pieces and couscous in some pita bread with plain Greek-style yoghurt or hummus (p. 56). You can freeze the marinated uncooked chicken drumsticks in a freezer-proof bag for up to 2 months. Simply thaw in the fridge overnight.

ALLERGIES/INTOLERANCES:
Gluten/wheat: instead of adding the couscous at step 3, toss the roast vegetables through some quinoa cooked in gluten-free chicken stock. **Dairy:** omit the feta or use a dairy-free alternative. **Nuts:** omit the pine nuts. **Vegetarian:** serve with feta-stuffed mushrooms or pan-fried haloumi.

tray-baked salmon *and* potatoes *with* creamy feta sauce

This tray bake is a firm favourite among our families and we love how easy it is to prep and cook while still providing big, punchy flavour! You can build on this truly versatile recipe once you have mastered it by using chicken thighs instead of the salmon and by switching up the veggies on the tray. The creamy feta sauce is also a must-try and can easily be doubled.

serves **4–6**
prep time: **10 minutes**
cooking time: **35 minutes**

500 g baby potatoes, halved
½ lemon
2 tablespoons olive oil
salt and ground black pepper, to taste
4 skinless, boneless salmon fillets (500 g)
2 bunches asparagus or head of broccoli, trimmed

spice rub

1 tablespoon olive oil
1 clove garlic, finely chopped
1 teaspoon dried oregano
1 teaspoon smoked paprika
pinch of salt and pepper

creamy feta sauce

170 g Danish feta
¼ cup (70 g) plain Greek-style yoghurt
½ lemon, juiced
small handful basil, finely chopped

Preheat the oven to 200°C (180°C fan-forced). Line a baking tray with baking paper.

Toss the potatoes and lemon half in olive oil and sprinkle with salt and pepper. Place onto the baking tray and bake for 20 minutes while you prepare the salmon.

For the spice rub, combine the ingredients in a shallow bowl. Dredge the salmon fillets through the mixture to coat (you can thread some cubes of the salmon onto blunt skewers for younger children, if you like). Place the salmon and asparagus or broccoli on the tray with the par-cooked potatoes. Cook for 15 minutes or until the salmon is cooked through and the potatoes are golden.

To make the creamy feta sauce, blitz all ingredients together in a blender until smooth and creamy. Serve dolloped on top of the salmon, potatoes and veggies.

baby serve: take ¼ cup cooked salmon and a piece of potato and mash or puree until you have your desired consistency, adding a little water or your baby's preferred milk if you require a thinner puree. Offer some whole pieces of the fish, asparagus or broccoli and potato as finger food.

toddler serve: for toddlers we like to thread small 2 cm cubes of salmon on a blunt skewer to cook in the oven with the adult serves. Offer the skewer or some mashed salmon pieces on the tasting plate with asparagus or broccoli and potato as finger food, and feta sauce on the side to 'dip'.

TIME-SAVING TIP: we skewer our salmon for the kids to make it family friendly, but you can simply bake the salmon pieces as they are.

STORAGE: store leftover cooked salmon in the fridge for 24 hours and briefly reheat in a frying pan until piping hot. Creamy feta sauce can be stored in an airtight container in the fridge for up to 2 days.

ALLERGIES/INTOLERANCES:
Dairy: omit the creamy feta sauce.
Vegetarian: omit the salmon and include extra veggies such as cauliflower and brussels sprouts. Toss through some cannellini beans or chickpeas for the last 5 minutes if desired.

read more reasons why we love skewers on p. 227

tray-baked salmon, p. 154

maple mustard lamb *with* crispy potatoes

An affordable midweek meal or a Sunday 'roast' to end any fabulous family weekend, this tray bake has no-fuss ingredients and minimal prep to keep everyone happy. For extra veg, try adding some broccoli or asparagus.

Place the maple syrup, mustard and 1 tablespoon of olive oil in a large bowl. Add the lamb chops and turn to coat. Marinate for at least 30 minutes (or up to 8 hours) in the fridge. Take the lamb chops out of the fridge for 10 minutes before they're due to go in the oven.

Preheat the oven to 220°C (200°C fan-forced). Line a large rimmed baking tray with baking paper.

Cut the potatoes in half. Place onto the prepared tray and toss in 1 tablespoon olive oil, along with the garlic. Bake for 25 minutes.

Remove the tray from the oven, add the brussels sprouts and drizzle with the remaining oil. Arrange the lamb chops on the tray, leaving a little space between each one. Return to the oven for 15 minutes, then add the tomatoes and cook for a further 10 minutes. Remove from the oven and allow to rest for 10 minutes before serving.

baby serve: for a spoon-fed meal, finely slice or mash the lamb with some potato and tomato, mixing through some of their favourite veggie puree too if you wish. Blend together for a smoother puree. For a finger-food option, refer to the toddler serve.

toddler serve: offer some sliced lamb, chopped roast potatoes and halved cherry tomatoes along with a serve of fruit. Avoid adding salt to the potatoes.

serves **4**
prep time: **10 minutes +**
    30 minutes marinating
cooking time: **50 minutes**

DF EF GF WF

1½ tablespoons pure maple syrup
1 tablespoon Dijon mustard
2½ tablespoons extra virgin olive oil
4 × 150 g lamb chump or loin chops
500 g baby potatoes
2 cloves garlic, crushed
6 brussels sprouts, trimmed
200 g truss cherry tomatoes

TIME-SAVING TIP: marinate the lamb in the morning before you head out for the day, or keep a stash of the marinated lamb in the freezer to cut down the prep work even more. It can't get any easier!

TIP: you may prefer to use lamb cutlets. These take around 20 minutes to cook and we recommend turning them halfway through.

STORAGE: keep leftovers in the fridge for up to 2 days. Leftover sliced lamb can be enjoyed with salad or with the tomatoes and some cheese in a toasted sandwich or quesadilla.

a brilliant breakfast tray bake

Whether it's for a family breakfast or breakfast-for-dinner, there is something for everyone in this recipe, even if it's just the sausage and toast. We love it because it's colourful and tasty and there's hardly any washing up.

serves 4–6
prep time: **10 minutes**
cooking time: **40 minutes**

8 small chipolatas,
    or 4 thin sausages
1 tablespoon extra virgin olive oil
4 medium flat brown or white
    mushrooms
75 g feta, crumbled
1 teaspoon finely grated lemon zest
squeeze of lemon juice
1 bunch spinach, trimmed
2 rashers bacon, rind removed,
    halved lengthways
4 eggs
200 g truss cherry tomatoes,
    or handful of cherry tomatoes
    (optional)
sourdough or whole grain toast,
    to serve (optional)

Preheat the oven to 200°C (180°C fan-forced) and line a large rimmed baking tray with baking paper.

Place the chipolatas on the tray, drizzle with a teaspoon of oil and bake for 10 minutes.

Meanwhile, remove the stalks from the mushrooms and drizzle a teaspoon of oil over the top side of the mushrooms. In a small bowl, combine the feta, lemon zest and juice. Finely chop 1 tablespoon of the spinach leaves and stir into the feta mixture. Place mushrooms top side down on a board and spoon feta mixture onto them, dividing evenly. Drizzle over the remaining oil.

Remove the baking tray from the oven and arrange the mushrooms and bacon between the sausages. Return to the oven and roast for 15 minutes or until golden.

Meanwhile, place the remaining spinach in a heatproof bowl and pour over some boiling water. Gently stir for 20 seconds or until wilted. Drain the spinach, rinse under cold water and squeeze out the excess liquid.

Divide the spinach into 4 portions, and make 4 little piles among the chipolatas, mushrooms and bacon, with a well in each to hold the eggs. Crack an egg into each well, add the tomatoes to the tray (if using) and bake for a further 12 minutes, or until the eggs are cooked to your liking and the tomatoes are tender.

Season with freshly cracked pepper and serve with toast.

baby serve: best offered to older babies or toddlers. Younger babies may enjoy some toast strips with ricotta, a small slice or two of sausage and some well-cooked egg alongside a serve of puree or finger-food fruit.

toddler serve: serve sliced sausage, a little bit of bacon and some spinach and egg on a tasting plate. Older toddlers may like to dip some toast in the egg, or have it spread with ricotta.

FUSSY EATING TIP: whether they're picking out the bacon or sausage to enjoy with some bread, dipping a toast finger into the egg yolk, or spooning out the feta from the mushroom, there are lots of ways to engage the reluctant eater when enjoying this delicious tray bake.

STORAGE: leftovers can be stored in the fridge for up to 2 days.

ALLERGIES/INTOLERANCES:
Gluten/wheat: choose gluten-free sausages and gluten-free bread for toast. **Egg:** omit the egg. **Dairy:** omit the feta. **Vegetarian:** omit the bacon and serve with vegetarian sausages and add some extra vegetables such as brussels sprouts and asparagus.

hoisin *and* ginger beef meatballs *with* vegetables

A tray-bake twist on the standard stir-fry! Save even more time and cut down the clean-up by prepping the meatballs, sauce and veggies in advance. Sure to be a hit with the whole family, this meal is a great way to offer veggies that kids enjoy while also introducing and maintaining exposure to veggies they may regularly refuse.

DF

serves **6**
prep time: **20 minutes**
cooking time: **30 minutes**

2 tablespoons hoisin sauce
¼ cup (60 ml) sweet chilli sauce
¼ cup (60 ml) kecap manis
⅓ cup (80 ml) light soy sauce
500 g premium beef mince
1½ tablespoons finely grated ginger
2 cloves garlic, finely chopped
2 eggs
¾ cup (90 g) dried breadcrumbs
1 red capsicum (pepper), sliced
1 yellow capsicum (pepper), sliced
1 carrot, sliced
extra virgin olive oil, for drizzling
400 g packet hokkien noodles, prepared according to packet instructions
200 g snow peas or sugar snap peas, trimmed

Preheat the oven to 220°C (200°C fan-forced). Grease a large rimmed baking tray or roasting pan.

In a small bowl, combine the hoisin, sweet chilli, kecap manis and soy sauce. Set aside.

In a medium bowl, combine the beef mince with the ginger, garlic, eggs and breadcrumbs. Add 2½ tablespoons of the sauce mixture. Mix well to combine and roll level tablespoons of mixture into meatballs.

Place the sliced capsicum and carrot onto the prepared tray or pan, lightly drizzle with a little oil and toss to coat. Top with the meatballs and drizzle over half the remaining sauce mixture. Bake for 20 minutes, or until the meatballs are cooked and golden.

Add the noodles, snow or sugar snap peas and the remaining sauce. Toss gently to combine. Bake for a further 10 minutes, or until the peas are vibrant and tender.

Serve in shallow bowls.

baby serve: offer appropriate elements of the tray bake, such as the meatballs, cooked vegetables and noodles, chopping to a size your baby is capable of picking up to eat. Alternatively, mash some of the meatballs with some cooked rice or mashed vegetables to spoon feed to your baby.

toddler serve: serve elements of the tray bake your toddler enjoys mixed together in a bowl, alongside a plate of a few things they may be learning to like. Alternatively, serve the meatballs, noodles and vegetables deconstructed on a tasting plate.

STORAGE: leftovers can be stored in an airtight container in the fridge for up to 2 days.

FUSSY EATING TIP: if you have a toddler- or child-friendly food-prep knife available, ask your child to help slice the capsicum. Other things they may be able to help with include peeling carrots, cracking eggs and rolling some meatballs.

ALLERGIES/INTOLERANCES: Gluten/wheat: check the ingredient lists of your sauces and choose gluten-free sauces. Use gluten-free breadcrumbs. Omit the hokkien noodles and toss through cooked rice noodles at step 6. **Egg:** replace the eggs with 2 'chia eggs' (p. 21). Substitute cooked rice noodles for hokkien noodles. **Vegetarian:** use sliced firm tofu in place of the beef meatballs.

storing leftovers correctly in quality airtight containers can help reduce household food wastage

fast-prep pasta bake, p. 173

fast meals

WITH SO MUCH MEAL PREP AND PLANNING GOING ON during the week, busy parents need to include some nights off in their schedule. Sometimes the chaos of family life causes even the best-laid plans to go awry at the last minute. But having a few fast meals up your sleeve means that you're prepared for these bumps in the road, without any of the unnecessary stress.

Fast meals might be simple, but they are the humble lifesavers of the week that will save you time as well as money on greasy takeaway and expensive top-up shops. Having a select number of pantry and fridge staples on hand will keep you cooking wholesome food in minutes and are a great way to use up leftovers from the weekly shop.

simple homemade 'fast food'

We believe in simple, wholesome food, and there's nothing wrong with including the basics in your meal plan each week. An egg on toast, baked beans, or breakfast for dinner all have their place in a busy household. Here are 10 easy ideas for when everyone is exhausted that don't even require a recipe:

1 Eggs with buttery toast

2 Baked bean toastie

3 Pasta with pesto

4 Porridge topped with fresh or stewed fruit

5 Tinned tuna and salad

6 Cheese on toast

7 BLAT – bacon, lettuce, avocado and tomato sandwich

8 Platter of raw veggies, sliced cold meats or tinned legumes, cheese, crackers and fruit

9 Baked potato with tuna or cheese

10 Hummus and salad wraps

make-something-from-nothing staples

You will find that our recipes include lots of pantry, fridge and freezer staples that allow you to make something from next to nothing. Swapping similar-textured veggies, using leftover meats and stirring through different proteins are all doable in our recipes. Keeping a few long-shelf-life staples on hand will mean you always have something for weeknights that are busy with activities or simply don't go to plan.

Have some staple items to use up and not sure where to start? Use our simple guide to find your staple and match it with a meal:

staple	what to make/serve with
Arborio rice	Baked risotto with garlic prawns (p. 168)
Coconut cream	Gado gado (p. 192)
Coconut milk	Butter chicken (p. 93)
	Coconut beef curry with vegetables (p. 98)
Corn chips	Leftover nachos (p. 106)
	Guacamole (p. 106)
Couscous	Chicken drumsticks and roast veggie couscous (p. 152)
Dried noodles	Veggie noodle muffins (p. 62)
Dried pasta	Broccoli and bacon carbonara (p. 174)
	Fast-prep pasta bake (p. 173)
	Creamy garlic chicken (p. 100)
	Stir through a frozen pesto (p. 58)
	Sausage ragu (p. 126)
	Lemony chicken and risoni soup (p. 130)
Dried red lentils	Vegetable red lentil lasagne with spinach (p. 144)
	Vegetable and red lentil soup (p. 145)
Eggs	Tomato and chorizo frittata (p. 180)
	Zucchini slice (p. 136)
	Zucchini nuggets (p. 138)
	Breakfast tray bake (p. 158)
	Classic caesar salad (p. 198)
Hokkien noodles	Hoisin and ginger beef meatballs with vegetables (p. 160)
Peanut butter	Gado gado (p. 192)
Potatoes	Barbecue mince and cheese-loaded baked potatoes (p. 118)
	Tray-baked salmon and potatoes with creamy feta sauce (p. 154)
Quinoa	Quinoa and marinated feta salad (p. 196)
Ready-rolled puff pastry	Vegetable curry puffs (p. 112)
	Pork and caramelised apple sausage rolls (p. 54)
	Chicken and leek pie with cauliflower potato mash (p. 124)
	Creamy fish pies (p. 109)
	Spinach and cheese 'croissants' (p. 52)
Rice	Rainbow rice salad (p. 60)
	Soy roast chicken (p. 114)
	Leftover chicken fried rice (p. 116)

staple	*what to make/serve with*
Tahini	Roast cauliflower and chickpea salad (p. 200)
	Rice Bubble and seed mini bars (p. 46)
Tinned brown lentils	Spiced lamb pastry pockets (p. 143)
Tinned chickpeas	Roast cauliflower and chickpea salad (p. 200)
Tinned red kidney beans	Mexican bean burrito bowl (p. 182)
Tinned tomatoes/passata	Melt-in-your-mouth meatballs (p. 146)
	Mexican beef with dumplings (p. 104)
Tinned tuna	Tuna and pesto balls (p. 58)
Tortillas	Sandwich press fold-ups (p. 170)
	Fish tacos with corn salsa and lime mayonnaise (p. 122)
	Mexican bean burrito bowl (p. 182)

supper or bedtime meals

Supper can be a daily or an occasional part of your meal schedule. Whether you offer supper will depend on your family, what time you eat dinner and your family members' appetites. Some children naturally have a greater appetite in the morning, and eat particularly well earlier in the day, and even after a small dinner may go to bed satisfied. Other children's appetites peak later in the day and they enjoy a good dinner and a bedtime snack too.

If you have a reluctant eater who regularly refuses dinner, we recommend you avoid offering uneaten dinner items or lunchbox leftovers for supper as this tends to only contribute to anxiety and fussy eating behaviours. We believe supper can be included in schedules in a positive way, free of pressure and without creating bad habits, and can even be an opportunity to help top up any nutrients that may have been missed throughout the day.

reasons to offer supper

- **Early dinner:** if your family enjoys an early dinner, at around 5–5.30 pm, and there are a couple of hours before bedtime, at say 7.30–8 pm, including a bedtime snack may be worthwhile.
- **Consistency:** if irregular suppers create tension at bedtime or anxiety in your child, including a small snack routinely can help keep them calm and help smoothen the transition.
- **Genuine hunger:** for children whose appetites peak later in the day, or for children on medication that affects their appetite and those experiencing growth spurts, supper can offer the additional energy and essential nutrients their growing bodies require.

- **Growth spurts and active days:** some days kids are more active than others or require more energy and nutrients to satisfy their needs, and an occasional supper snack can help provide these.
- **Overnight or early waking:** there are many reasons for this, but if it happens consistently and they complain that they are hungry, a small snack containing carbohydrates and protein at bedtime may help.

simple supper rules

If you do offer supper it's important to treat this bedtime snack just like another mealtime. It's not bribery for eating dinner or a reward for good behaviour. Keep it positive. We have a couple of basic rules for keeping supper simple and relaxed:

1 Offer supper at least 45 minutes after dinner time. Avoid offering it to kids who ask for it immediately after their dinner, especially after food refusal.

2 Keep the meal simple and not too exciting. We aren't cooking or creating an extravagant meal here. Supper should serve its purpose of filling and satisfying a hungry tummy quickly. If your child refuses what's on offer, they're probably not that hungry.

supper options

When serving supper we like to choose simple, no-fuss, filling foods that don't require much energy to eat or effort to prepare. Plus, if you keep the meal simple, children tend to only ask for it when they really need it.

Great foods to try are:

- yoghurt, on its own or sprinkled with seeds or muesli
- a piece of fruit
- Weet-Bix, cooked oats or wholegrain cereal
- a small bowl of custard
- a small glass of warm milk
- a slice of cheese and a few crackers
- a nut butter sandwich

NOTE As with all meals, children should only eat what they need and not be forced to finish. When your child listens to their body, they will eat as much as they require, and this becomes a healthy habit for both everyday and sometimes food. Enjoy seeing one bite left on their plate and rest assured your hard work is paying off!

keeping supper positive

When we respect our children's hunger and fullness cues and offer supper in a respectful and simple way, we may find it doesn't necessarily need to be an everyday meal and can come and go with those unseen developmental or nutritional needs. Here are a couple of questions we're often asked about supper:

what if my older child needs supper but my younger child doesn't?

If an older sibling needs and enjoys a bedtime snack and a younger sibling wants the same but may not need it, you can try to resolve this in one of two ways. Firstly, if the older sibling goes to bed later, perhaps wait until the younger child has gone to bed before offering the snack. Alternatively, you can offer the younger child a smaller portion of the same snack. Initially the excitement will encourage engagement and interest but you may find that this interest wears off and they no longer care for supper very often. Or they may genuinely enjoy the snack and the time spent with their sibling.

what if my child refuses dinner and holds out for supper?

There are many children who refuse dinner, or who eat little because they simply aren't hungry. They go to bed happy, sleep well and wake ready to enjoy a good breakfast. For these children there is no need for supper. Others may begin to hold out for it, if they are only offered it on evenings when they refuse their meal. This can lead to more frequent food refusal. So the first option is to phase out supper and include more liked foods – such as bread, pasta, fruit or even desserts – with dinner, particularly dinners that are challenging or that they are still learning to like. This is particularly effective if there is only a short window between dinner and their bedtime. The other option is to offer supper consistently as a separate mealtime – not just when they refuse food and not immediately after dinner. Transitioning to a daily bedtime snack creates a firm routine, reduces anxiety and may in fact lead to your child becoming more engaged with the refused foods.

It's important to remember that you are responsible for what's on offer at supper. It's not a time to take requests. If it's a piece of fruit or cheese and crackers that's on offer, they can take it or leave it. You provide, they decide. Just be mindful to provide a liked food, as continually offering foods they are learning to like can contribute to any ongoing mealtime anxiety.

baked risotto *with* garlic prawns

For many families, risotto is a crowd-pleaser. You can mix and match different ingredients to produce a varied meal each time. However, standing over the stove and stirring isn't achievable on a busy evening. Introducing the baked risotto. Pour it all in, pop it in the oven and voila! Enjoy your favourite meal with minimal effort.

EF

serves **4**
prep time: **10 minutes**
cooking time: **50 minutes**

2 tablespoons unsalted butter

1 brown onion, finely chopped

1 zucchini (courgette), coarsely grated

1 sprig thyme

3 cloves garlic, finely chopped

¾ cup (150 g) arborio rice

2½ cups (625 ml) salt-reduced vegetable stock, heated

½ cup (40 g) finely grated parmesan or ½ cup (60 g) grated cheddar cheese + extra to serve

1 tablespoon olive oil

16 peeled uncooked prawns

oven-warmed baguette and green salad, to serve

Preheat the oven to 180°C (160°C fan-forced).

Heat 1 tablespoon of butter in a large ovenproof saucepan or flameproof casserole dish over medium heat. Add the onion, zucchini, thyme and 2 chopped garlic cloves. Cook for 5 minutes or until soft and starting to caramelise. Add the rice and hot stock and stir to combine.

Cover tightly with foil or a lid and bake for 45 minutes or until the stock is absorbed and the rice is cooked through.

Gently fold through the parmesan or cheddar cheese and 1 tablespoon of butter.

To cook the prawns, heat the olive oil in a frying pan over medium–high heat. Add the prawns and stir-fry for 2 minutes or until golden and almost cooked through. Reduce the heat to low, add the remaining garlic and continue to fry for a further 2 minutes. Remove from the heat.

Top the risotto with the garlic prawns and sprinkle with extra cheese. Serve with the baguette and salad.

baby serve: take ¼ cup of cooked risotto, mash any lumps to ensure an even texture, stir through 1 tablespoon of their preferred milk and serve. Offer a prawn as finger food to munch on.

toddler serve: once the risotto is cool enough to touch, roll teaspoon-sized amounts of mixture into balls. Serve on a tasting plate with some chopped prawn, bread and fresh fruit.

STORAGE: keep leftover risotto in an airtight container in the fridge for up to 3 days. Alternatively, freeze for up to 3 months. The leftover cooked prawns can be stored in the fridge and enjoyed within 24 hours.

OPTIONAL EXTRAS: love this risotto but want to mix it up? Try omitting the prawns and roasting some sweet potato or pumpkin cubes in the oven while the risotto is cooking, or stirring through a small tin of tuna or leftover roast chicken (p. 114) when you add the cheese.

ALLERGIES: Gluten/wheat: use a gluten-free stock. **Dairy:** use olive oil instead of butter. Omit the cheese. **Vegetarian:** omit the prawns and sauté some sliced mushrooms with the zucchini. Alternatively, stir through some roasted sweet potato or pumpkin with the cheese.

sandwich press fold-ups

Sandwich press fold-ups are a simple and delicious way to use up leftover meals and meats. You can use any leftover cooked minced, shredded or casserole meats from the meals within this book. Simply omit the ham and get creative – there are endless ways to enjoy these simple fold-ups.

(EF)

serves **4**
prep time: **10 minutes**
cooking time: **15 minutes**

4 large flour tortillas
4 slices (120 g) ham
   (or leftover meat or veg)
2 cups (240 g) grated cheddar cheese
1 cup baby spinach leaves
2 tablespoons whole-egg aioli or
   mayonnaise
sliced avocado and side salad,
   to serve (optional)

Take your tortillas and make a cut from the middle top down to the centre (see pic). Add your chosen meat to one quarter, the cheese to another quarter, the spinach to another quarter and the aioli to the last quarter. Fold them up into triangles and place on the sandwich press. Close, press and cook until golden brown and the cheese has melted.

Serve with some sliced avocado, or a side salad if desired.

baby serve: omit the ham for babies and instead use cooked shredded meats, mashed roast veggies or baked beans. Slice into strips or small triangles and serve as finger food to your baby alongside some vegetables and fruit. Offer a small serving of a spoon-fed meal too, if they prefer this texture over finger foods.

toddler serve: serve the triangle sliced and alongside some finger-food vegetables and fruit.

FILLINGS WE LOVE: baked beans and cheese; Mexican beef (p. 105) and rice; shredded soy roast chicken (p. 114) and cheese; Sweet shredded pork and slaw (p. 90); roasted vegetables and couscous.

NOTE: if you don't have a sandwich press you can simply use a frying pan. Heat the frying pan over medium heat. Drizzle some olive oil and cook the fold-ups on both sides until golden brown.

STORAGE: best served fresh.

ALLERGIES/INTOLERANCES:
Gluten/wheat: use gluten-free tortillas. Egg: omit the aioli or mayonnaise. Dairy: omit the cheese. Vegetarian: try these fold-ups with roasted vegetables or beans.

chicken mince stir-fry

Without a single thing you need to dice, slice or chop, this is the ultimate quick stir-fry for busy weeknights.

serves **4**
prep time: **5 minutes**
cooking time: **7 minutes**

2 tablespoons olive oil
500 g free-range chicken mince
2 cloves garlic, crushed
200 g sugar snap peas, trimmed
2 tablespoons salt-reduced soy sauce
1 tablespoon dark soy sauce
   (or extra salt-reduced soy sauce)
1 tablespoon sweet chilli sauce
1 tablespoon fish sauce
2 teaspoons sugar
lime wedges, to serve (optional)
cooked rice or noodles, to serve

Heat the oil in a wok or frying pan over medium–high heat. Add the chicken mince and cook, breaking up any lumps, for 5 minutes. Stir through the garlic and sugar snap peas.

Add the sauces and sugar and cook, stirring, for a further 2 minutes. Add a tablespoon or two of water to loosen the sauce, if you prefer.

Serve with lime wedges, if desired, and cooked rice or noodles.

baby serve: serve a spoonful of the stir-fry on top of some noodles or mashed through some rice and extra pureed veggies. Offer a sugar snap pea or noodles as finger food too. To avoid the high-salt sauces, remove some of the cooked chicken mince for your baby before adding the sauces for the rest of the family.

toddler serve: serve the stir-fry with, or alongside, some rice or noodles with a few sugar snap peas.

MEAL PLANNING TIP: the sugar snap peas and sauces can be prepped in advance to shave more time off your meal prep. Or just grab a handful of veggies from your veggie grab box (p. 28).

FUSSY EATING TIP: sugar snap peas are so easy to grow from seeds or seedlings in the garden, or a pot, and they taste so fresh, sweet and crisp.

Give growing them a go with young children – they're bound to give a fresh-picked one a try, and this is a fantastic bridging step to other similar veggies such as green beans and snow peas.

STORAGE: keep leftover stir-fry in an airtight container in the fridge for up to 2 days.

ALLERGIES/INTOLERANCES:
Gluten/wheat: choose gluten-free fish sauce and soy sauces.
Vegetarian: replace the chicken mince with extra veggies such as white onion, bok choy or gai lan, capsicum and a tin of corn spears. Add some tofu if you like; omit the fish sauce.

This is a super-quick pasta bake you can throw together at the end of the week when all that is left is a bare fridge and a few pantry staples. It's perfect for when you are low on time and motivation.

Preheat the oven to 200°C (180°C fan-forced).

Cook the pasta according to packet instructions. Drain well and return to the saucepan. Add the pasta sauce, half the cheese and any of the optional protein or veggies you like. Stir to combine.

Pour the mixture into an 8-cup (2 litre) capacity baking dish and top with the remaining cheese. Bake for 30 minutes or until the cheese is golden.

baby serve: pull apart some of the pasta bake to offer to your baby as finger food alongside some finger-food veggies and fruit. If they enjoy spoon-fed meals, chop or mash the pasta bake into smaller portions with or without some veggie puree or extra pasta sauce for a smoother texture. Alternatively, offer the pasta bake as finger food alongside a spoon-fed portion of veggies and/or fruit.

toddler serve: serve a portion of the pasta bake on a tasting plate with some veggies and a portion of fruit. Alternatively, serve with some salad or vegetables in the middle of the table, family-style, for your toddler to choose from. Refer to the fussy eating tip for more serving options for reluctant eaters.

BONUS: Slow cooker tomato and basil pasta sauce
Add 2 finely chopped onions, 2 crushed cloves garlic, four 400 g tins no-added-salt chopped tomatoes, ⅓ cup (95 g) no-added-salt tomato paste, 1 tablespoon balsamic vinegar, 2 teaspoons sugar, 2 bay leaves and 2 teaspoons dried basil to the bowl of a slow cooker. Stir to combine. Cover and cook on LOW for 6 hours or HIGH for 3 hours. Alternatively, you can cook for 15 minutes in a pressure cooker, allowing the pressure to release naturally for 10 minutes before manually releasing the pressure completely. When the sauce has cooled, transfer to a blender or food processor and process until smooth. This makes around 7 cups (1.75 litres). Store in an airtight container in the fridge for up to 3 days, or freeze in portions for up to 3 months.

fast-prep
pasta bake

serves **6–8**
prep time: **10 minutes**
cooking time: **about 40 minutes**

500 g spiral or penne pasta
2 cups (420 g) slow cooker pasta sauce (see below) or 400 g jar good-quality tomato and basil pasta sauce
3 cups (360 g) grated cheddar cheese
Optional protein: 1 cup (160 g) leftover shredded chicken, 185 g tin Italian-style tuna, drained, or 400 g tin chickpeas, rinsed and drained
Optional veggies: 60 g chopped spinach, 1 punnet (200 g) chopped cherry tomatoes, 1 zucchini, coarsely grated, ½ cup (60 g) peas

STORAGE: keep leftover pasta bake in the fridge for up to 3 days. Alternatively, freeze unbaked portions in airtight containers for up to 3 months.

ALLERGIES/INTOLERANCES:
Gluten/wheat: use gluten-free pasta.
Dairy: if only some require dairy free, reserve some of the pasta mixed with the pasta sauce and set aside

to serve separately before adding the cheese and baking the pasta bake. If everyone requires dairy-free, omit the cheese.

broccoli *and* bacon carbonara

This is a quick, tasty and light yet creamy pasta sauce that cooks in the same amount of time as the pasta, and that is versatile enough to suit whatever you may have in the fridge. Transform the scraggly mushrooms, use the last of the peas, and even add leftover sliced sausages in place of the bacon.

serves **4**

prep time: **10 minutes**

cooking time: **10 minutes**

300 g dried pappardelle, linguine or your preferred pasta

2 tablespoons olive oil

3 rashers bacon, trimmed and chopped

¾ cup (70 g) chopped broccoli florets

3 eggs

¼ cup (20 g) finely grated parmesan cheese, plus extra to serve

ground black pepper

Bring a large pot of water to the boil over high heat, add the pasta and cook according to packet instructions.

While the pasta is cooking, heat the oil in a large frying pan over medium heat. Add the bacon and broccoli and cook for 5 minutes, or until the bacon has browned and crisped up to your liking, and the broccoli is tender and vibrant in colour. Turn off the heat.

Whisk the eggs in a small bowl with the parmesan cheese and season with a little pepper.

When the pasta is cooked, drain, reserving ¼ cup (60 ml) of the cooking liquid. Add the pappardelle to the pan with the bacon and broccoli, along with a spoonful or two of the cooking liquid, and the egg. Toss everything together until the egg is just set and creamy, but not scrambled.

Serve in bowls and season with extra parmesan and pepper.

baby serve: chop the pasta and broccoli, and some bacon if you wish, into small pieces and spoon feed to your baby. For a smoother texture, mix through a few spoonfuls of veggie puree with the pasta. Serve some longer lengths of linguine and bits of broccoli alongside their spoon-fed meal to explore and enjoy as finger food.

toddler serve: serve a small bowl of linguine carbonara to your toddler. Or deconstruct and serve as per the fussy eating tip below.

FUSSY EATING TIP: deconstructing the sauce for children still learning to like bacon, broccoli or creamy sauces may help to sensitively stretch their preferences to new flavours and more complex textures. As you prepare the carbonara, reserve (or set aside) some of the bacon, broccoli and pasta before combining with the egg. Serve these separately, or on the side of their preferred pasta, to allow your child to explore all the elements without pressure.

TIME-SAVING TIP: chop the bacon and broccoli, crack the eggs and grate the parmesan in the morning or during 'nap time', and store them, covered, in the fridge to save precious minutes in the evening.

ALLERGIES/INTOLERANCES:
Gluten/wheat: use gluten-free pasta. Egg: use ½ cup (125 ml) thickened cream instead of the egg. At step 4, over low heat, add the cream instead of the egg, then the parmesan, pasta and all of the reserved pasta water. Cook, stirring regularly, until the liquid has reduced into a thick creamy sauce. Add the extra parmesan, season with pepper and serve.
Dairy: omit the parmesan cheese, and try adding a teaspoon or two of nutritional yeast for a cheesy flavour.
Vegetarian: omit the bacon, sauté some mushrooms with the broccoli and add some peas and chopped spinach to wilt along with the pasta.

examples of how to sensitively stretch your child to enjoy new foods and flavours

easy roasted fish parcels *with* couscous

Fish is always a winning choice when you are short on time. These delightful and nutritious little parcels can be prepped and assembled earlier in the day, so you can simply pop them in the oven as the pre-dinner chaos descends.

serves **4**
prep time: **15 minutes**
cooking time: **25 minutes**

400 g tin no-added-salt
    chopped tomatoes
1 cup (200 g) wholemeal couscous
1 small (110 g) zucchini (courgettes),
    sliced
1 small red onion, finely sliced
250 g cherry tomatoes, halved
1 lemon, zest finely grated,
    cut into wedges
1 tablespoon olive oil
salt and ground black pepper
    (optional)
4 × 120–150 g firm white boneless fish
    fillets (such as flathead, snapper
    or thawed frozen basa fillets)
dill or flat-leaf parsley sprigs

Preheat the oven to 180°C (160°C fan-forced). Tear four 35 cm long pieces of foil and four 35 cm long pieces of baking paper. Place a sheet of baking paper on top of each piece of foil and lay out on a clean benchtop.

Spoon the tinned tomato onto the centre of each piece of baking paper, dividing it evenly.

In a medium bowl, combine the couscous, zucchini, onion, cherry tomatoes and lemon zest. Drizzle over the olive oil, squeeze over some lemon juice and season with pepper, if desired.

Spoon the couscous and vegetables on top of the tomatoes, top with the fish and scatter over the dill or parsley. Season the fish with salt and pepper, if desired.

Seal the parcels by bringing the two longer sides together and folding tightly, then tucking the ends underneath. Carefully place the parcels onto a large baking tray. Bake for 20–25 minutes. The fish should be cooked through and the couscous tender. Serve with the remaining lemon wedges.

baby serve: mash together the fish, couscous and vegetables and spoon feed to your baby. Flake some fish and offer as finger food with some of the vegetable pieces.

toddler serve: serve the couscous in a bowl, with the fish flaked on top. Alternatively, deconstruct and offer on a tasting plate with a serve of fruit.

FUSSY EATING TIP: for children who might be overwhelmed by a veggie-loaded parcel, you can begin by serving this recipe with plain couscous. Once they warm to the parcels, try serving the veggies on the side. In the final step you can begin to add small amounts of their favourite veggies to the couscous as per the recipe. For children who love to dip, you can add one alongside this meal. Tartare sauce or aioli work well, and encourage children to try something new alongside something familiar.

STORAGE: leftover fish and couscous can be stored in an airtight container in the fridge for up to 2 days.

ALLERGIES/INTOLERANCES:
Gluten/wheat: use cooked quinoa instead of couscous. Vegetarian: try steaming some extra vegetables and serve with some pan-fried firm tofu or legumes.

beef skewers *with* honey-mustard sauce

This sweet sauce is everything! Drizzling it over the classic beef skewers takes them to the next level. We love to enjoy these skewers by sliding the cooked meat off onto fresh pita bread and crunchy cucumber slices. For a more wintery meal you can serve the skewers with fluffy basmati rice and peas and, as always, drizzled with the delicious sauce.

(EF)

makes **8 skewers**

prep time: **10 minutes +**
    optional marinating time

cooking time: **10 minutes**

⅓ cup (95 g) + 1 tablespoon Dijon
    honey mustard
1 tablespoon olive oil
500 g sirloin or rump steak, fat
    trimmed, cut into 2 cm cubes
½ cup (125 ml) cooking cream
pita bread, to serve
sliced cucumber, to serve

You will need 8 metal skewers for this recipe. Pre-soak in water for 10 minutes if you're using regular bamboo skewers.

Mix 1 tablespoon of the mustard and the olive oil in a shallow bowl. Add the beef cubes and toss to coat. Cook straight away, or cover and refrigerate for up to 24 hours to marinate the meat. (If you are making for your baby, omit the mustard marinade on their serve of meat.)

Thread the marinated beef onto the skewers, leaving a small gap between each piece. Heat a barbecue hot plate or a frying pan over medium–high heat. Cook the skewers for 10 minutes, turning to cook evenly, or until slightly charred and cooked to your liking. Remove from the heat and allow to rest.

To make the sauce, place the remaining honey mustard with the cream in a saucepan over medium heat. Stir until combined and heated through.

Slide the beef off the skewers and serve on fresh pita bread with sliced cucumber, drizzled with the creamy sauce.

baby serve: combine ¼ cup of finely chopped meat with ¼ cup mashed sweet potato or other puree, to create a textured meal for your baby. Serve alongside some steamed vegetables and fruit.

toddler serve: thread the beef onto a small blunt bamboo skewer for your toddler to enjoy on their tasting plate along with torn pita bread, sliced cucumber and chopped fruit. Alternatively, dice the meat into small manageable pieces.

MONEY-SAVING TIP: choose the right cuts of meat if cooking on the grill. We like to use middle-of-the-range cuts such as sirloin or rump as they are more economical than expensive steak cuts, while still being tender and juicy. You can also halve the amount of meat used in this recipe and alternate the beef cubes with vegetables such as capsicum, button mushrooms or zucchini.

STORAGE: store leftover cooked beef skewers in the fridge for up to 2 days. The sauce is best served fresh.

ALLERGIES/INTOLERANCES:
Gluten/wheat: use gluten-free pita bread. **Dairy:** use coconut cream instead of cooking cream or serve with hummus (p. 56) instead of the sauce. **Vegetarian:** thread cubed firm tofu, haloumi and vegetables such as button mushrooms, zucchini and capsicum onto the skewers.

With their deliciously crunchy crumb, these marinated morsels are so tasty and tender they're a perfect stepping stone for children learning to like meat. We love to make these nuggets in bulk and flash freeze them (p. 20), to have a stash on hand for when we need them.

Place the soy sauce, oyster sauce, garlic, ginger and cornflour in a large bowl and stir to combine. Add the chicken and mix well to combine. Cover and marinate in the fridge for at least 4 hours, or overnight.

Preheat the oven to 220°C (200°C fan-forced) and line 2 baking trays with baking paper.

Place the breadcrumbs in a large bowl or freezer bag, add the chicken in batches, and toss well to coat in the crumbs. Repeat with the remaining chicken until all the pieces are coated. Place the crumbed chicken onto the prepared trays in a single layer.

Generously spray the chicken with oil. Bake for 20 minutes, turning halfway through cooking, until the chicken is golden brown and cooked through.

Serve the nuggets with coleslaw, mashed potatoes and your favourite dipping sauce, if you like.

baby serve: omit the sauces for your baby's nuggets to reduce the salt content. Halve or quarter the nuggets depending on the age of your baby, and serve alongside some finger-food vegetables and fruit and/or some appropriate sides.

toddler serve: serve the nuggets alongside any sides. Slice the nuggets if you need to and serve with toothpicks to engage the more reluctant eater.

homemade baked chicken nuggets

makes **approx. 50**
prep time: **20 minutes**
    (+ 4 hours marinating time)
cooking time: **20 minutes**

2 tablespoons light soy sauce
1½ tablespoons oyster sauce
2 cloves garlic, finely chopped
2 teaspoons finely grated ginger
2 teaspoons cornflour
1 kg chicken thigh fillets,
    cut into bite-sized pieces
3 cups (185 g) panko or fresh
    breadcrumbs
spray olive oil
coleslaw (p. 92) and mashed
    potatoes, to serve (optional)
dipping sauce, to serve (optional)

TIP: any leftovers are delicious served in lettuce cups, topped with chopped tomato, cucumber and your preferred sauce.

STORAGE: keep leftover cooked nuggets in an airtight container in the fridge for up to 2 days. A portion of the nuggets can be set aside uncooked, flash frozen (p. 20) and stored in an airtight container in the freezer for up to 3 months.

ALLERGIES/INTOLERANCES:
Gluten/wheat: use gluten-free sauces and breadcrumbs.
Vegetarian: try marinating firm tofu sliced into rectangles as an alternative to the chicken.

tomato *and* chorizo frittata

Eggs are a fast and nutritious family meal option when you're short on time. Frittata is a wonderful and delicious meal-in-minutes that you can add into your rotation along with boiled and scrambled eggs. Leftovers make for a satisfying lunch the next day, too.

serves **4–6**
prep time: **10 minutes**
cooking time: **25 minutes**

2 tablespoons extra virgin olive oil
1 red onion, chopped
1 small red capsicum (pepper), finely sliced
1 × 125 g chorizo, cut in half lengthways, sliced (or good-quality sausage from the butcher for babies and young toddlers)
6 eggs
¾ cup (180 ml) milk or cream
salt and ground black pepper
2 roma tomatoes, cut into thin wedges
75 g feta
flat-leaf parsley, to garnish (optional)
crusty bread and tossed mixed salad, to serve

Heat the olive oil in a 28 cm ovenproof frying pan over medium–high heat. Add the onion, capsicum and chorizo and cook, stirring occasionally, for 5 minutes, or until the chorizo starts to brown.

Meanwhile, in a medium bowl, whisk together the eggs and milk or cream. Season and set aside.

Add the tomatoes to the pan, stirring gently for 1 minute to soften slightly. Reduce the heat to medium, pour over the egg and crumble over the feta.

Cover the pan with a lid or large baking tray, reduce the heat to medium–low and cook for 10 minutes, or until the egg is set around the edges and the middle is beginning to set. Meanwhile, preheat the grill to medium–high heat.

Remove the lid or baking tray from the frying pan and transfer the pan to the grill. Cook for around 7 minutes, or until the frittata is golden brown and the eggs are set.

Carefully remove from the grill (the handle will be very hot) and stand for a few minutes. Garnish with parsley, if desired. Slice and serve with crusty bread and salad.

baby serve: slice the frittata into finger-sized portions for a baby 6–9 months, and chopped into bite-sized pieces for a baby 9–12 months. Serve alongside some finger food or mashed vegetables and fruit.

toddler serve: serve some chopped frittata on a tasting plate with some bread and finger-food vegetables and fruit.

MEAL PLANNING TIP: frittata is a great meal to include at the end of the week. Use up the last of the veggies and adapt this frittata to whatever leftovers you might have in the fridge. Mushrooms, a few spinach leaves, corn kernels and zucchini are all winning additions.

STORAGE: keep leftover frittata in an airtight container in the fridge for up to 2 days.

ALLERGIES/INTOLERANCES:
Gluten/wheat: choose a gluten-free chorizo. **Dairy:** use dairy-free milk or cream and omit the feta. **Vegetarian:** omit the chorizo.

mexican bean burrito bowl

You won't miss the meat in this fast and fresh midweek meal! Mix and match your preferred veggies and try sliced avocado instead of (or as well as) spinach, and add some coriander sprigs. Toast the corn kernels in a frying pan for 3–4 minutes for a charred flavour too. Any leftovers make for a delicious lunch!

Pour 3 cups (750 ml) of water into a medium saucepan. Add the rice and salt. Stir, cover and bring to the boil, then reduce the heat to low and simmer for 10–12 minutes or until the water has been absorbed. Remove from the heat and stand, covered, for 10 minutes for the rice to finish cooking.

While the rice is standing, heat 1 tablespoon of oil in a large frying pan over medium–high heat. Add the carrot and onion and cook for 4 minutes or until softened. Add the tomato paste, garlic and Mexican spice mix and cook for a further 1 minute, until fragrant.

Add the beans and 1 cup (250 ml) water. Stir over medium heat for 1–2 minutes to heat through and to thicken.

In a medium bowl, combine the corn and tomato, then toss with the remaining olive oil and the white vinegar.

To serve, divide the rice among bowls, top with the bean mixture and sprinkle over the cheese. Top with the spinach and the corn and tomato mixture. Serve with lime wedges, yoghurt or sour cream and warmed tortillas or corn chips, if desired.

baby serve: combine a spoonful or two of the bean mixture with some rice and stir through some chopped or mashed tomato, corn and spinach. Top with some cheese and a little yoghurt and offer as a spoon-fed meal.

toddler serve: serve together in a bowl, deconstruct on a tasting plate, or roll some of the bean mixture and rice, with a few veggies, yoghurt and cheese, tightly in a tortilla to offer as a wrap.

serves **4–6**
prep time: **15 minutes**
cooking time: **20 minutes**

1¼ cups (250 g) basmati rice
pinch of salt
1½ tablespoons extra virgin olive oil
2 carrots, coarsely grated
1 brown onion, diced
⅓ cup (95 g) no-added-salt tomato paste
2 cloves garlic, chopped
2 tablespoons homemade Mexican spice mix (p. 104) or store-bought taco/burrito seasoning
400 g tin black beans, drained and rinsed
400g tin red kidney beans, drained and rinsed
2 corn cobs, steamed and kernels removed, or 300 g tinned corn kernels, drained
1 tomato, diced
2 teaspoons white wine vinegar
½ cup (60 g) grated cheddar cheese
60 g baby spinach leaves, roughly chopped
1 lime, cut into wedges, to serve
plain Greek-style yoghurt or sour cream, to serve (optional)
tortillas or plain corn chips, to serve (optional)

MEAL PLANNING TIP: skip the store-bought spice mix for all your favourite Mexican meals and make a big batch of our Mexican spice mix (p. 104). Store in an airtight jar in the pantry. It's a game changer.

STORAGE: leftover rice and beans can be stored in an airtight container in the fridge for up to 3 days or in the freezer for up to 3 months. The leftover dressed salad ingredients can be stored in the fridge, and are best enjoyed the next day.

ALLERGIES/INTOLERANCES:
Gluten/wheat: choose gluten-free tortillas or corn chips. Check any ready-made spice mixes for allergens. Dairy: omit the cheese and yoghurt or sour cream, or choose a dairy-free variety.

salads

Hands up if you'd like your family to enjoy more salads! Whether you're serving them as a main meal or as a side, we've made veggies the hero in this chapter and are giving you all the tips to make salads engaging, fun and delicious for the kids. Just watch them dig in and give all those naturally vibrant colours a try.

When you're beginning to incorporate a greater variety of veggies into your meal plan, it helps to consider your family's food preferences to boost enjoyment. This of course can present a challenge when each family member has slightly different tastes. But with a few tricks up your sleeves, a little creativity and some delicious recipes to boot, you can make veggies exciting and tasty and have the kids coming back for more and more.

Why veggies are so good for our health and wellbeing:

- **They are great sources of vitamins and minerals:** these protect our bodies against sickness and disease in different ways. No one vegetable can do the job alone, which is why a variety of veggies in a range of colours is so important.

- **They are rich in antioxidants and natural plant chemicals:** these not only provide their rich colour and vibrancy, but also promote overall health and wellbeing and protect our bodies against heart disease, site-specific cancers and other lifestyle diseases.

- **They are high in both soluble and insoluble fibre:** this is so important for good gut health, which in turn supports the immune system and our mood, promotes regular and healthy bowel movements, and may reduce the risk of bowel cancer.

what a serve of veggies looks like

- ½ cup cooked green or orange vegetables (such as broccoli, spinach, carrots or pumpkin)
- ½ cup cooked dried or tinned beans, peas or lentils (preferably with no added salt)
- 1 cup leafy green or raw salad vegetables (such as lettuce, baby spinach or cucumber)

- ½ cup sweetcorn kernels
- ½ medium potato or other starchy vegetables (such as sweet potato, taro or cassava)
- 1 medium tomato

how many serves we need

The minimum recommended number of servings each day ranges from 2–3 serves for those 1–2 years of age, to 2½ serves for those 2–3 years of age, to up to 5 serves for those aged 9 and above. For men, 6 serves a day are recommended for those aged 19–50, 5½ serves for those aged 51–70 and 5 serves for those 71 and above. Women aged 19 and above are recommended to enjoy a minimum of 5 serves per day, and breastfeeding women a minimum of 7½ serves per day.

½ cup cooked green or orange veggies

what a serve of veggies looks like

½ cup cooked dried or tinned beans, peas or lentils

1 cup leafy green or raw salad vegetables

1 medium tomato

½ medium potato

½ cup sweetcorn kernels

how to hero veggies

There are loads of ways, at and away from the table, to engage and inspire kids to enjoy vegetables. Here are our favourites:

1 **shop with your kids:** this may not be our favourite pastime, but it is hugely valuable to kids' interest in veggies, and seeing the abundant displays of vegetables in all shapes and sizes is great for exposure. You can begin conversations about which vegetables you are choosing and what they might be used for in this week's meal plan – lessening the surprise at the dinner table. Talk about vegetables they may not have tried and ones they'd like to give a go. Veggie shopping is a hugely sensory activity with lots of colour, people, smells and noise, so if your kids find it a little overwhelming, you might like to try smaller supermarkets or your local farmers' market. Even unpacking the groceries can be beneficial for little kids if online shopping is your vibe.

2 **garden with your kids:** this is a quieter and calmer but still fabulous sensory experience that allows kids to get their hands dirty, get messy and enjoy quality time with a parent, grandparent or carer outdoors. Planting herb and veggie seeds and seedlings is a great way to engage them with foods they may not be so interested in trying or have lost interest in. To get started, try growing something they love, something they like and something they are learning to like. For kids who thrive on responsibility, being given the regular tasks of watering and looking after their seedlings might inspire them to try the fruits, or rather the veggies, of their labour. Homegrown sugar snap peas have never tasted so sweet and basil has never smelt so good.

3 **cook with your kids:** this inspires interest and engagement with vegetables in a safe and secure environment without any pressure to try them. This non-threatening exposure in the kitchen may help to increase interest when you reach the table too. There are many simple tasks that even young toddlers can help with – picking vegetables from the fridge, washing them, peeling them with appropriate peelers and chopping them with toddler-suitable knives. Other tasks they might be able to help with include arranging the veggies on the platter, tossing or mixing the elements together, or threading veggies on skewers. (Be mindful to always supervise your children with skewers and snip off the sharp end for toddlers.) These simple interactions might lead to a sneaky nibble or munch on a new veggie or two. Don't make a fuss and see what happens at the table.

4 **serve veggies to your kids:** kids can't give veggies a try if you don't offer them, so remember to offer, offer and offer again. It could be days, weeks or even years until they try a particular vegetable, but it's important that it's offered from time to time. While they're learning to explore and like mixed salads, try deconstructing portions to serve alongside them. They might choose only their favourite elements, or they might be inspired to choose a new food too. All of our salads can be deconstructed and they offer new and exciting ways to encourage kids to give veggies a try.

5 **eat with your kids:** have you ever noticed that your kids often prefer to eat from your plate rather than their own? Sitting down to eat mixed and varied salads of your own with different dressings is another form of exposure without pressure. Whether they choose some from their own plate or have a simpler version to explore, offer them some from your plate or let them try yours if they ask. So prioritise family mealtimes, role model positive eating behaviours and provide safe and secure mealtimes free of pressure.

creative serving suggestions

- **Sauces and dressings:** these add a huge flavour boost, and tangy, salty and sweet dressings appeal to the taste preferences of kids who need a sensory hit at mealtimes. Dressings can make a great dipping sauce for veggies and can provide a stepping stone to mixed salads or interaction with veggies.

- **Favourite ingredients:** including cheese cubes, avocado slices, crunchy croutons, crispy bacon bits and even fruit slices such as pear, apple and mango in your favourite salads – whether they're deconstructed or mixed – is likely to engage even the fussiest of eaters. They might just go for the cheese or the fruit, but over time, with continued exposure without pressure, they are likely to choose a broader variety.

- **Salad skewers:** alternating loved salad ingredients with salad ingredients they are learning to like can have almost every kid running to take a look. Whether they help to make them or simply eat them, salad skewers are well worth a try.

- **Build-your-own salads:** salad platters and deconstructed mixed salads allow your family members creative control to pick and choose what they like, and how much, from what's on offer. We know this creates safety and security and reduces anxiety at mealtimes, which in turn inspires engagement with and enjoyment of food. If your child is not yet inspired to build their own salad, perhaps ask them to build a salad for you. Be excited about what they come up with, and you never know, it might not be long before they make one for themselves.

- **Treasure-hunt salads:** when presenting a mixed salad, without pressuring them to eat anything, try a treasure hunt and have fun with a mealtime! You can ask them: Can you find something green? How about something crunchy? Now something soft? Something you like? How about something you are learning to like? Not every child will enjoy this, so if they become anxious or show frustration, end the game and switch to something else, and give this a go another time.

- **Novelty utensils:** there's nothing like kids' chopsticks, mini tongs, ice-cube trays or silicon muffin trays to boost engagement with salads and veggies tenfold. Be sure to include these from time to time to bring an element of simple fun to mealtimes.

.

Did you know? The healthy fats in many salads, such as extra virgin olive oil, and the nut butters in dressings, avocados, nuts and seeds, can help boost the absorption of some essential nutrients found in vegetables.

fruit counts too

For the reluctant veggie eater, remember that fruits offer many of the same nutrients veggies do. So if you are struggling with vegetables, try serving a fruit or two of similar colours to the veggies that are also on offer. For example, if you have:

- **red cabbage – serve blueberries**
- **zucchini – serve cucumber or honeydew melon**
- **green beans – serve kiwifruit**
- **sweet potato – serve orange**
- **pumpkin – serve rockmelon**
- **yellow capsicum – serve mandarins**
- **cherry tomatoes – serve strawberries**
- **lettuce – serve grapes**
- **carrot – serve mango**
- **potato – serve banana**

5 meal planning tips to enjoy more veggies

1. Plan your meals to accommodate a variety of vegetables throughout the week – both kids and adults can get bored if they eat the same veggies prepared in the same way for lunch and dinner each and every day. Start the habit of offering a salad with dinner each night from when they are young. You can use leftovers the next day in sandwiches or lunchboxes.

2. Plan to prepare a variety of vegetables in different ways throughout the week. Raw veggie sticks are a great, nutritious and very easy option. They're one that the kids will usually accept, but it's also important to offer veggies in a range of mixed salads, and at other times steamed or roasted.

3. Choose seasonal veggies for better taste and quality. They're often cheaper too.

4. Wash and prep veggies as you unpack your groceries and fill your veggie grab box (p. 28) – peel the husks from corn cobs, and wash and remove stickers from apples and pears, etc. Taking a few minutes to do this will encourage you to eat them and likely reduce food wastage too.

5. Peel and chop veggies for upcoming meals whenever you can (p. 28).

reducing fruit and veggie waste

1. **meal-plan:** while it's lovely to impulse-buy gorgeous leafy bunches of greens from your grocer, unless you have a planned use for them, they often go limp and get thrown out. Instead, make a note and remember to include a recipe for that bunch of silverbeet or spinach and buy it next time.

2. **wash, prep and store:** prepping that veggie grab box (p. 28) encourages you to offer those capsicum, celery and carrot sticks and green beans to your family more often. Take the time to learn how your fridge works or invest in quality vegetable storage containers to appropriately store your veggies to lengthen their 'shelf' life.

3. **choose seasonal:** seasonal fruits and vegetables are usually from local producers and are often better quality, and you are more likely to eat and enjoy them. Often out-of-season or imported fruits and veggies are expensive, lack flavour and texture, and are more likely to go to waste.

4. **use leftover and limp veggies:** include a weekly recipe that easily accommodates leftover veggies – a stir-fry (p. 230), frittata (p. 180), tray bake (p. 151), risotto (p. 168) or casserole (p. 128) is perfect for this. Even our smoothie bags (p. 37) can accommodate a straggly veggie or two.

5. **compost:** if you have to throw anything out, a compost bin is so valuable for reducing household waste going to landfill. There are many varieties to suit spaces of all sizes, even those indoors.

how to store fresh herbs

We use fresh herbs for added flavour in so many of our meals and salads. To extend their shelf life and maintain their texture and vibrancy, here are our top storage tips for our favourite herbs:

- **Basil:** place the roots, or trimmed stems, in a vase or jar of cold water and leave on the kitchen bench or in the fridge for up to a few days. Loosely cover the leaves with a plastic bag if you have one available.
- **Bay leaves:** use bay leaves straight from the tree, if you have one, or freeze in a reusable freezer-proof bag or an airtight container for up to 3 months. Alternatively, hang a bunch until they are dry and store in an airtight container.
- **Chives:** wrap, unwashed, in paper towel and store in the fridge in a reusable ziplock bag for up to 2 days.

- **Dill, mint, marjoram, oregano, thyme:** wrap, unwashed, in paper towel and store in the fridge in a reusable ziplock bag or airtight container.
- **Parsley:** place the stalks in water, loosely cover the leaves with a plastic bag and store in the fridge for a few days. Alternatively, pick the leaves, wash and dry them, then store them in a paper-lined reusable ziplock bag or airtight container in the fridge.
- **Rosemary, sage:** store in a reusable ziplock bag or airtight container in the fridge.

If your fresh herbs are starting to go limp and you have no urgent use for them, chop them up and sprinkle them into an ice-cube tray, then top them with olive oil and freeze. Add these cubes to sauces and soups or even pasta and rice dishes for added flavour. Or, for basil, try our favourite pesto on p. 58.

gado gado

This flavourful salad can be enjoyed as a main dish and can be deconstructed beautifully for reluctant eaters, or for those who are exploring new tastes and textures. Try using the peanut sauce as a dip for the range of colourful proteins and vegetables on offer.

To make the peanut sauce, place all the ingredients in a small bowl and mix well to combine. Set aside.

Bring a small saucepan of water to the boil over high heat. Add the eggs and cook for 7 minutes, or 8–9 minutes for hard-boiled eggs. Transfer to a bowl of cold water until cool enough to handle. Peel and halve.

Meanwhile, heat the oil in a large frying pan over medium–high heat. Add the tofu and fry for 3 minutes each side or until brown and crispy, then transfer to a plate. Add the potatoes to the pan and cook for a few minutes or until they have warmed through and are starting to crisp up. Transfer to the plate with the tofu.

Arrange all the elements on a large platter. Serve drizzled with the peanut sauce, or with the sauce on the side, if you prefer, for everyone to serve as they wish, or in small ramekins for kids who may prefer to dip.

baby serve: mash some tofu, potato and hard-boiled egg with a little bit of peanut sauce and serve alongside appropriate finger-food elements of the vegetables available, such as cucumber, capsicum, green beans or cherry tomatoes as well as the tofu, potato and egg.

toddler serve: serve a selection of tofu, potato, egg and vegetables on a tasting plate with some peanut sauce on the side.

serves **4**

prep time: **15 minutes**

cooking time: **10 minutes**

DF

2 eggs

1 tablespoon olive oil

200 g firm tofu, chopped into small bite-sized pieces

4 baby potatoes, cooked and quartered

1½ cups (90 g) shredded iceberg lettuce or cabbage

60 g baby spinach leaves

1 cucumber, halved lengthways and diagonally sliced

1 carrot, halved lengthways and diagonally sliced

½ cup (100 g) cherry tomatoes, halved

½ red capsicum (pepper), sliced

prawn crackers, to serve (optional)

lime cheeks, to serve

peanut sauce

½ cup (125 ml) coconut cream

½ cup (140 g) peanut butter

2 tablespoons kecap manis

1 tablespoon palm sugar or soft brown sugar

1 teaspoon fish sauce

juice of 1 lime

1 clove garlic, crushed

MEAL PLANNING TIP: this salad is a great one to enjoy when you have leftover roast potatoes. Prepare extra for a roast or tray bake the night before, and enjoy the leftovers the next day in this delicious salad. Use a variety of vegetables from whatever is available – anything goes! Include your veggie grab box for inspiration if you need to reduce any wastage.

TIME-SAVING TIP: make the sauce, slice the tofu and slice any vegetables earlier in the day to make preparing this salad a breeze at mealtime.

STORAGE: keep leftovers in the fridge for up to 2 days.

ALLERGIES/INTOLERANCES:
Gluten/wheat: use gluten-free soy sauce or tamari instead of kecap manis. **Egg:** omit the egg. **Nuts:** if alternative nuts are tolerated, choose a cashew and/or almond butter in place of the peanut butter. If no nuts are tolerated, try a sweet chilli sauce or Kewpie mayonnaise as an alternative to the peanut sauce. **Vegetarian:** omit the fish sauce from the peanut sauce.

layered asian chicken *and* vegetable salad *with* soy mayonnaise dressing

serves **6**

prep time: **20 minutes**

cooking time: **20 minutes**

500 g free-range chicken breast
    fillets

270 ml tin coconut milk

200 g green beans, trimmed,
    sliced in half

1 head (280 g) broccoli, cut into florets

100 g dried rice vermicelli noodles

400 g tin corn kernels, drained

1 red capsicum (pepper), diced

1 baby cos lettuce, finely shredded

coriander sprigs or chives,
    to garnish (optional)

soy mayonnaise dressing

½ cup (125 g) whole-egg
    mayonnaise

½ cup (125 g) plain Greek-style
    yoghurt

2 cloves garlic, finely chopped

3 teaspoons light soy sauce

1½ teaspoons white wine vinegar

1 tablespoon chopped coriander
    leaves or chives

A colourful, layered salad to engage the fussiest of salad eaters, this dish is delicious served as part of a family barbecue or when entertaining friends. Have a few sets of tongs ready so everyone can tuck in and choose their favourite veggies.

Place the chicken in a small saucepan that will fit the fillets quite snugly. Pour over the coconut milk and add enough water to cover. Cover with the lid and bring just to the boil, then reduce heat to low and simmer for 10–12 minutes. Turn the heat off and stand for 10 minutes to finish cooking. Transfer chicken to a plate and leave to cool. Once cool enough to handle, finely shred the chicken and set aside.

Meanwhile, bring a large saucepan of water to the boil over medium–high heat. Add the beans and broccoli and cook for 2–3 minutes, just until bright green. Drain and refresh under cold water. Drain well.

Soak the noodles according to packet instructions, then drain and refresh under cold water. Cut into shorter lengths with kitchen scissors.

Mix together the corn and red capsicum in a small bowl.

To make the dressing, place all the ingredients in a small bowl and mix well to combine.

To assemble, arrange the cos lettuce on a large platter and top with the noodles, then arrange the beans, broccoli, corn and capsicum in layers. Top with the chicken. Drizzle over the dressing and garnish with coriander sprigs or chives, if desired.

baby serve: shred the chicken and mash or chop with some of the noodles and veggies, such as broccoli, corn and capsicum. Stir through some yoghurt or some of their favourite veggie puree. Offer some appropriate elements as finger food too.

toddler serve: offer some of the salad elements deconstructed on a tasting plate or allow your child to select some of the elements from the salad on their own using a pair of small tongs and with supervision.

SALAD PREPARATION TIPS:

1. This salad is a crowd-pleaser. All the ingredients can be pre-prepared so all you have to do is assemble it when serving.

2. The chicken can be pre-cooked and stored in an airtight container in the fridge for up to 24 hours. If preferred, simply cook the chicken in water or some light stock, or for those super busy days, buy a barbecue chicken and shred it.

3. For a crunchy noodle salad option, use a couple of packets of fried noodles instead of the rice noodles. Scatter them over the top just before serving.

4. Feel free to use any combination of vegetables that you may have available. Try cherry tomatoes, cucumbers, radishes or snow peas.

5. If you don't have time to prepare the soy mayonnaise dressing, try a good-quality Asian dressing as an alternative.

FUSSY EATING TIP: it's easy to deconstruct the salad further to engage reluctant eaters who may be overwhelmed by seeing all the veggies touching. Try reserving a little bit of each of the elements and arrange them either separately on a plate or in a variety of small bowls.

Having this on offer next to the main salad can help break it down even further. Watch as they gradually explore the small bowls and individual ingredients.

STORAGE: keep leftovers in an airtight container in the fridge for up to 2 days.

ALLERGIES/INTOLERANCES:
Gluten/wheat: choose a gluten-free soy sauce or tamari for the dressing. **Egg:** choose an egg-free mayonnaise. **Dairy:** omit the yoghurt. **Vegetarian:** omit the chicken and serve with cooked firm tofu or legumes.

quinoa *and* marinated feta salad

We love to serve a portion of each salad element alongside the mixed salad to inspire the kids to engage and interact with a range of nutritious foods they love, as well as some they might be learning to love. This salad is perfect served alongside our Lemon and oregano chicken skewers (p. 229) or Fennel and rosemary lamb (p. 226), or toss some cannellini beans or chickpeas through it for a complete vegetarian meal.

(V) serves **4–6**
prep time: **20 minutes**
cooking time: **40 minutes**

300 g pumpkin, cut into 2–3 cm cubes
1 tablespoon extra virgin olive oil
½ cup (95 g) quinoa
60 g baby spinach leaves
½ cup (100 g) marinated feta cubes
1 Lebanese cucumber, halved
    lengthways and sliced
squeeze of lemon juice, to serve

Preheat the oven to 200°C (180°C fan forced) and line a baking tray with baking paper.

Place the pumpkin on the baking tray and toss with the olive oil. Bake for 40 minutes, or until tender.

Meanwhile, rinse the quinoa well in a fine mesh sieve under cold running water, then place in a small saucepan with 1 cup (250 ml) water. Bring to the boil over medium–high heat, then cover, reduce the heat to low and simmer for 10 minutes. Turn off the heat and allow the quinoa to sit, still covered, for a further 3–4 minutes. Remove the lid and fluff with a fork.

Transfer the quinoa to a large serving bowl and set aside to cool. Toss through the pumpkin, baby spinach, feta and cucumber, then drizzle with a squeeze of lemon juice. If the feta is not marinated, toss through a drizzle of extra virgin olive oil too.

baby serve: mash some quinoa with the pumpkin, a pinch of finely chopped spinach, and avocado if you have some, to spoon feed to your baby. Offer alongside some cucumber and pumpkin as finger food.

toddlers: serve a portion of the salad to your toddler, or deconstruct some elements for them to interact with and explore, or to assemble their own mini mixed salad from. Include any extra veggies you know they love and accept to encourage enjoyment.

FUSSY EATING TIP: to encourage kids to interact with less familiar foods, ask them to create a salad for you using the unmixed ingredients, or try a treasure hunt using tongs to pick out ingredients in the mixed salad. If they're willing to engage, this is a great time to ask them questions such as 'What does it smell like? Is it smooth or crunchy? Can you give it a lick?' They might surprise you and surprise themselves when they enjoy a new veg or two.

STORAGE: keep any leftover salad in an airtight container in the fridge for up to 2 days.

ALLERGIES/INTOLERANCES:
Dairy: omit the feta and add some avocado and a drizzle of extra virgin olive oil to the salad.

classic caesar salad

The whole family can enjoy this classic caesar salad as a light meal or as a simple side to one of your favourite marinated meats (see p. 219 for marinades) or beef skewers (p. 179). It's also a great meal to enjoy as a family as you can role model how to eat and savour a more challenging meal. The kids will be much more keen to try it after watching you!

serves **4–6**
prep time: **20 minutes**
cooking time: **10 minutes**

½ **ciabatta loaf, torn into 2 cm pieces**
1–2 **tablespoons olive oil**
4 **rashers bacon, trimmed**
1 **large cos lettuce, leaves torn**
½ **cup (40 g) finely grated or shaved parmesan**
2 **hard-boiled eggs, quartered**
2 **anchovy fillets, drained and chopped (optional)**

caesar dressing
½ **cup (125 g) whole-egg mayonnaise**
¼ **cup (20 g) finely grated parmesan**
1 **tablespoon lemon juice**
1 **small clove garlic, crushed**
½ **teaspoon Dijon mustard**
½ **teaspoon Worcestershire sauce**

Preheat the oven to 180°C (160°C fan-forced) and line a baking tray with baking paper.

Drizzle the torn ciabatta with the olive oil, toss to coat and bake for 10 minutes or until golden and crispy. Set aside to cool.

Meanwhile, heat a non-stick frying pan over medium heat. Fry the bacon for a few minutes either side until crispy. Drain on paper towel, then chop into small pieces.

For the dressing, whisk together the ingredients until smooth and creamy. This can be made in advance and kept in the fridge until needed.

To assemble the salad, place the lettuce in a large bowl, pour over the dressing and toss thoroughly. Add the croutons, bacon, parmesan, egg, and anchovy fillets (if using). Toss to combine.

baby serve: offer some boiled egg as finger food alongside a spoon-fed portion of veggies and/or fruit.

toddler serve: serve the salad deconstructed on a tasting plate with some veggies and a portion of fruit. Alternatively, serve a variety of salad elements or vegetables in the middle of the table, family-style, for your toddler to choose from.

FUSSY EATING TIP: this salad is easily deconstructed, so why not try serving the individual elements to your more reluctant child so they can explore and create their own version in their own time?

STORAGE: store the dressing in an airtight container in the fridge for up to 3 days.

ALLERGIES/INTOLERANCES:
Gluten/wheat: use gluten-free bread and sauces. **Egg:** omit the egg and use an egg-free mayonnaise. **Dairy:** omit the parmesan and use a dairy-free mayonnaise. **Vegetarian:** omit the bacon, anchovies and Worcestershire sauce.

roast cauliflower *and* chickpea salad

This hearty and filling salad with two dressings to choose from will keep you coming back time and time again, and is perfect for 'bring a plate' barbecues, or to use up leftover veggies. We love that this salad can be served as a meal on its own or as a side to one of our simple marinated meats (p. 219).

Preheat the oven to 200°C (180°C fan-forced) and line 2 baking trays with baking paper.

Break the cauliflower florets into small popcorn-sized pieces and place in a bowl with the chickpeas. Drizzle over the olive oil, sprinkle with the spices and toss to combine. Transfer to the trays and roast for 25 minutes, or until tender and golden brown. Set aside to cool.

Meanwhile, in a large salad bowl, combine the mixed leaves, parsley, cucumber and cherry tomatoes.

To make either dressing, combine all ingredients in a bowl and whisk until completely smooth, adding ⅓ cup (80 ml) water for the lemon tahini dressing.

Toss the cooled roasted cauliflower and chickpeas in with the salad. Add a little of the dressing and toss to combine. Top the salad with avocado and feta, and serve remaining dressing on the side.

baby serve: mash ¼ cup of the cauliflower with a little avocado and 1 tablespoon of your baby's preferred milk, and spoon feed to your baby. Serve alongside roasted cauliflower, cucumber slices and avocado sticks as finger food.

toddler serve: you could try serving each element of the salad in a large ice-cube tray or muffin tin complete with dipping sauce (dressing) at the end.

FUSSY EATING TIP: the path to variety involves repeated exposure to unfamiliar foods alongside familiar and liked foods in a supportive, safe mealtime environment. Sitting together as a family to enjoy this salad will help build the foundation for future success. Offering a plate of safe foods such as fruit or bread alongside this meal provides your child with the security and comfort they need to try to explore new foods when they are ready.

STORAGE: keep any leftover salad in the fridge for up to 2 days. The dressing can be stored in an airtight container in the fridge for up to 3 days.

ALLERGIES/INTOLERANCES: Dairy: omit the feta.

serves **6–8**
prep time: **15 minutes**
cooking time: **25 minutes**

1 head cauliflower
400 g tin chickpeas, drained and rinsed
2 tablespoons extra virgin olive oil
1 teaspoon smoked paprika
1 teaspoon ground turmeric
¼ teaspoon garlic powder
6 cups (360 g) mixed leaves, such as baby spinach leaves, cos lettuce
½ bunch flat-leaf parsley, leaves finely chopped
2 Lebanese cucumbers, cut into chunks
10 cherry tomatoes, halved
1 avocado, sliced
100 g feta, crumbled

lemon tahini dressing
⅓ cup (90 g) tahini
¼ cup (60 ml) lemon juice
2 cloves garlic, crushed
½ teaspoon ground cumin
salt and ground black pepper, to taste

or

creamy honey-mustard dressing
¼ cup (60 ml) extra virgin olive oil
1 lemon, juiced
¼ cup (90 g) honey
2 tablespoons Dijon mustard
2 tablespoons tahini
2 tablespoons apple cider vinegar
pinch of salt (optional)

desserts

Sweet foods are a normal part of a balanced, varied and healthy diet. Our attitude to the serving and eating of dessert is important because it allows us to really create a positive approach to food for our families.

Creating a positive attitude around eating foods of all types is essential. Trying to restrict one food over another because of its nutritional value, or offering one food as a reward over another, can create all sorts of unnecessary food hierarchies – hierarchies that put desserts and sweeter, less nutritious foods above more nutritious ones.

Incorporating sweet foods into your weekly meal plan can make a balanced approach more achievable if desserts are something your family is not used to. When children are exposed to and encouraged to enjoy different foods in a judgement-free environment, they will naturally develop a healthy attitude when making food choices now and in the future. Here's how you can incorporate dessert mindfully and positively into your family's routine:

include baking and dessert in the meal plan

Planning a rotation of sweet snacks for the week, to either top up your baking box (p. 28) or for dessert, can be just as important as planning the main meal. It helps to reduce your mental load, additional grocery shops and food wastage. Along with a well-stocked baking box, having a seasonal fruit grab box (p. 27) on hand can help make your sweet choices for lunchboxes, snack platters and family mealtimes varied and delicious. Preparing a premix (p. 69) every couple of weeks can remove some of the stress and mess of getting a sweet snack ready in a hurry. Our Cake in a mug (p. 78) is set to be a sure-fire favourite with the kids and will bring variety to your weekly dessert or afternoon tea routine.

try dessert with dinner

To some this may sound unusual, but for us it makes perfect sense, especially when combined with tasting plates (p. 87) or deconstructed mealtimes (p. 86) and the Division of Responsibility (p. 8). Serving dessert with dinner can significantly reduce anxiety as it provides a familiar food that is easy to eat, satisfies any 'hangries' quickly and facilitates enjoyment.

If dessert with dinner is a new concept and mealtime strategy for your family, you might find that the novelty encourages the dessert to be eaten and enjoyed first. However, as it becomes commonplace, dessert might no longer be the first thing to be picked and you might notice a renewed interest in the other foods on offer. Dessert will perhaps start to be eaten midway or at the end of a mealtime, or nibbled on throughout – and sometimes not even all of it will be eaten.

5 examples of everyday desserts

- **Fresh fruit:** our usual go-to 'dessert with dinner' option is a nutritious choice. Fruit is high in vitamin C and adds colour and familiarity to the plate or table, as well as helping to boost iron absorption from other foods on offer.

- **Oat biscuits or seed slices:** high in fibre and a source of satisfying and long-lasting energy, these can be a nutritious choice for an everyday dessert. Baked porridge squares (p. 74), Raspberry and white chocolate blondies (p. 80) and even Rice Bubble and seed mini bars (p. 46) are good options.

- **Chocolate and kidney bean cupcakes (p. 48):** with the goodness of legumes and not a lot of added sugar, these appealing cupcakes can attract the kids' attention from a long way off. Try offering half a muffin, or make mini-muffins, for those with small appetites, so as not to fill up their tummies too much.

- **Simple egg custard (p. 214):** eggs are a nutritious option for children and provide 11 essential vitamins and minerals, as well as being a good source of protein and energy.

- **Yoghurt:** this is a rich source of calcium and protein, and natural and plain Greek-style yoghurts in particular are also free of added sugars. However, be mindful of how frequently calcium-rich foods such as milk and yoghurt are offered as a side at mealtimes. They can reduce the absorption of iron and children's appetite for other nutritious foods. Instead, serve them mostly at snack times or supper.

make it its own mealtime

If dessert with dinner doesn't suit your routine then simply make it its own mealtime, but without the bribery. Dessert can be offered regardless of whether your child has refused dinner, nibbled at a few bits and pieces or cleared their plate and enjoyed seconds. It's a new mealtime, a new opportunity to test and reinforce the Division of Responsibility (p. 8) and encourage your child to tune in to their hunger and fullness cues. Dessert doesn't need to be extravagant – an everyday dessert (such as those listed above), a slice of our simple yet delicious fresh Ginger and yoghurt cake (p. 215) or a scoop or two of vanilla ice-cream will do the trick. Simply sit down, be mindful and enjoy what you have chosen to eat together.

ditch the bribery

Bribery may initially work and may bring you the reward of your child trying a new food or two, but at what cost? Have you noticed the bribes getting bigger, your expectations getting smaller, mealtime stress rising and confrontations becoming more frequent?

If so, we highly recommend you switch your approach. Try bringing forward the reward and including it as part of the mealtime by serving dinner with dessert (as above), even if it is chocolate or ice-cream, without reward or consequence. As with all change there will naturally be a period of adjustment, but the desserts can become simpler, more nutritious and less frequent if you prefer.

recognise hunger and fullness

As with all foods and all mealtimes, it's important to build trust with your child and to reinforce feelings of hunger and fullness. Knowing when they are hungry, enjoying a variety of food from what's on offer, and knowing when to stop are skills to be nurtured and encouraged. Be sure to practise these skills with your children with desserts and sweet foods too.

choose positive words

Your child's relationship with food is hugely influenced by your own feelings and attitudes towards eating, as well as your words. Interact with foods and talk about them the way you would like your child to. Keep it positive, even if the food is something you might not enjoy. Please be mindful to not use any words that may associate guilt or restriction with food.

keep it consistent

Creating a consistent and positive approach to mealtimes provides a sense of safety for children. If they know a sweet food – even if it is usually fruit – is always served at dinner, or that dessert is routinely offered on weekends, for example, this gives them a feeling of security that these foods will be available and are to be enjoyed. These items then become 'just food' and no longer sit on a pedestal above other more nutritious foods.

create connection

Desserts bring joy. They bring friends and family together and are a source of celebration. And they help us to celebrate all things big and small. Our One-bowl chocolate sheet cake (p. 208), Pavlova platter (p. 212) and Rocky road ice-cream cake (p. 216) are perfect for sharing. A touch more effort and a little sweeter, these desserts take pride of place at birthdays and barbecues and are there to be enjoyed.

one-bowl chocolate sheet cake

You made a wish and it came true! A simple, light and fluffy chocolate cake that only uses one bowl. Here is another cake recipe to add to your perfect-every-time collection. Enjoy, and don't forget to share your clever birthday cake creations with us.

Preheat the oven to 180°C (160°C fan-forced). Grease a 33 cm × 23 cm × 5 cm rectangular slice tin (or small roasting pan) and line with baking paper.

In a large bowl, whisk together the eggs, buttermilk, oil and vanilla to combine.

Add the sugar and salt to the wet ingredients. Sift in the flour, cocoa powder, bicarbonate of soda and baking powder. Mix well until there are no lumps.

Carefully add 1 cup (250 ml) boiling water and mix until well combined. Pour the mixture into the prepared tin and bake for 30 minutes or until a skewer inserted into the centre of the cake comes out clean. Remove from the oven and cool in the tin for at least 20 minutes before turning out onto a wire rack to cool completely.

To make the chocolate buttercream, combine the icing sugar, butter and vanilla in the bowl of an electric mixer. Beat on high speed until pale and creamy, about 4–6 minutes.

Scrape down the sides and bottom of the bowl. Add the cooled melted chocolate and beat until well combined. Add the cream and beat for another 2–4 minutes or until it is light and fluffy.

Spread the icing over the cooled cake, decorate with 100s & 1000s, if using, and serve.

* Take the butter out of the fridge about 30 minutes before making.

makes 1 cake
prep time: 15 minutes
cooking time: 30 minutes

2 eggs
1 cup (250 ml) buttermilk
½ cup (125 ml) canola or vegetable oil
2 teaspoons pure vanilla extract
1½ cups (330 g) caster sugar
1 teaspoon salt
1¾ cups (260 g) plain flour
¾ cup (75 g) cocoa powder
1½ teaspoons bicarbonate of soda
1½ teaspoons baking powder
natural 100s & 1000s, to serve
   (optional)

makes 2½ cups (420 g)

chocolate buttercream

1 cup (125 g) icing sugar, sifted
180 g salted butter, slightly cold
   and cut into cubes*
1 teaspoon pure vanilla extract
150 g milk chocolate, melted
   and cooled
2 tablespoons thickened cream

NUTRITION NOTE: when your kids are savouring their slice of cake (or two!), it's good to remember that all foods are just food. Some might be more nutritious and offered more frequently, and some less nutritious and offered only sometimes, but all food is there to be enjoyed. So make sure you take the time to enjoy your slice too.

STORAGE: store in an airtight container in the fridge for up to 3 days. Alternatively, to freeze, once the cake has cooled completely (unfrosted), wrap well in plastic film and then with foil and place in a freezer bag. Freeze for up to 3 months. To serve, thaw in the fridge overnight, still wrapped. Top with frosting once fully thawed.

Store any leftover buttercream in a freezer-proof bag in the freezer for up to 2 months. We love using the extra buttercream on the Chocolate and kidney bean cupcakes (p. 48).

ALLERGIES/INTOLERANCES: Gluten/wheat: use a gluten-free flour and baking powder. Egg: try 2 'chia eggs' (p. 21) or 1 mashed overripe banana as a substitute for the eggs. Dairy: omit the buttermilk and try your preferred dairy-free milk with 1 tablespoon white vinegar or lemon juice. Omit the buttercream.

lemon curd parfait *and* lemon curd shortbread slice

Lemon curd is a delightful recipe to use up any lemons you might have, or simply to satisfy those zesty cravings. The curd can be spread on toast or used to create our delicious shortbread slice or parfait – the kids will love to help with these in the kitchen.

makes **2½ cups (760 g)**
prep time: **10 minutes**
cooking time: **15 minutes**

1½ tablespoons finely grated
lemon zest
1¼ cups (310 ml) fresh lemon juice
1½ cups (330 g) caster sugar
5 eggs, lightly beaten
200 g unsalted butter, cut into small
cubes

lemon curd

Combine all the ingredients in a medium saucepan over medium–low heat and stir to melt the butter. Reduce the heat to low and stir continuously for 12–14 minutes, or until the mixture thickly coats the back of a wooden spoon.

Strain the curd into a glass bowl and cover the surface with plastic film. Place in the fridge to chill.

MONEY-SAVING TIP: when making a recipe that uses a fresh ingredient in bulk, always look for imperfect picks. Most major supermarkets have bags of bulk fruits and vegetables at very reasonable prices.

TIP: around 5–6 lemons are required to make the curd. It's best made in advance and allowed to cool before being used in the slice or parfait.

STORAGE: keep leftovers in the fridge for up to 3 days.

ALLERGIES/INTOLERANCES:
Dairy/egg: mix 1 cup (250 ml) lemon juice with ⅓ cup (50 g) arrowroot starch or cornflour. Combine with 1½ tablespoons finely grated lemon zest and 800 ml coconut cream, sweetening to taste with caster sugar or maple syrup. Bring to a gentle simmer over medium–low heat and stir continuously until the mixture thickly coats the back of a spoon.

lemon curd and strawberry parfait

Pour the cream into the bowl of an electric mixer, add the icing sugar and whisk on medium–high speed for 3–4 minutes or until thickened.

Using 6 × 1½-cup (375 ml) capacity glasses, layer in half the biscuit crumbs, curd, cream and strawberries. Repeat the layers, then chill in the fridge until you are ready to serve.

makes **6**
prep time: **15 minutes**

600 ml thickened cream
½ cup (60 g) icing sugar
250 g packet plain biscuits, crushed
1½ cups (450 g) lemon curd
250 g strawberries, hulled and chopped

STORAGE: keep the parfait in the fridge and enjoy within 1–2 days.

ALLERGIES/INTOLERANCES: Gluten/wheat: use gluten-free biscuits. Egg: use the dairy- and egg-free curd. Dairy: use the dairy- and egg-free curd and a dairy-free whipping cream.

lemon curd shortbread slice

Preheat the oven to 180°C (160°C fan-forced). Line a 20 cm × 30 cm slice tin with baking paper, extending over the two long sides.

In a medium bowl, combine the sugar, coconut and flour. Make a well in the centre, add the butter and stir to combine.

Evenly spread the mixture into the prepared tin. Use the back of a metal spoon to press and smooth it down, ensuring the mixture reaches the sides of the tin. This prevents the curd from seeping.

Bake for 20 minutes or until golden, then cool for 10 minutes.

Reduce the oven to 150°C (130°C fan-forced). Evenly spread the curd onto the shortbread base, leaving a 5 mm space around the edges. Bake for a further 10–15 minutes, until just set. Leave to cool completely – the curd will set more as it cools.

Using a sharp knife, cut into 24 rectangles, or 32 smaller squares. Wipe the knife with a wet cloth after each cut to help get cleaner slices.

Serve topped with icing sugar, desiccated coconut or fresh berries.

makes **24 larger rectangles,**
   or 32 smaller squares
prep time: **15 minutes**
cooking time: **35 minutes**

1 cup (220 g) caster sugar
½ cup (40 g) desiccated coconut
2 cups (300 g) plain flour
200 g unsalted butter, melted
1½ cups (450 g) lemon curd
icing sugar, desiccated coconut,
   or fresh berries, to serve

STORAGE: keep the slice in an airtight container in the fridge for up to 5 days. Take the slice out of the fridge around 15 minutes before serving.

ALLERGIES/INTOLERANCES: Gluten/wheat: use gluten-free flour. Egg: use the dairy- and egg-free curd. Dairy: use the dairy- and egg-free curd and use coconut oil instead of butter in the base.

pavlova platter

Whether you want to impress some guests or just want a special night in with the family, pavlova is a good choice for dessert. It's all about having fun and enjoying food with the people you love. With this recipe you can make a classic round pavlova topped with an abundance of fresh fruit – or try our crowd-pleasing pavlova platter with mini pavs and a pick 'n' mix selection of toppings.

Perfecting the pav is far easier than it looks, so we hope you will give it a try. Here are some of our tips for creating a pavlova that is perfectly formed while being crisp on the outside and gooey in the middle:

- The bowl of your mixer should be very clean. You can use a small amount of white vinegar on a paper towel to wipe the inside of the bowl. This adds a little acid and helps to stabilise the meringue. It also removes any residual fat from the bowl from previous uses.

- Separate the yolks and whites of your eggs when they're cold and then allow the whites to come to room temperature. It is easier to do this when the eggs are cold.

- Save your yolks to make a curd or our delicious homemade custard (p. 214).

---

makes **12–15 mini pavlovas or 1 × 20 cm regular pavlova**
prep time: **30 minutes**
cooking time: **50 minutes for mini pavlovas, 1½ hours for regular**

5 egg whites
1¼ cups (275 g) caster sugar
3 teaspoons gluten-free cornflour, sifted
1 teaspoon white vinegar

Preheat the oven to 170°C (150°C fan-forced). Line a large baking tray with baking paper.

Place the egg whites in a large, clean bowl of an electric mixer. Mix on medium–high speed until soft peaks form. Continuing to whisk the egg whites, slowly add the sugar, 1 tablespoon at a time. Once all the sugar has been incorporated, continue whisking until thick and glossy. Use a clean spatula to gently scrape down the sides of the bowl a couple of times. You'll know when it's done because the sugar will be completely dissolved. You can test this by rubbing a small amount of mixture between your fingertips. If it feels grainy, there is undissolved sugar.

Add the cornflour and vinegar to the egg-white mixture. Beat on low speed or carefully fold with a spatula until just mixed through and combined.

To make the mini pavlovas, spoon the mixture evenly onto the prepared baking tray, using a slightly heaped ¼ cup for each meringue. Leave a 5 cm space between each one. Use the back of a spoon to make an indentation in the centre of the meringue to act as your 'bowl' for the toppings later.

Reduce heat to 115°C (95°C fan-forced) and bake for 50 minutes – do not open the oven during this time. The mini pavlovas should be dry and crisp to touch. Turn off the oven and allow the mini pavlovas to cool completely in the oven.

Continued →

platter serving suggestions

Place the cooled mini pavlovas on a platter and arrange the sauces, toppings and fruit in small bowls around them. Let your guests pick 'n' mix the ingredients to create their own perfect pavlova.

- **Fruit:** 2 cups of chopped fruit such as fresh berries, kiwifruit, mango, passionfruit pulp.

- **Whipped cream:** 1½ cups (375 ml) single (pouring) cream. Whisk cream until soft peaks form.

- **Sauces:** caramel sauce, chocolate sauce, lemon curd (p. 210), passionfruit curd, strawberry coulis or custard (see below).

- **Toppings:** toasted coconut flakes, sprinkles, Maltesers, grated chocolate.

FUSSY EATING TIP: the perfect pavlova platter will have something for everyone. It might be pavlova and cream for some, fruit and chocolate for others, or perhaps a little bit of everything.

BAKING NOTES: if you would like to make 1 regular pavlova, draw a 20 cm circle in the middle of a piece of non-stick baking paper. Link a baking tray with the baking paper, pencil side down. Once you have made the meringue, scoop it out into the circle, piling it high. Carefully spread the meringue to the edge of the circle and shape the pavlova. Bake for 1½ hours. Turn the oven off and leave the door closed. Allow the pavlova to cool inside the oven. Top with whipped cream and seasonal fruits, and drizzle with passionfruit pulp. Once topped, serve immediately.

STORAGE: store mini pavlovas in an airtight container for up to 3 days.

ALLERGIES/INTOLERANCES:
Egg: use the liquid drained from a 400 g tin of chickpeas as a replacement for the egg whites.
Dairy: use a dairy-free whipping cream or a dairy-free Greek-style yoghurt.

makes **2 cups (500 ml)**
prep time: **2 minutes**
cooking time: **15 minutes**

2 cups (500 ml) milk
1 teaspoon pure vanilla extract
4 egg yolks
1 tablespoon gluten-free cornflour
1½ tablespoons caster sugar or maple syrup

simple egg custard

Place the milk and vanilla extract in a saucepan over medium heat and heat until just below boiling point.

Place the egg yolks, cornflour and sugar in a large heatproof bowl and whisk well to combine.

Slowly pour the milk into the egg yolk mixture, whisking continuously.

Return the mixture to the saucepan and cook over medium–low heat, stirring continuously to make sure the custard doesn't stick to the bottom of the pan, for 5–10 minutes until the custard has thickened and coats the back of a spoon.

STORAGE: serve immediately or store in the fridge for up to 2 days.

ginger *and* yoghurt cake

Like all things nice, this cake has a lovely balance of sugar and spice, making it a delicious addition to afternoon tea, dessert or celebrations.

Preheat the oven to 160°C (140°C fan-forced) and line the base of a 22 cm springform tin with baking paper.

Place the yoghurt, syrup, oil and eggs in a large mixing bowl and whisk well to combine. Stir in the ginger and sugar.

Sift in the flour, bicarbonate of soda and cinnamon and stir until just combined.

Pour the mixture into the prepared tin and bake for 1 hour, or until a skewer inserted into the centre comes out clean. Allow the cake to cool in the tin for 10 minutes before removing and transferring to a wire rack to cool completely.

Dust with icing sugar to serve, if you like.

makes **1 x 22 cm cake**
prep time: **15 minutes**
cooking time: **1 hour**

¾ cup (210 g) plain Greek-style yoghurt
½ cup (125 ml) golden syrup
½ cup (125 ml) light-flavoured extra virgin olive oil
2 eggs
2 tablespoons finely grated ginger
½ cup (110 g) caster sugar
2 cups (300 g) plain flour
1 teaspoon bicarbonate of soda
1 teaspoon ground cinnamon
icing sugar, to serve (optional)

FUSSY EATING TIP: from engagement and enjoyment of ginger cake, you can stretch reluctant eaters to ginger in other forms such as in soups and noodle stir-fries.

TIP: if you don't have any fresh ginger, use 1 tablespoon ground ginger.

STORAGE: keep the cake in an airtight container at room temperature for up to 5 days. To freeze, once the cake has cooled completely, wrap well in plastic film and then with foil and place in a freezer bag. Freeze for up to 3 months. To serve, thaw in the fridge overnight, still wrapped.

ALLERGIES/INTOLERANCES:
Gluten/wheat: use gluten-free flour.
Egg: use 2 'chia eggs' (p. 21) or ½ cup (125 ml) apple puree. Dairy: substitute the yoghurt for a dairy-free natural-flavoured yoghurt, or increase the oil to 1 cup (250 ml).

rocky road ice-cream cake

Making your own homemade ice-cream cake is not only a lot of fun, but you'll also know exactly what's in it – reducing some of the artificial colours and additives found in store-bought varieties. The kids will love to get involved in hiding all sorts of goodness in this cake. We love adding broken-up biscuits, halved raspberry lollies, crushed peanuts and shredded coconut.

makes **1 x 20 cm cake**
prep time: **20 minutes + 30 minutes**
    chilling
freezing time: **6 hours minimum**

150 g Scotch Finger biscuits
50 g unsalted butter, melted
2 litres chocolate ice-cream
½ cup (140 g) crunchy pure
    peanut butter
100 g marshmallows,
    cut into chunks

hard-set chocolate drizzle
80 g milk chocolate, chopped
1 teaspoon coconut oil

Line the base and sides of a 20 cm springform tin with baking paper.

Finely crush the biscuits in a food processor. Add the melted butter and pulse until incorporated. It should hold together when pressed. Firmly press the biscuit mixture into the base of the prepared tin. Place in the fridge for at least 30 minutes to set.

Place the ice-cream in a large bowl and allow it to soften slightly for about 10 minutes at room temperature. Layer about one-third of the ice-cream on top of the biscuit base. Top with one-third of the peanut butter and marshmallows, arranging evenly over the surface. Repeat this layering with half the remaining ice-cream, peanut butter and marshmallows. Scoop on the remaining ice-cream and top with the remaining peanut butter and marshmallows. Cover and freeze for 6 hours or until firm.

To make the chocolate topping, place the chocolate and coconut oil in a microwave-safe bowl. Microwave on high in 30 second increments until chocolate is soft. Stir until smooth and completely melted. Let it cool for 5–10 minutes. Remove the cake from the freezer and release it from the springform tin. Transfer it to a serving plate and drizzle the cooled, melted chocolate over the cake. Return to the freezer until ready to serve.

TIP: you'll need to make this cake a day ahead to allow it to set. But you can also make it days ahead of any celebration, helping to keep the party-planning chaos at bay.

NOTE: remove cake from the freezer 10 minutes before slicing, to soften slightly.

ALLERGIES/INTOLERANCES:
Gluten/wheat: use gluten-free biscuits. Dairy: choose a dairy-free ice-cream. Swap the butter for coconut oil or another mild-flavoured oil. Nuts: omit the peanut butter.

make-in-a-minute marinades

Simple recipes that pack a big, delicious punch at mealtimes, our marinades can be made in minutes, can be added to a variety of proteins and vegetables to improve flavour and texture for kids learning to eat, and are a huge time-saver in the kitchen. Add some to your meal plan today and they'll become your new favourites.

We know many children who love a meat-and-three-veg meal and many who prefer more textured meals and minced meats. And then there are a few in between, who enjoy a little of A and a little of B. These flavourful marinades are designed to suit all families, all children and all food preferences. They can be offered with a range of proteins and vegetables to sensitively stretch the more reluctant eater from foods and flavours they love to new textures and tastes.

Aversion to meat, and vegetarian proteins such as tofu and tempeh, can be a common concern for parents of little kids, and marinades can help us to make the transition a little easier. Some children are sensation-seekers who love big, bold flavours such as the sourness of citrus, the tang of spices, the saltiness of Asian sauces and the sweetness of sugar. Our marinades combine many of these elements to boost the flavour profile of meats and other proteins, making mealtimes more enjoyable.

why kids may be averse to meat

Understanding why kids may be averse to meat can help you consider their preferences and adapt how you serve meat to young children still learning to eat.

- **Too chewy:** children who are still learning to like meat often come to the table already uninterested in trying it or engaging with it. They may then be discouraged further by meat that looks tough, and that takes a lot of work to chew before they can swallow it.

- **Too tired:** after a busy day playing and learning new skills, kids often lack the energy to engage with foods of varying textures and flavours. If it's hard work to eat, and not something they enjoy just yet, they're likely to refuse it.

- **Underdeveloped jaw strength and oral motor skills:** many kids refuse meat because they simply don't have the ability to eat it. Kids need practice with a range of meat and food textures to build up their jaw strength, oral motor skills and confidence.

- **Too busy:** if they're busy playing imaginative games with their toys, or exploring and having fun outside, our guess is that they're often going to say they 'don't like it' without even having seen it or given it a go. Giving them some notice before mealtimes, setting aside toys so they can focus on the food, and offering liked foods as well as new or challenging ones all help to encourage a child to the table.

- **Colours too dull, and uneven:** some children love being stimulated at mealtimes with bright colours. The often brown, beige and white colours of red meat, chicken and fish may not tickle their fancy, and the uneven browning of meats, charred from the barbecue or grill, can deter them even further.

- **Dislike the flavour:** repeated refusal of meats can impart an aversion to their taste of meat foods. Even as their oral motor skills and chewing ability improve, kids will often refuse meat based on the expected taste.

- **Dislike the smell:** for children who are very sensitive to smells, walking into the kitchen or dining room, or even outside as the barbecue is on, can put them right off a meal.

how we can sensitively stretch children to enjoy meat

- **Family mealtimes:** this is our number-one strategy. Role modelling appropriate eating behaviours and enjoyment of a wide variety of foods is essential. You can have fun with this too and include games to engage the kids. For example, you can ask, 'What does it smell like?', or compare taking mouse nibbles and monster bites. Or have chewing competitions – if they do take a bite of meat, you can ask, 'How many chews can you chew it for?' or 'Can you chew it for 20 chews?', offering sips of water to help with managing the food bolus in their mouth and their ability to swallow it. And remember to skip the bribes (p. 206).

- **Skewers:** threading marinated sliced or diced chicken, beef, lamb, fish or tofu onto skewers to barbecue or grill can immediately increase engagement with meat. Skewers are easy to pick up, you can spin them around when holding them at each end, and from there kids might find an interesting part to smell, lick or bite. Baby steps! You can thread almost anything onto a skewer, even foods that have already been cooked, such as crumbed chicken tenderloins – kids love nibbling around the crispy edges. From little nibbles they learn to take bigger bites. You might like to alternate meat with pieces of food they enjoy, such as the cooked schnitzel with cheese and/or cucumber. Note: please blunt the edges of skewers when offering them to young toddlers, and they're best not offered to babies.

- **Toothpicks:** small, bite-sized pieces of tender cooked meats offered on toothpicks are a great stepping stone too. When kids reach out to grab one, it's one step closer to their mouth – even if they only smell it. Toothpicks are a great way to manage mouthfuls for toddlers and preschoolers who might otherwise overstuff their mouths with food, struggle to chew and have to spit the food out. Note: please supervise the use of toothpicks when offering them to young toddlers, and they're best not offered to babies.

- **Tasting plates:** some children might not enjoy the focus on a food, and it can be better to offer a bit of meat at mealtimes without bringing any attention to it at all. A tasting plate, with a few foods you know they like and enjoy, and a little of a food or two they are learning to like, can reduce anxiety and increase their interest and engagement.

- **Deconstructed mealtimes:** similar to tasting plates, deconstructed family mealtimes involve presenting all the elements of a meal in the middle of the table and everyone choosing what and how much they'd like to eat from all the foods on offer. If your child doesn't choose any meats, you might like to ask them to serve you some, or to pass particular plates around the table. This encourages connection between family members, increases interaction with new and refused foods without pressure or expectation to eat, and reduces any fear the child might have around food and mealtimes.

- **Marinated meats:** marinating meats can significantly increase acceptance by boosting or changing the flavour profile. This will greatly help kids who refuse meat based on its smell and taste. You can also stretch them from foods they might like, such as teriyaki salmon, to teriyaki chicken or beef (p. 230). Marinating meats can also tenderise the meat and make it easier for little kids to bite and chew. Our lemon and oregano marinade (p. 229) tenderises chicken thighs beautifully. We highly recommend you give it a go.

- **Shredded meats:** for very reluctant meat eaters, shredded meats are a nice step on from minced meats. They require little effort to chew, and for kids who love saucy or more textured meals you can really adapt them in many ways. For bolognese lovers, you can try a delicious shredded beef version, or try Mexican-flavoured shredded beef for burritos or nachos. Shredded meats are delicious in toasted sandwiches and burgers too (see our shredded pork recipe on p. 90). After saucy shredded meats, you can try finely chopped and barbecued, grilled or roasted shredded meats in some of these meals (try shredding some of the meat from our homestyle Beef, sweet potato and kale casserole, p. 128), and then move on to serving the meat separately, without the sauce. Small stepping stones to big mealtime wins.

- **Allow children to spit out food:** spitting out food is all part of learning to eat, particularly when the food is hard to chew or has a more challenging texture. Children often need to feel they can safely get food out of their mouth before they feel they can safely swallow it. If they spit food out time and time again, the attempts at chewing are at least helping to improve their jaw strength and oral motor skills. However, if you are at all concerned about their oral motor skills and chewing ability please seek the advice and recommendations of a speech pathologist specialising in feeding difficulties.

- **Blowing bubbles:** the simple fun game of blowing bubbles is a fantastic way to develop your child's eating skills. It strengthens the small muscles in their mouth as they try to pucker their lips to blow the bubbles.

vegetarian protein options

It's not all about meat. Many families enjoy a vegetarian diet for religious, cultural, ethical, environmental, nutritional and/or personal reasons. Other families enjoy regular meat-free meals, with the advantages of saving money, helping the environment, an increased vegetable intake and encouragement to try new foods. In addition to vegetables and grains, dairy foods, eggs, tofu, tempeh, legumes and nuts are all sources of high-quality protein that would otherwise be provided by meat, poultry and fish. Throughout the book we have provided some vegetarian suggestions for meat-containing meals, and feature and recommend ways to match our marinades with vegetarian protein sources. Our Salads chapter (p. 185) also discusses some wonderful strategies to inspire and encourage the enjoyment of a wide variety of vegetables.

meal planning tips with marinades

Marinades are your new best friend when it comes to preparing quick, easy and nutritious meals for your whole family.

- **On the double:** try doubling the recipe and freezing half for your future self. Many of our marinades are suitable for the freezer, and you can even freeze them mixed with the prepared meat too. Just like a dump bag (p. 89) but for the barbecue!

- **Time-saver:** meat becomes more tender and more infused with flavour the longer you marinate it, so it is great to do meal prep the night before, in the morning before you go to work, or during 'nap times'. All of a sudden last-minute dinner prep will be a breeze on busy afternoons.

- **Increase variety:** you will boost the variety of meals your family accepts when you find a marinade they love – even if it's just the one! If they love teriyaki beef and rice (p. 230), try teriyaki salmon and noodles. Or give lemon and oregano chicken skewers (p. 229) and salad, or lemon and oregano roast chicken and roast veggies a go.

- **Leftover love:** use large cuts of meat for your marinades, such as for our fennel and rosemary butterflied leg of lamb (p. 226) or lemon and oregano roast chicken (p. 229) recipes. Or make a larger quantity – for example, a double batch of tandoori chicken (p. 224), and repurpose the leftovers into a new meal the next day, such as chicken pastries, fried rice or toasted sandwiches. More leftover inspiration can be found in our Dinner + Leftovers chapter (p. 103).

- **One meal only:** there's no need to prepare a different meal for the kids. Our homemade marinades are super quick to make, and often use pantry and kitchen-garden staples and basic ingredients without nasty additives or preservatives, making them appropriate* to offer to babies as young as 6 months, those with allergies and intolerances, and the whole family generally!

*Be careful of the sodium content of our teriyaki (p. 230) and Asian-inspired (p. 227) marinades – they're best for older babies and toddlers and beyond.

tandoori

This super quick and easy tandoori marinade is mild and flavourful, perfectly suited to salmon or chicken. It works equally well with firm white fish if this is a preference for your family, or on tofu, for vegetarians.

makes ⅓ **cup (80 ml)**
prep time: **5 minutes**

1 teaspoon garam masala
1 teaspoon ground turmeric
½ teaspoon Kashmiri chilli powder
    or mild chilli powder, to taste
    (optional)
2.5 cm piece ginger, finely grated
4 cloves garlic, crushed
2 teaspoons extra virgin olive oil
¼ cup (70 g) plain Greek-style or
    natural yoghurt

Combine the spices, ginger, garlic and olive oil in a small bowl and mix well to combine.

Add the yoghurt and stir to combine.

FUSSY EATING TIP: for kids with sensitive tastebuds who are learning to like spices, try adding extra yoghurt to the marinade or serve additional yoghurt alongside the meal as a dip for the salmon or meat.

HOW WE LOVE IT: cover 4 × 200 g salmon fillets or 500 g chicken breast or thigh fillets in the marinade and marinate in the fridge for at least 2 hours. Cook the salmon under a hot grill for 7 minutes, turning halfway through, or until cooked to your liking; or slice into 2–3 cm pieces, thread onto skewers and barbecue over medium heat for 3-4 minutes each side, or until cooked to your liking. Barbecue or cook the chicken on a chargrill pan over medium heat for 8–10 minutes each side, or until cooked through. Serve alongside some basmati rice, steamed vegetables or salad and extra yoghurt.

STORAGE: keep the tandoori marinade in an airtight container in the fridge for up to 2 days.

ALLERGIES/INTOLERANCES:
Dairy: use coconut cream in place of the yoghurt.

fennel
and
rosemary

A butterflied leg of lamb, marinated well and cooked on a barbecue or in the oven, is a winner dinner in both summer and winter months and best shared with friends. The lamb slices are also a great finger food for young babies and toddlers, who often love the flavours. Leftovers are delicious in toasties, salads or wraps the next day too. You could also try using a rack of lamb or backstrap fillets, or even chicken pieces, firm white fish fillets or cuts of beef suited to grilling/roasting.

F **DF** **V** **EF** **GF** **WF**

makes **about 100 ml**
prep time: **5 minutes**

2 tablespoons rosemary leaves
1 tablespoon fennel seeds
1 teaspoon ground black pepper
¼ teaspoon sea salt
5 cloves garlic, roughly chopped
⅓ cup (80 ml) extra virgin olive oil

Place the rosemary, fennel, pepper, salt and garlic in a mortar and pestle and pound to a coarse paste. Add the olive oil and mix well to combine. Use on your chosen cut of meat.

MEAL PLANNING TIP: schedule leftover lamb toasted sandwich fold-ups (p. 170) in the meal plan for the next evening. Yum!

STORAGE: keep the marinade in an airtight container in the fridge for up to 24 hours, or freeze for up to 3 months.

HOW WE LOVE IT: to prepare a butterflied leg of lamb, cut slits in the skin side of the lamb and rub the marinade all over. Cover and refrigerate for at least 30 minutes, removing the lamb from the fridge about 15 minutes before you cook it. Heat the oven to 180°C (160°C fan-forced). Place the lamb in a large roasting pan and cook for 45 minutes for medium. To cook on the barbecue, heat a covered barbecue to high heat. Place the lamb flesh-side down on the grill or flat plate. Close lid and cook for 10 minutes. Turn the lamb over so the skin side is facing down and cook with the lid closed for a further 15 or 25 minutes for medium-rare or medium, depending on the thickness of your lamb and heat of the barbecue. Enjoy leftover lamb slices in salads, wraps or sandwich press fold-ups.

OTHER SERVING SUGGESTIONS: use to marinate lamb racks, smaller lamb fillets and steaks, or even try a whole chicken to roast, or chicken thighs.

This is a delightfully sweet and salty marinade that works well when cooking meats fast over high heat. To achieve the best results we love to use this marinade on fast-cooking cuts of meat such as riblets or cubed chicken, lamb or beef, or even salmon threaded onto skewers.

Place the onion, garlic and brown sugar in a small food processor and process to a smooth paste. Add the sauces and oil and process briefly until combined.

asian-inspired marinade

makes ½ cup (160 g)
prep time: 5 minutes

1 small white onion, chopped
1 clove garlic, crushed
1 tablespoon brown sugar
1 tablespoon fish sauce
1 tablespoon salt-reduced soy sauce
1 tablespoon olive oil

MEAL PLANNING TIP: marinated and grilled or barbecued meats are a great addition to the meal plan on evenings when you have busy afternoons of activities or work scheduled. They are also perfect for weekends when you have been enjoying the outdoors.

HOW WE LOVE IT: to prepare, thread 500 g of your chosen meat onto bamboo skewers (soaked in water for 30 minutes). Lay in a shallow dish and pour over the marinade. Turn to coat, cover and refrigerate for at least 1 hour. Preheat the barbecue or a large frying pan. Cook for 10 minutes, turning frequently, until cooked to your liking. Allow to rest for a few minutes before serving.

STORAGE: keep in an airtight container in the fridge for up to 1 week, or freeze for up to 3 months.

ALLERGIES/INTOLERANCES:
Gluten/wheat: choose gluten-free fish sauce and soy sauce or use tamari as an alternative.

This is a must-make marinade. It's so quick to prepare, so tasty and tangy, and it tenderises chicken beautifully. It gives a big flavour boost to veggies too.

Combine all the ingredients in a small bowl and mix well to combine.

lemon *and* oregano

makes **about ¼ cup (60 ml)**
prep time: **5 minutes**

¼ cup (60 ml) extra virgin olive oil
½ lemon, zest finely grated
3 cloves garlic, crushed
1 teaspoon dried oregano
1 teaspoon sumac or sweet paprika, or 1 tablespoon lemon juice (optional)

F
DF
V
EF
GF
WF

FUSSY EATING TIP: offering food on skewers, or bite-sized bits of meat on toothpicks, can increase kids' interest and engagement in a new or regularly refused food in an instant.

TIME-SAVING TIP: double the marinade ingredients and freeze a portion, with or without your chosen protein, in a small airtight container or reusable freezer bag.

HOW WE LOVE IT: toss 500 g chicken thigh fillets, cut into bite-sized pieces, in the marinade and refrigerate for at least 2 hours (or up to 8 hours). Thread onto bamboo skewers (soaked in water for 30 minutes). Cook on a barbecue grill over medium–high heat for 15 minutes, turning occasionally, until the chicken is brown and cooked through.

TRY: haloumi, zucchini, capsicum and cherry tomato skewers for a vegetarian option, or combine with the chicken for a mixed variety. The marinade works beautifully on a whole chicken, chicken pieces, lamb fillets or lamb skewers for something different. Lemon and oregano prawns are worth a try too.

STORAGE: keep in an airtight container in the fridge for up to 3 days, or in the freezer for up to 3 months.

teriyaki

Sweet and salty, this is a marinade that suits the taste preferences of little kids. You can use it to encourage acceptance of meats and fish. For example, if they like teriyaki chicken, try teriyaki beef or tofu as a stepping stone to other meat and/or fish dishes.

makes ¼ cup (60 ml)
prep time: **5 minutes**
cooking time: **15 minutes**

¼ cup (60 ml) light soy sauce,
  salt-reduced if possible
¼ cup (60 ml) mirin
2 tablespoons brown sugar
¼ teaspoon finely grated ginger
  (optional)

Place all the ingredients and ¼ cup (60 ml) water in a small saucepan over medium–high heat and stir until the sugar has dissolved. Bring to the boil.

Reduce the heat to low and simmer for 10 minutes, or until thickened slightly. The marinade will continue to thicken as it cools.

NUTRITION NOTE: be mindful of sodium content, choose reduced-salt sauces wherever possible, and serve only on occasion to young babies and toddlers.

STORAGE: keep in an airtight container in the fridge for up to 5 days, or freeze for up to 3 months.

HOW WE LOVE IT: combine half the marinade with 500 g sliced rump steak and marinate in the fridge for 2–3 hours. Heat 1 tablespoon olive oil in a wok over high heat and cook the meat in batches until just browned. Be careful not to overcook. Remove from the wok and set aside. Heat another tablespoon of oil in the wok, add some trimmed 10 cm spring onion pieces and red capsicum (pepper) strips, and stir-fry for a few minutes. Return the beef to the wok with the remaining teriyaki marinade and cook, stirring, for a further few minutes until the beef is cooked to your liking and the veggies are coated in the sauce. Serve with steamed rice. Use any veggies you like, such as onion wedges, snow peas, sugar snap peas or broccolini.

Our teriyaki sauce also works beautifully with sliced chicken breast or thigh fillets, chicken drumsticks, sliced tofu and salmon fillets.

ALLERGIES/INTOLERANCES:
Gluten/wheat: choose a gluten-free soy sauce or use tamari as an alternative.

bibliography

Australian Institute of Food Safety, foodsafety.com.au.

Derbyshire, E. J., 'Flexitarian diets and health: A review of the evidence-based literature', *Frontiers in Nutrition*, vol. 3, 2017.

Food Standards Australia New Zealand, foodstandards.gov.au.

Gaunt, A., J. Beaton and S. Buckle, *One Handed Cooks: Boosting Your Basics: Making the most of every family mealtime – from baby to school age,* Penguin Random House, Melbourne, 2019.

Gaunt, A., J. Beaton and S. Buckle, *One Handed Cooks: How to raise a healthy, happy eater – from baby to school age*, Penguin Random House, Melbourne, 2016.

Griffiths, G. and D. Stapleton, *Sense-ational Mealtimes!: Making sense of tricky mealtime behaviour, fussy/picky eating and feeding difficulties,* 2013, sense-ationalmealtimes.com.au.

Hammons, A. J. and B. H. Fiese, 'Is frequency of shared family meals related to the nutritional health of children and adolescents?', *Pediatrics*, vol. 127, 2011, pp. 1565–74.

Huntley, R., White Paper: 'Because family mealtimes matter', Ipsos Australia, 2008.

'Infant feeding guidelines' and 'Australian dietary guidelines', National Health and Medical Research Council (NHMRC), nhmrc.gov.au.

Manno, C. J., C. Fox, P. S. Eicher and M. E. Kerwin, 'Early oral-motor interventions for pediatric feeding problems: What, when and how', *Journal of Early and Intensive Behavior Intervention*, vol. 2, 2005, pp. 145–159.

Meat Free Monday, meatfreemondays.com.

Satter, E. M., 'The feeding relationship', *Journal of the American Dietetic Association*, vol. 86, 1986, pp. 352–56.

Satter, E. M., 'The Satter Eating Competence Model (ecSatter) works' and 'Raise a healthy child who is a joy to feed', ellynsatterinstitute.org.

Skafida, V., 'The family meal panacea: Exploring how different aspects of family meal occurrence, meal habits and meal enjoyment relate to young children's diets', *Sociology of Health & Illness*, vol. 35, 2013, pp. 906–23.

'SOS approach to feeding', sosapproachtofeeding.com.

Toomey, K., 'Feeding strategies for older infants and toddlers', *Pediatric Basics: The journal of pediatric nutrition and development*, 2002, vol. 100, pp. 2–11.

acknowledgements

We have been developing the ideas within this book in our homes and with our wonderful online community for so long, and we are thrilled that it's finally here. This book is one that we hope will live on the bench with food-splattered pages, and we can't wait to share the magic of family mealtimes as we all cook along together.

We are so grateful to our incredible agent at Curtis Brown, Pippa Masson, who once again helped bring our vision to life. From the initial jumbled proposal of our very best ideas to something real that will bring joy, organisation and delicious food to so many. We thank you as always for believing in us.

Our sincere thanks to the team at Penguin Random House, particularly Isabelle Yates, who has enhanced our vision and then improved it with her wisdom. You are always so polite and tolerant of our behind-the-scenes chaos, made even more intense this time with many months of homeschooling and interrupted Zoom calls. To our editors, Tracy Rutherford and Melissa Lane: your hard work has been so inspiring, piecing this puzzle together so beautifully and taking such care to understand each and every recipe. To designer Adam Laszczuk for designing a book we will be proud to have on our benchtops for many years to come. To Julian Mole at Post Pre-press for his help with typesetting, and to proofreader Lucy Heaver. And to our publicist Tessa Robinson and marketer Braden Bird, and everyone else at PRH who has supported this book.

To our stylist Jerrie-Joy Redman-Lloyd, who styled our food to perfection. Shooting during a pandemic was no easy task but you took it on with such ease and professionalism. Your sense of humour over burnt chicken and willingness to adapt to whatever was placed in front of you made for a very relaxed and enjoyable shoot. We adore the colour and vibrancy you have brought to the pages of this book.

We are so fortunate to be able to work with the best and want to thank the following brands for supplying some of the props. Bonnie and Neil for the most delightful linens, napkins and tea towels. Mud Australia, Batch Ceramics and The Corner Booth Annandale for so many of the incredible props you can see within these pages. To our friends at Solidteknics who supplied the baking trays and skillets that help cook our food to perfection. Le Creuset for your timeless casserole pots, frying pans and woks that stand out within these pages. To our local Harris Farm Markets for supplying us with the most abundant box of fresh seasonal produce to style our food.

To Wendy Quisumbing for bringing some new inspiration to this recipe collection and for your expertise in cooking in bulk for young children and busy families. You are always such a pleasure to work with.

To Kate Thomassian, a very much valued member of our team. For your brilliance in coming up with new and clever ways to help organise busy parents and your delicious premix recipes that will soon feature in decluttered pantries across Australia.

To our parents David, Cathy, Neil, Margie, Peter, Victor, Sarah, Rob and Jan: for your love, support and endless hours of last-minute babysitting when one hand just wasn't enough.

And finally to our families, our inspiration and grounding. To Allie's children Harry, Amelia and Archer, for your kissable cheeks and endless belly laughs, and husband Henry for testing countless meals and helping decide if they're 'book worthy'. To Jess's children George, Hamish, Louis and Jude, for your boundless energy and limitless love, and husband Charlie for all your hugs and high fives. To Sarah's husband Joe, for always being a constant source of love and encouragement. Thank you for all your support in everything that we do.

Allie, Jess and Sarah xxx

index

VIKING

UK | USA | Canada | Ireland | Australia
India | New Zealand | South Africa | China

Viking is part of the Penguin Random House group of companies
whose addresses can be found at global.penguinrandomhouse.com

Penguin
Random House
Australia

First published by Viking in 2022

Photography © Sarah Buckle
Cover design by Adam Laszczuk © Penguin Random House Australia Pty Ltd
Internal design by Adam Laszczuk © Penguin Random House Australia Pty Ltd
Styling by Jerrie-Joy Redman-Lloyd
Typeset in 10/12.9 pt Chaparral Pro by Post Pre-press Group, Australia

Printed and bound in China by RR Donnelley

A catalogue record for this
book is available from the
National Library of Australia

ISBN 978 1 76104 264 5

penguin.com.au

We at Penguin Random House Australia acknowledge that Aboriginal and Torres Strait Islander
peoples are the Traditional Custodians and the first storytellers of the lands on which we live and work.
We honour Aboriginal and Torres Strait Islander peoples' continuous connection to Country, waters,
skies and communities. We celebrate Aboriginal and Torres Strait Islander stories, traditions and
living cultures; and we pay our respects to Elders past and present.